# LEARNING DISABILITY:
## Uncover the Myths

# Learning Disability: Uncover the Myths

*Editors*

**Amita Bajpai**
**Meenakshi Dwivedi**

KALPAZ

ISBN: 978-93-5128-235-8

Price: ₹ 990

First Published, 2017

*Published by*

Kalpaz Publications
C-30, Satyawati Nagar,
Delhi – 110052
E-mail: kalpaz@hotmail.com
Ph.: 9212142040

*Printed at:* G. Print Process, Delhi

**Cataloging in Publication Data—DK**
Courtesy: D.K. Agencies (P) Ltd. <docinfo@dkagencies.com>

**Learning disability :** uncover the myths / editor, Meenakshi Dwivedi.
pages cm
Includes bibliographical references.
ISBN 9789351282358

1. Learning disabilities—India. I. Dwivedi, Meenakshi, editor.

LC4706.I5L43 2016 DDC 371.90954 23

# Contents

# Foreword

The people associated with teaching and learning fraternity are always looking for information of all sorts about the issues related to the education of all type of children whether normal or special. There is often an urgent demand for certain information on the new concepts and trends related to the educational problems of these children that seemingly should be, but some reasons were not conveniently available. This book ***Learning Disabilities: Uncover the Myths*** may serve as portals to information that we need right away. The editor of this book ***Professor Amita Bajpai*** with her co-editor ***Dr Meenakshi Dwivedi*** has made an earnest effort to consolidate the expertise, research findings and recommendations by the authors in the form of the present book.

This book aims to provide insight to its readers all the information about learning disabilities at a single platform. The content of the book is systematically presented in seventeen chapters. The detailed description of the concept, causes, diagnosis, types, problems, strategies, intervention etc. is provided in the book. This book has two purposes: firstly to serve as a text for several courses like D.Ed, B.Ed, M.Ed and research running in various teacher training institutes and universities and secondly to provide a reference manual for professionals working in the field of Learning Disabilities. Whether you are an undergraduate or postgraduate student, a doctoral or postdoctoral fellow, professor or a lay person, you will find a body of extensive information within the covers of this book.

***Professor Amita Bajpai***, the editor of this book is an academician and a person having a proven capacity in the field of education. The co-editor ***Dr Meenakshi Dwivedi*** being a UGC Post-doctoral Research Fellow has a keen interest in the field of research. You have in your hands the fruit of their labour, enthusiasm and research aptitude which

I believe will provide a pleasurable experience to the readers. Undoubtedly the book because of its features and new vision shall gain popularity. I therefore, have no hesitation in recommending this book to all associated with the world of teaching and learning. The Faculty of Education will certainly be pleased to see this book. Faculty should obtain a copy and put within easy reach of their students. When students ask where they can find the best content about learning disabilities……Just point them out towards this book. The sooner they become accustomed to using it as an information source, the better off their research and understanding of learning disabilities will be.

— **Professor S. B. Nimse**
*Vice Chancellor*
*University of Lucknow*
*Lucknow*

# Acknowledgements

First and foremost, I want to thank all of the learned contributors to this book: ***Professor Deepa Rani Saxena, Dr Arpana Godbole, Dr Arvind Sharma, Dr Sitaram Pal, Dr Akanksha Singh, Dr Chhaya Soni, Dr Rashmi Singh, Dr Deepa Awasthi, Dr Vandana Singh, Dr Preeti Jaiswar, Sunil Kumar Bhagat, Waseem Zahra, Rashmi Tiwari, Priyam Shukla, Priyanka Srivastava, Hans Raj.*** Their profound knowledge on learning disability has made this endeavour taken its shape. Conceiving of, assembling, co-authoring and editing this book has provided me with a special opportunity to work with each of these amazing individuals. Through this joint effort, my enormous admiration for them and their work has grown even greater and it has been a tremendous honour to work together.

I am also obliged to the distinguished panel of reviewers, consist of ***Dr S K Shukla***, *Retired Faculty, Depart ment of Education, University of Lucknow,* ***Professor R J Singh***, *Ex Vice Chancellor, Kashi Vidyapeeth*, ***Professor Ranu Uniyal,*** *Director, Women Studies, University of Lucknow* and ***Aruna Pandey***, *Co-ordinator, Chetna Institute for Special Children* who invested their precious time and hard work in evaluating the contributions from various authors and further guided them to make their writing focused, clear and appropriate for this book.

More gratitude than I could ever express is also due to ***Dr Meenakshi Dwivedi,*** my talented co-editor and lovely student. She thoroughly edited multiple drafts of the manuscript and improved it significantly, in substance, structure and style.

Nevertheless, I take this opportunity to express the profound gratitude from my deep heart to my parents, family, colleagues and friends for their encouragement and continuous support when and where required. Lastly, I would like to thank God. I could never have done this without the faith I have in you, the Almighty.

**—Amita Bajpai**
*(Editor)*

# Authors' Introduction

1. **Professor Amita Bajpai**

   ***Professor, Department of Education, University of Lucknow, Lucknow, Uttar Pradesh, India.***

   (Contributed Article: Education for Learners with Dyslexia)

   Professor Amita Bajpai is the professor in the Department of Education, University of Lucknow. She is M.Sc. (Chemistry), M.Ed, Ph.D (Education). She has been the first JRF-SRF in the Department of Education, University of Lucknow. She has received the gold medal for obtaining the highest marks in B.Ed. She has been the director, Directorate of Distance Education, University of Lucknow. She has been the Co-ordinator (Academic) for the B.Ed. inservice programme at University of Lucknow. She has been the incharge of curriculum construction for two-year M.Ed. course. She has also developed the learning material for the B.Ed. through distance mode. She is the author of two textbooks in education named *Vishisht Balak and Shikha ke Samajshastriya Aadhar.* She contributed several research papers in many national and international journals. Till date seventeen Ph.Ds are awarded under her supervision. She has the vast experience as an administrator. She performed many duties like Proctor duties. She was the coordinator of Joint Ph.D examination 2014-15 of University of Lucknow. She also has been the deputy co-ordinator for the UP Joint Entrance Examination for B.Ed. 2010-11. Presently, she is the member of the Core team- Admission and the Hostel Provost.

2. **Dr Meenakshi Dwivedi**

   ***UGC Post-Doctoral Research Fellow, Department of Education, University of Lucknow, Lucknow, India and Member of Learning Disability Worldwide, United States of America.***

(Contributed Articles: Dyscalculia: Maths Learning Disabilities, Dyspraxia: Understanding the Hidden Disorder, Learning Disability Worldwide)

Author is currently a Member of US based International Association named 'Learning Disability Wordwide' and UGC Post-doctoral Research Scholar in Department of Education, University of Lucknow, Lucknow, India. She is working on the Project for the Education of students suffering from Autistic Syndrome Disorder. The title of the project is *'A Study to Improve Communication Skills in Children with Autistic Syndrome Disorder through an Intervention Programme in Inclusive School Settings'*. She has completed her doctoral thesis on the topic '*Pains and Gains of Mainstreaming: A Study of Visually Impaired Students Studying in Higher Education'*. She is post graduate in Education, Mathematics and Physics. She has also worked as Assistant Professor (B.Ed) for approximately seven years. She has participated and presented the papers in sixteen national/international seminars and conferences including 102nd Indian Science Congress. She has participated in four national level workshops too. More than seventeen research papers and articles written by her on various issues have been published in reputed national/international journals. She has also contributed five chapters for different edited books. The teaching and research work of the author is focussed on Special Education, Psychology and Mathematics.

3. **Professor Deepa Rani Saxena**

   ***Professor, Department of Education, Mahila Mahavidyalaya, Banaras Hindu University, Varanasi, Uttar Pradesh, India.***

   (Contributed Article: Learning Disability: An Overview)

   Author is currently Professor of Education, Department of Education, Mahila Mahavidyalaya, Banaras Hindu University, Varanasi. She has written a book on "Environment and Psychology of Prospective Teachers". She is recipient of major research project of UGC (2009) *"Environment, Professional Ethics and Teacher Education Programmes in Bihar, Madhya Pradesh and Uttar Pradesh"*. She successfully submitted her research report in 2012. She has got published many papers and articles in reputed national and international journals. Her specialised areas are Professional Ethics, Environment, Human Rights Education, Text Books and Content Analysis.

## 4. Hans Raj

***Research Scholar, Faculty of Education, Banaras Hindu University, Varanasi, Uttar Pradesh, India.***

(Contributed Article: Learning Disability: An Overview)

Author is currently a Research Scholar (UGC-SRF) in Department of Education, Banaras Hindu University, Varanasi. He is doing research in the field of creativity and teaching methodology. He has participated and presented the papers in more than 25 national/ international seminars and conferences. More than 10 research papers and articles written by him on various issues have been published in reputed national/international journals. He has also contributed one Article for National Magazine.

## 5. Dr Chhaya Soni

***Assistant Professor, Faculty of Education, Banaras Hindu University, Varanasi, Uttar Pradesh, India.***

(Contributed Article: Identification of Learning Disability)

Dr Chhaya Soni is working as Assistant Professor in faculty of education (K), Banaras Hindu University, Varanasi, (U.P.). She is UGC-NET qualified and completed her doctorate degree from University of Lucknow, Lucknow. She is post graduate in Economics, Hindi and Master in Education. She has experience in teaching field approximately seven years. She has participated and presented the papers in nine international and thirty five national conferences. She has also participated in one international and six national workshops. Her areas of interest are psychology, language teaching and special education. Four research scholars are doing doctoral research under her supervision.

## 6. Dr Arvind Sharma

***Associate Professor and Co-ordinator in Department of Mental Retardation, Faculty of Special Education, Dr Shakuntala Misra National Rehabilitation University, Lucknow, Uttar Pradesh, India.***

(Contributed Article:Learning Disability: Challenges in Identification and Assessment)

Author is currently working as Associate Professor and Co-ordinator in Department of Mental Retardation, Faculty of Special Education, Dr Shakuntala Misra National Rehabilitation University, Lucknow. He has completed his doctoral thesis on Language Disabilities of Learning Disabled Children studying in primary schools. He is post graduate in Special Education (Learning Disability), Special Education (Mental Retardation), Zoology and PG Diploma in Computer programming, Office management and Mental retardation. He has got highest marks in post graduate in Special Education (Learning Disability) with other awards like Best Research Paper award, VIFRA Young Scientist award. He has authored of a book on Learning Disability published by International Publisher from Germany. He has participated and presented research papers in 22 International seminars/conferences, 28 National seminars/conferences. He has published more than 30 research papers in International and National Journals and 20 articles in different other publications. He is visiting expert of Rehabilitation Council of India (RCI), New Delhi and member in Board of Examiners of different Foreign and Indian Universities. He has membership of various professional bodies of International and National level and Associate Editor of Different International and National level Journal/e-journal He has participated in curriculum development in the field of Special Education of different Universities and has evaluated fifteen Ph.D these, more than 25 Dissertations at master's level and currently guiding five Ph.D in Special Education.

7. **Dr Rashmi Singh**

***Assistant Professor, Department of B. Ed., Maharana Pratap Government PG College, Hardoi, Uttar Pradesh, India.***

(Contributed Article: Learning Disabled: Understanding the Misunderstood)

Author is Assistant Professor, Department of B.Ed. in Maharana Pratap Government PG College, Hardoi, Uttar Pradesh. She is Ph.D. (Education), M.Sc. (Chemistry) and M.Ed. She has also qualified UGC-JRF (Education). Her achievements involve PC Banerjee Award for "Best Research Production of the Year- 2013" for her Doctoral thesis, Smt. Kailashwati Memorial Gold Medal-2006 for being 'Best Woman Student' obtaining the highest percentage of marks in B.Ed. She has participated and presented her research papers in more than 20 national and international seminars and conferences. Her publication work involves six articles in various reputed national and international journals and three chapters in edited books on various educational and social issues. Her keen interest areas include gender and women education and other burning issues related to field of education and sociology.

**8. Dr Deepa Awasthi**

***Ph.D-Education, University of Lucknow, Lucknow, Uttar Pradesh, India.***

(Contributed Article: 3 R of Learning and Learning Disability: Challenges and Possibilities)

Dr Deepa Awasthi is Doctorate in Education and Post Graduate in Education, Sociology and Economics. She has qualified UGC – JRF in Education and Sociology as well and has equal command on both the subjects. She has participated and presented her research papers in more than 50 national and international seminars and conferences. She also has five edited books on various educational and sociological issues to her credit. Her publication work also involves 12 chapters in edited books, 04 research papers in form of conference and seminar proceedings and 17 research paper and articles in various journals of national and international repute. Her keen interest areas include gender and other issues related to field of Education and Sociology.

**9. Dr Vandana Singh**

***Assistant Teacher, Government Primary School, Sitapur, Uttar Pradesh, India.***

(Contributed Article: Dyslexia: A Reading Disorder)

Author is working as Assistant Teacher in Government Primary School, Sitapur, Uttar Pradesh. She is postgraduate in Economics, Education and Psychology. She has qualified UGC-NET examination and completed her doctoral thesis in special education where she prepared a module for the effective education of backward children studying in junior high school. She also has the teaching experience of about seven years as teacher educator. Her keen areas of interest include primary education and special education and psychology. She has participated in twenty national and seven international seminars so far. She has also worked as the counsellor (B.Ed.) of Jamia Milia Islamia University, New Delhi, directorate of distance education.

**10. Sunil Kumar Bhagat**

***Assistant Professor, Department of Education, GSRM Memorial PG College, Lucknow, Uttar Pradesh, India.***

(Contributed Article: Dyslexia: A Reading Disorder)

Author is working as Assistant Professor, Department of Education in GSRM Memorial PG College, Lucknow, Uttar Pradesh. He is post graduate in History and Education. He qualified UGC NET and JRF exams in education. He is pursuing Ph.D. from Department of Education, University of Lucknow, Lucknow, Uttar Pradesh. He is having approximately seven years teaching experience for teaching the classes B.Ed. and M.Ed. He is also working as the counsellor (B.Ed.) of Jamia Milia Islamia University, New Delhi, directorate of distance education. He has participated and presented the papers in fifteen national and five international seminars. Apart from it, he has attended two national workshops too. His areas of interest in teaching and research are higher education and research methodology.

**11. Dr Preeti Jaiswar**

***Guest Faculty, Department of Education, Khwaja Moinuddin Chishti Urdu Arbi Farsi University, Lucknow, Uttar Pradesh, India.***

(Contributed Article: Supporting Learners with Dyslexia)

Author is presently working as guest faculty, Department of Education, Khwaja Moinuddin Chishti Urdu Arbi Farsi University, Lucknow. She has completed her Ph.D. in Education and qualified

UGC NET. She has worked for three years as Assistant Professor in education at graduation level and has done four years of extensive research work as Rajiv Gandhi National Senior Research Fellow. She has written and got published six research articles in various national journals on various topics. She has participated and presented Research in thirteen National and three International seminars, workshops and conferences. Her areas of interest in teaching and research are higher education and primary education.

**12. Dr Akanksha Singh**

***Assistant Professor, Faculty of Education, University of Allahabad, Allahabad, Uttar Pradesh, India.***

(Contributed Article: Dysgraphia : When Writing Hurts)

Dr Akanksha Singh is presently working as Assistant Professor in Department of Education, University of Allahabad. She did her B.Ed., M.Ed. and Ph.D. from I.A.S.E., Faculty of Education, University of Lucknow. She has received two gold medals in M.Ed. for being best student of the faculty. She worked as UGC-JRF and SRF and UGC Post-doc Research Fellow at Faculty of Education, University of Lucknow. She has also worked as Assistant Professor in Heeralel Yadav Balika Degree College, Lucknow, in Amity University, Lucknow and in Khwaja Moinuddin Chisti Urdu Arbi Farsi University, Lucknow. Her areas of specialisation are Philosophical foundations of Education, Educational Administration and Qualitative Research Methodology. She has presented plenty of research papers using Phenomenological research method. She also holds postgraduate degrees in Ancient Indian History, Philosophy and Business Administration.

**13. Waseem Zahra**

***Research Scholar, Department of Education, University of Lucknow, Lucknow, Uttar Pradesh, India.***

(Contributed Article: Attention Deficit Hyperactivity Disorder and Social Skill Development)

Author is a Senior Research Scholar in Department of Education, University of Lucknow. She is currently conducting a research on

'Preparedness of Teachers for Inclusive Education' for the fulfillment of her doctoral thesis. She is postgraduate in Biochemistry. She has also worked as Assistant Professor (B.Ed.) for approximately one year. She has participated and presented the papers in various national/international seminars and conferences. More than seven research papers and articles written by her on different issues have been published in reputed national/ international journals. She has also contributed two chapters for edited books. The teaching and research work of the author is focussed on Inclusive Education and Psychology.

**14. Rashmi Tiwari**

***Vice Principal, Tender Hearts School, Kursi Road, Lucknow, Uttar Pradesh, India.***

(Contributed Article: Psychological Problems of Pre-adolescent Learning Disabled Students)

The author is presently working as Vice Principal at Tender Hearts School, Kursi Road, Lucknow. She holds Post Graduate degree in Chemistry (Physical) and Biology (Zoology). She completed her Master in Education and completed the dissertation on the topic *'A Comparative Study of the Moral Behaviour of Students of General and Public Schools'*. She has worked as TGT and PGT for fifteen years. Her areas of interest include psychological and behavioural Problems in school going children.

**15. Dr Sitaram Pal**

***Assistant Professor, Department of Hearing Impairment, Dr Shakuntala Misra National Rehabilitation University, Lucknow, Uttar Pradesh, India.***

(Contributed Article: Auditory Problems and Remedial measures for Children with Learning Disabilities)

Author is presently working as Assistant Professor, Department of Hearing Impairment, Faculty of Special Education, Dr Shakuntala Misra National Rehabilitation University, Lucknow. He has completed his Ph.D. in Special Education. He holds Post Graduation degree in Sociology, Education and Special Education (Hearing Impairment). He has worked as lecturer in special education for the course of Diploma in special education and B.Ed. in special education approximately 10 years and 2 years of teaching and research in M.Ed. special education. He has written three books in the field of special education and rehabilitation. He has written more than two dozen articles in Hindi and English for the education and rehabilitation of children with special needs. He has participated and presented the papers in 12 national and seven International seminars and conferences. Presently he is reviewer of four international journals in education and humanities. five research articles have been published in various national and international journals on different topic with reference to special education and rehabilitation. He has also developed Study Learning Material (SLM) of Uttar Pradesh Rajarshi Tondon Open University and Dr Baba Saheb Ambedkar Open University, Ahmedabad. The interested area of teaching and research is early identification, early intervention and inclusive education of children with special needs.

**16. Priyam Shukla**

***TGT (English), Delhi Public School, Jankipuram, Lucknow, Uttar Pradesh, India.***

(Contributed Article: Learning Disabled vs Low Achievers)

Author is presently working as TGT (English) at Delhi Public School, Jankipuram, Lucknow. She has the Master degree in English Literature. She has completed her Master in Education and completed a dissertation on the topic, *'A Case Study of the Special Schools for Autistic Students'*. She has presented her Research Paper entitled *'Role of Community in Providing Education to the Autistic Children'* at the National Conference on Role of Community Psychology in Creating Well Being Under the aegis of Community Psychology Association of India held at University of Lucknow. She has been working as a TGT and PGT for more than thirteen years. Her areas of interest include Special Education and Autism.

**17. Dr Arpana Godbole**

***Associate Professor, Department of Education, University of Lucknow, Lucknow, Uttar Pradesh, India.***

(Contributed Articles: Psychological Problems of Pre-adolescent Learning Disabled Students, Learning Disabled vs Low Achievers)

Author is working as Associate Professor in the Department of Education, University of Lucknow, Lucknow. She did her Ph.D. in Education. Her area of research is Social Psychology. She did her post-graduation in Education and Sanskrit from University of Lucknow. She has the teaching experience of more than twenty six years. She has written a book on School Organisation. Several research papers are written and got published by her. Many students are pursuing research under her supervision. Presently she is teaching research methodology and measurement and evaluation. She is a key member in developing two-year M.Ed. curriculum of faculty of Education, University of Lucknow. As an administrator, she has worked as the deputy co-ordinator for the UP Joint Entrance Examination for B.Ed. 2010-11. She was the deputy co-ordinator of Joint Ph.D. examination 2014-15 of University of Lucknow.

**18. Priyanka Srivastava**

***Research Scholar, Department of Education, University of Lucknow, Lucknow, Uttar Pradesh, India.***

(Contributed Articles: Learning Disability and Assistive Technology)

Author is currently a Research Scholar in Department of Education, University of Lucknow. Her research area is Special Education. She has completed M.Ed. (Hearing Impairment) from Ali Yavar Jung National Institute for Hearing Handicapped, Mumbai University, Mumbai. She is post-graduate in History. She has done Bachelor in Science with the subjects Zoology, Botany and Chemistry. She has also worked as Assistant Professor (B.Ed.-HI) for one year in Nehru Gram Bharti University, Allahabad. She has participated and presented approximately 21 papers in national/ international seminars and conferences. Four Research papers and articles written by her on various issues have been published in reputed refereed journals. She has also contributed one chapter for an edited book of international publication. The teaching and Research work of the author is focussed on Special Education, Psychology, Educational Policies and Science.

# Introduction

Learning disabilities are a group of disabilities characterised by persistent and significant difficulties in learning academic skills such as reading, writing and maths. This edited book entitled as **"Learning Disability: Uncover the Myths"** has seventeen chapters covering the history, concept, nature, types, identification, assessment, causes, intervention techniques which are discussed in detail. It provides a clear understanding of the characteristics, causes, prevalence and approaches to evaluation of learning disabilities and other developmental disorders. Although the book is oriented towards the teaching profession, it is targeted at all professionals in the health sector i.e. pediatricians, neurologists, psychiatrists, speech and language pathologists, in the field of education it targets to teacher educators, specialist teachers and non-specialist teachers.

## Content Glimpses

In the first chapter of this book **'Learning Disability: An Overview'** author ***Professor Deepa Rani Saxena and Hans Raj*** have defined the concept of learning disability through various definitions. They presented an overview based on studies done in the field of learning disability on behavioural pattern of learning disabled students. The problem of perception, difficulty in memorisation and speaking fluently, limited attention span and poor retention and self-concept are precisely shown by the individuals with learning disabilities. It is emphasised that extensive-exploratory and phenomenological studies are required to categories learning disability in terms of child's estimated academic potential and his or her actual level of academic performance, so that, deficit can be known and norms may be established.

In the next chapter **'Identification of Learning Disability'** author ***Chhaya Soni*** tried to describe the different aspects and strategies for identifying learning disabled children/students. Tests which are used in assessment have been categorised as norm-referenced and criterion-referenced. She also presented a rating scale for identifying the learning disabled children. Different Models i.e. Ability Model, Skill Model that are helpful in assessment of these children are discussed in detail. Besides it, diagnostic model- skill and ability is also helpful for screening of learning disabled student.

In the third chapter of the book **'Learning Disability: Challenges in Identification and Assessment'** the author ***Arvind Sharma*** threw light upon few challenges regarding identification and assessment of Learning Disabilities. He described that the primary issues in the identification and assessment of Learning Disability appear to be the construction and validation of identification tools, identification criteria, identification of reasons for the occurrence of a particular Learning Disability, identification of co-occurrence of other deficits along with Learning Disabilities in an individual. He has also mentioned that the lack of awareness in the community, parents and teachers about learning disabilities and also regarding the provisions available for them, is yet another issue.

The fourth chapter of the book is **'Learning Disabled: Understanding the Misunderstood'** drafted by ***Rashmi Singh.*** The author here tried to uncover several myths regarding learning disability and attempted to present this concept in totality so that one can diagnose learning disabled students correctly and provide them special education accordingly. She described the causal factors of learning disabilities. She explained that in terms of learning disabled students there is concept of "habilitation" instead of rehabilitation because here a function has not lost which has to be regained but the individual has born with certain neurological disorder. This habilitation involves special education programme which covers many therapies including training in social skills.

The fifth chapter of the book is titled as **'3 R of Learning and Learning Disability: Challenges and Possibilities'** written by ***Deepa Awasthi.*** The author explained the concept of three R (Reading, Writing and Arithmetic) which was given by Sir William Curtis in 1795, in terms of learning disabled students. The three R's are considered to be the core skills which are needed by all the learners during his/her education. Therefore, the author described the types of learning disability associated with the three R's i.e. Dyslexia, Dysgraphia and Dyscalculia. She suggested some measures for teachers and parents so that learning disabled children can learn in a better way with proper support by their parents and teachers. They can help these learners in organising their work as well in study and can suggest significant ways to overcome their weaknesses.

The sixth chapter is on the topic **'Dyslexia: A Reading Disorder'** which was jointly written by***Vandana Singh and Sunil Kumar Bhagat.*** In this chapter, the authors explained the concept, symptoms, types, causes, diagnosis and treatment for dyslexia in detail. They advocated for a comprehensive evaluation which is needed to diagnose this problem. Children with reading disorder overcome their difficulties if they receive appropriate treatment at early age because early intervention is a key to prevent the problems associated with reading disability. They suggested how to improve reading outcomes of students with or at risk for reading disorders on the basis of some research studies.

The seventh chapter of the book titled as **'Education for Learners with Dyslexia'** which is penned by ***Amita Bajpai.*** The author explained about the main educational effects of dyslexia like Reading and perceptual difficulties, Writing problems etc. She also suggested classroom strategies for students with Dyslexia as schools can implement academic accommodations and modifications to help students with dyslexia succeed. The measures related to Accommodations involving materials, Accommodations involving interactive instruction, Accommodations involving student performance, Computers and literacy skills are discussed in detail. The brief success story of some exceptional, versatile and creative dyslexic persons is also mentioned who were recognised and were appropriately supported in their life span.

The next chapter of the book is titled as **'Supporting Learners with Dyslexia'** author of which is ***Preeti Jaiswar.*** She discussed symptoms of dyslexia in children at different level of schooling like kindergarten level, Middle School Level, High School Level. According to her Dyslexia does not affect only reading and writing ability of the child but also other skills and activities like social skills, listening ability, memorising ability, time management and navigation too. The author suggested for the professional help to these children by teachers, doctors, psychiatrist etc. in order to help them in improving their affected skills and activities. The parents are also advised to praise their child even on small efforts which will help in building child's self-esteem and confidence.

In the sequence the ninth chapter of the book is titled as **'Dysgraphia: When Writing Hurts'** authored by ***Akanksha Singh***. She discussed the learning disorder of written expression i.e. Dysgraphia in detail. Along with the concept, types of dysgraphia, ways to assessment are discussed in detail in the chapter. A sample checklist is also provided for dysgraphia. Four types of Educational Interventions can be used for eliminating the Dysgraphia which are Self-learning, Self-monitoring, Relaxation and Refreshment and Mental - movement exercises. The author emphasised on the use of cursive writing which eliminates the necessity of picking up a pencil and deciding where to replace it after each letter. She added that dysgraphia learners benefit by using computer software that encourages them to add graphics, colour and other fun aspects to their story.

The tenth chapter of the book is entitled as **'Dyscalculia: Maths Learning Disabilities'** composed by ***Meenakshi Dwivedi.*** The author defined dyscalculia in psychological, biological and pedagogical contexts described the criteria required to diagnose students with dyscalculia and delineate practical methods and instructional designs that can be implemented in the classroom to address the specific learning needs of dyscalculia learners. The author also defined Dyslexic Dyscalculia where the problem manifests primarily in reading difficulties which then lead to mathematical problems for the child. Instructional Modifications Designed to accommodate dyscalculia learners are also provided that can be incorporated into the classroom.

The next chapter is about dyspraxia named as **'Dyspraxia: Understanding the Hidden Disorder'** which is authored by ***Meenakshi Dwivedi.*** This chapter deals with the concept, symptoms in different age groups and causes of dyspraxia which is also known as

Developmental Co-ordination Disorder (DCD), Motor Learning Difficulties, Perceptuo-Motor Dysfunction. The concept of verbal dyspraxia is also explained where children have difficulty in making and co-ordinating the precise movements required for the production of clear speech. Although dyspraxia is a lifelong condition, motor co-ordination may improve with age yet early recognition enables a child's special educational and social needs to be identified. In the special segment the author defined how dyspraxia affects the handwriting of the learner as this happens due to poor motor skills, perceptual dysfunction and erratic organisation and motor planning.

The twelfth chapter of the book titled as **'Attention Deficit Hyperactivity Disorder and Social Skill Development'** is written by ***Waseem Zahra.*** Here the author wrote that children with attention deficit and hyperactivity disorder (ADHD) lack the necessary social skills to develop good interpersonal relationships. The training of social skills become a "hidden curriculum" — rule that students are held accountable for but are never explicitly explained or taught. On the basis of research findings she explained the effectiveness of social skills training for students with ADHD which leads to improvement in students' social skills. She advocated that parents need to take the long view of social problems and to map out a plan to solve them quite as carefully and thoughtfully as they would consider academic or health problems.

The thirteenth chapter deals with the **'Psychological Problems of Pre-adolescent Learning Disabled Students'** drafted collectively by ***Arpana Godbole and Rashmi Tiwari.*** They emphasised that the self-concept, attributions, anxiety, depression and suicide among pre-adolescents with learning disabilities is examined through researches for the purpose of detecting consistency of indicators concerning these emotional and developmental variables. The emotional development of many pre-adolescents with learning disabilities is not notably positive and these students appear to be at increased risk for severe depression and suicide. The outlook of teachers, parents and society was also discussed elaborately as handling pre-adolescents with learning disabilities requires a lot of patience, research and integrated effort of parents and other family members and teachers too.

The fourteenth chapter of the book is **'Auditory Problems and Remedial Measures for Children with Learning Disabilities'** written by ***Sita Ram Pal.*** He explained that children and adults who have Central Auditory Processing Disorder (CAPD) are a heterogeneous group of people who have difficulty using auditory information to communicate and learn due to the impact on the brain's ability to filter and interpret sounds. He clearly described the difference between hard of hearing and auditory processing disorders as Auditory Processing Disorders (APD) is not the inability to hear. It's the inability to interpret, organise, or analyse what's heard. A checklist is also designed to help in assessing whether a child has CAPD.The need of additional support by parents, speech-language pathologists, teachers and tutors is also acknowledged.

The fifteenth chapter of the book is **'Learning Disabled vs Low Achievers'** written by ***Arpana Godbole and Ms Priyam Shukla***. The chapter deals with the concept of learning disabled learners and low achievers. Along with the differences and similarities between these two are discussed in detail. The author described that learning disability is entirely intrinsic in nature while low achievement is basically extrinsic in nature. Learning disability has no relation with IQ whereas low achievers possess low IQ level. But they both require separate and one to one approach while receiving the teaching learning instructions.

The sixteenth chapter of the book is titled as **'Learning Disability and Assistive Technology'** authored by ***Priyanka Srivastava.*** She wrote that assistive devices and assistive technologies are important in enabling Persons with learning disabilities to 'live independently'. She categorised the types of technologies in Low-tech Technology and High-tech Technology and then explained in detail about the assistive devices for reading, writing, speaking, memory etc. available for these learners. There is a distinct and important role for both assistive technologies and special educators to play in the educational process. Collectively, the vast range of technology conditions before these learners can result in positive outcomes for students with Learning Disability.

The last but not the least the seventeenth chapter is entitled as **'Learning Disabilities Worldwide'** authored by ***Meenakshi Dwivedi.*** Here it is presented the status of learning disabilities in some countries like UK, US, China, Canada, Korea and India where societies adapt their structures to ensure that all children, irrespective of age, gender and disability, can enjoy their basic human rights without discrimination of any kind. It is found that there are several agencies across the world in government and non-government sector working in the field and contributing for elimination rather detection of this classroom disorder. Interestingly, many institutions facilitate early intervention in the child's academic life so that he/she learns the strategies and skills necessary to cope with it better.

# Chapter - 1

# Learning Disability: An Overview

— *Professor Deepa Rani Saxena and Hans Raj*

**Abstract**

*Learning disability is a general term that is related to specific kinds of learning problems. LDs vary in severity and may interfere with the acquisition and use of language, speaking, reading, writing, mathematical calculations etc. LD is also related to organisational skills, social and psychological factors. It is very common and affects one to five per cent of the people. LD is due to genetic and other congenital or neurobiological factors. In this chapter, we have discussed the conceptual framework of learning disability and its various types. After describing various kinds of learning disabilities, some suggestions have been provided based on previous studies in the field of learning disability. These suggestions will be very helpful for teachers as well as parents in creating supportive atmosphere for better adjustment and development of learning disabled students.*

***Keywords:*** *Learning disability, Organisational skills, Conceptual framework, Neurobiological factors.*

## Introduction

The term 'disability' is derived from the Latin prefix '*dis*' meaning negation, separation, lack of or opposite of and the Latin '*habilitas*', meaning fitness and '*habere*', indicating to have or to be easily handled. Today, disability is usually regarded as a negative attribute which indicates the lack of power or ability to do something.

According to US department of Education office of Special Education Programme (2000), "The Central concept of Specific Learning Disabilities (SLD) involves disorders of learning and cognition that are intrinsic to the individual. These disorders each significantly affect a relatively narrow range of academic and performance outcomes. SLD may occur in combination with other disabling conditions, but they are not due to other conditions, such as mental retardation, behavioural disturbances, lack of opportunities to learn or primary sensory deficits" (Bradley, 2002).

According to **Kirk and Kirk (1971),** learning disability is not minor or temporary difficulties in learning but with a severe discrepancy between ability and achievement in educational performance.

**Stevens (1962)** defined disability as a loss of function; impairment as tissue damage or disease and handicap as the burden which is imposed on the learner when confronted with educational situations which cannot be resolved by reason of body dysfunction or impairment.

Consequently, learning disability is the problems of learning which observed in speaking, reading, writing, mathematical calculations etc. these learning problems are not due to hearing, visual impairment, mental retardation or socio-economic problems. It is very difficult to obtain accurate data on the prevalence of school children whose academic performance is below expectations, but informed estimates have placed their numbers as high as 20 per cent of school age population. It may be one of the important causes of school dropouts where parents and teachers both of them are unable to understand that child has learning trouble.

## Types of Learning Disability

The most common types of learning disabilities involve problems with reading, writing, mathematical operations, reasoning and speaking. Rama (1992) has given the description of different types of learning disabilities. The descriptions are given in Table 1.

**Table 1: Types of Learning Disabilities and Major Problems Encountered**

| *Types of disabilities* | *Major/Primary Problems* |
|---|---|
| **1. Oral Language disabilities** | |
| (a) Dysphasia | Partial inability to comprehend the spoken word and to speak. |
| (b) Aphasia | A loss of ability to comprehend manipulates or expresses words in speech, writing or gestures. |

*(Cond...)*

| | |
|---|---|
| **2. Reading Disabilities** | |
| (a) Dyslexia | Partial inability to read or to understand what one reads silently or aloud. |
| (b) Alexia | Loss of ability to read/ write the printed language. |
| **3. Writing disabilities** | |
| (a) Disgraphia | Disgraphia refers to the partial inability to write. |
| (b) Agraphia | Agraphia refers to the total inability to write. |
| (c) Revisualisation Problems | It is the inability to re-visualise the image of letters or words. |
| (d) Formulation and Syntax Disorders | Formulation disorder refers to the inability to organise the ideas into a clear concise pattern of words. Syntax disorder refers to the difficulty in ordering the words to form phrases clauses or sentences. |
| **4. Spelling Problems** | Most of the learning disabled children have spelling problems. |
| **5. Arithmetic Disabilities** | Problems related to mathematical operations. Dyscalculia is a term for problems concerning mathematics, a student may do well in social science and language, but he may fail in tests involving fractions and percentages. |
| **6. Social-skill Disabilities** | Social skills disabilities are frequently a characteristic of student with behaviour problems. |

Since, none of these disabilities have certain definitions. Lack of knowledge of scope, their factors and unavailability acknowledge model on learning disability is one of the prime reasons to lag behind it. Each of the learning disability required its positive and negative aspects of their characteristics. So that early intervention, diagnosis and remedy may be provided on time. Individual difference is another reason to generalise the findings of learning disability. It is a bio-psycho-social behavioural problem where assessment of intellectual potential is in itself question. Lastly, most of the time learning disabled children is considered due to developmental lag. Thus, today learning disabled children are poorly understood by teachers, parents and society.

## An Overview Based on the Studies in the Field of Learning Disability

To identify the students with learning disability is a challenging task because there is no single symptom that we can look to as proof of a problem. Generally, the problem of perception, difficulty in memorisation and speaking fluently, limited attention span and poor retention and self-concept are shown by the individuals with learning disabilities.

**Chhabra (2009)** investigated on delinquency in relation to learning disabilities, personality and family environment and found that 89.2 per cent delinquents were learning disabled. He further reported positive relationship between learning disability and family environment.

**Kumar (2007)** explored psycho-neurological aspects of learning disabilities and reported that psycho-neurological functions are related to learning disability. He further conveyed that learning disabled children are overactive or more impulsive and deficient in attention and memory in comparison to non-disabled children.

**Iqbal and Gupta (2006)** studied on self-esteem and adjustment of children with learning Disabilities. The result showed that the children with learning Disabilities had lower Self-esteem in comparison to normal children in the domain of general-self, home parents and total self-esteem. However, no significant differences were found between those two groups on social self-peer and school academic domain of self-esteem. Further they reported that children with learning Disabilities had significantly poorer adjustment than normal children in all the areas assessed, i.e., educational, emotional, social and also in total adjustment.

**Jacob (2004)** conducted a study on effects of deficits in scientific skills on achievement in science of the learning disabled at the primary school level. The results were found as follows: (i) 20 percentages of the population are learning disabled and (ii) found significance difference between learning disabled (LD) and non-disabled (ND) children with respect to their achievement in Malayalam, mathematics, science process skills, intelligence and achievement in science which shows the superiority of non-disabled children.

According to the characteristics of learning disabled children are as follows: (i) a repeated history of academic failure in educational pursuits. (ii) Motivational abnormality (iii) a vague, almost free-floating anxiety (iv) Erratic, uneven behaviour. (v) Incomplete evaluation (vi) Inadequate education. Learning disabled students have average or above average intelligence but they have difficulties in learning in certain specific areas as like- reading, writing, speaking language, arithmetic, reasoning power etc. the problems of learning disability is found at any stage of life from early childhood to adults.

**Gibney et al. (2002)** examined the attention disorders with measures of neuro-cognitive functioning. The result was found that there are more attentional difficulties in learning disabled subjects in comparison to non-learning disabled children.

**Defort (2002)** studied on construction and validation of a test of writing competency and reported that participants with learning disabilities showed significantly more difficulty organising sentences in a logical sequence than their non-disabled peers.

**Vijayanthi and Meera (1997)** studied on problems of primary level learning disabled and suggested for establishing the guidance centres in schools to identify learning disabled students.

**Sood (1994)** explored the personality correlates of learning disabled children and found relationship between certain personality factors like self-concept, social maturity, reasoning ability, general anxiety and learning disability.

**Srivastava and Afiah (1992)** focused on the identification of the learning disabled and assessment of their ability in reading, writing, spelling, language and arithmetic. Further, they reported that there was no significant difference between boys and girls in their disabilities in reading, arithmetic, language and spelling but sex had a definite bearing on the writing disability of the learning disabled.

**Vasanthi (1992)** studied on Mathematics learning disabilities in relation to certain psychological, social and educational factors among class VII pupils. The result indicated that Mathematical learning disabilities have negative relation to intelligence and socio-economic status and have positive relation to behaviour problems.

**Mohapatra (1991)** conducted a study on the problems of reading, memory and attention processes of normal and reading disabled children. He found that the normal and the reading disabled children did not differ with respect to their intelligence and the normal children made significantly less error than reading disabled children.

**Tripathi, Tripathi and Srivastava (1991)** studied on "Learning disability: Some behavioural manifestations". The results were found as follows: (i) Significant difference was found between LD and NLD students in their competence, (ii) LD and NLD students had significant differences on length-assessment task and (iii) NLD students demonstrated a high level of iconic memory whereas the LD students could not tackle the task very successfully.

**Kamhi and Johnson (1982)** reported that specific language impaired children have more difficulties with grammatical morphemes and complex syntactic constructions than the similar age non-language impaired children.

## Suggestions

On the basis of above studies, some suggestions for teaching and better adjustment of the students with learning disability are given as following:

1. The learning disabled students should be taught by special teachers with special curriculum.
2. Teachers should familiar with the learning disabled students' interests, achievement level, aptitudes, abilities, strengths, weaknesses, learning styles, knowledge base, developmental level, motivational values, cultural and community background before using any new and special teaching techniques and strategies.
3. The teacher should make teaching more and more interesting by using different types of teaching learning materials.
4. Provide extra time to solve questions and home works and reduce number of questions.
5. Provide opportunities for self-learning and success in a supportive classroom atmosphere to help in building self-esteem and self-confidence.
6. Use number lines, fact sheets and allow use of calculator for improving computational skills.
7. Provide peer reader or reading technology and audio books for improving decoding problems.

8. Provide regular practice and re-practice and allow peer assistance.
9. Brainstorm vocabulary and provide correct spelling in advance for improving writing skills.
10. Make flexibility in the classroom teaching procedures.
11. Make use of self-correcting materials that provide instant feedback without embarrassment.
12. Use simple vocabulary as possible as in teaching lesson for learning disabled students.
13. Teachers should use Computer and various Electronic Medias for teaching in word processing and other skill development.
14. They should be identify and diagnose all types of learning disabilities in the early stage of children so that proper guidance can be provided.
15. The parents of the children should aware about learning disability so that early remedial steps against the disability problems can be taken.
16. Teachers should improve their teaching style through special workshops, seminars, specialised reading, action research and practice in the field of special education.
17. School administrators should conduct periodical meetings and face-to-face discussions about what opportunities could be exploited and arrived at a commitment to specific goals for better learning of the children with learning disabilities.
18. Research oriented effort is necessary to launch and improve the process of guiding teaching-learning process related to learning disabled students. So the administrators or educational agencies should provide special and experimental projects for teachers.

## Conclusion

Thus, above analysis clearly indicates that learning disabilities (LDs) are a group of neurological or brain-based problems that adversely affect the acquisition, retention, understanding or use of information. Therefore, it becomes necessary to organise the classroom environment properly to make it more conducive and supportive for learning disabled students.

Learning disabled children need the support of a multidisplinary team. It consists of regular teachers, specialists, psychologists, physicians and counsellors. Teacher has the prime role in identifying the learning disability of a child and implementing appropriate remedies. A teacher should use different teaching methods and strategies in the class for improving learning habits in LD students. The parents can also play an active role in identifying and diagnosing the problems of LD in their children and can provide proper care and direction to help them this problem.

Research in this area is still very limited in extent and scope. Future efforts can be done in the field of diagnosis and remediation, a more precise taxonomy of the behaviours which comprise the problems labelled learning disability and more effective research on the basis component of learning disability of various types. Similarly, in the field of psycho-social problem of LD children to find out underlying causes of the learning difficulty can be accomplished.

Extensive-exploratory and phenomenological studies are required to categories learning disability in terms of child's estimated academic potential and his or her actual level of academic performance, so that, deficit can be known and norms may be established. Research studies in this area are time taking and difficult task needs longitudinal study to determine characteristics of various learning disability.

## References


- Babu, S.K., Prasad, V. and Rao, D.B. (2004). *Reading Disabilities.* New Delhi: Sonali Publication.
- Bradley, R. L. Danielson and D.P. Hallahan (Eds.) (2002). *Identification of Learning Disabilities*: Research to Practice, Mahwah, N.J. : Erlbaum.
- Chhabra, N. (2009). *Delinquency in relation to learning disabilities, personality and family environment.* Ph.D. thesis, Department of psychology, Guru Nanak Dev University, Amritsar. Retrieved from http://shodhganga.inflibnet.ac.in/handle/10603/20592.
- Cushenbery, Donald C. (1972). *Remedial Reading in the Secondary School.* New York: Parker.
- Defort, A.L. (2002). Construction and validation of a test of writing competency. *Dissertation Abstracts International, Section A: Humanities and Social Science, 63*(1 -A), 80.

- Douglas D.C. (1996, Aug.). *Teaching strategies for students with diverse learning needs.* Retrieved from http://www.nebraskasocialstudies.org/pdf/tsfswdln.pdf
- Gibney, L.A. et al. (2002). *Diagnosing attention disorders with measures of neurocognitive functioning.* International Journal of Neurosciences, 112 (5), 539-564.
- Iqbal and Gupta, L. (2006). *Self-esteem and Adjustment of Children with learning Disabilities,* Disabilities and Impairment, *20* (1), pp. 37-44.
- Jacob, J. P. (2004). *Effects of deficits in scientific skills on achievement in science of the learning disabled at the primary school level.* Ph.D. thesis of education, School of pedagogical sciences, Mahatma Gandhi University, Kottayam. Retrieved from http://shodhganga.inflibnet.ac.in
- Kamhi, A. and Johnston, J. (1982). *Towards an understanding of retarded children's linguistic deficiencies in M. Lahey language disorders and language development.* New York: Macmillan.
- Kirk, S.A. and Kirk, W. D. (1971). *Psycholinguistic Learning Disabilities: Diagnosis and Remediation,* Urbana, IL: University of Illinois Press.
- Kumar, S. S. (2007). *Psycho-neurological aspects of learning disabilities.* Ph.D. thesis, department of psychology, University of Calicut. Retrieved from http://shodhganga.inflibnet.ac.in/handle/10603/22741
- Kumaran, D. and Menon, M. (2002). Development and validation of rating scale for screening the learning disabled, *Recent Researches in Education and Psychology.* Vol. 7, p. 59.
- Mangal, S.K. (2010). *Advanced Educational Psychology* (2nd Ed). New Delhi: PHI Learning.
- Ministry of Children and Youth Services, Ontario. (2009). *A Handbook on Learning Disabilities.* Ontario: Author. Retrieved September 23, 2015 from http://www.childdevelop.ca/sites/default/files/files/WAM%20LD%20handbook.pdf
- Ministry of Education, Province of British Columbia. (2011). *Supporting Students with Learning Disabilities: A Guide for Teachers.* Columbia: Author. Retrieved September 23, 2015 from http://www.bced.gov.bc.ca/specialed/docs/learning_disabilities_guide.pdf
- Poonam, (1990). *A study of social and psychological factors in families with handicapped children.* Fifth Survey Educational Research, New Delhi: NCERT.
- Rama, S. (1992). *Handbook of Learning Disabilities*, Regional College of Education, Mysore: NCERT.
- Sood, P. (1994). Personality co-relates of learning disability. *Journal of the Indian Academy of Applied Psychology*, Jan.
- Stevens, G. D. (1962). *Taxonomy in special education for children with body disorders.* Pittsburgh: Department of Special Education and Rehabilitation, University of Pittsburgh.

- Tripathi, L. B., Tripathi, A. N. and Srivastava, A. N. (1991). Learning Disabilities: Some behavioural Manifestations, *Fifth Survey of Educational Research*. New Delhi: NCERT.
- University of Guelph. (2000). *Creating Opportunities for Successful Learning: A Handbook for Faculty on Learning Disability Issues.* Retrieved September 23, 2015 from https://www.uoguelph.ca/tss/resources/pdfs/lophandbook.pdf
- Vasanthi, R. (1992). *Mathematical learning disabilities in relation to certain Psychological, socio and educational factors among call 7th pupils*, Indian Educational Review, 30 (2).
- Werts, M.G., Cullatta, R.A. and Tompkins, J.R. (2011), *Fundamentals of Special Education*. New Delhi: PHI Learning Pvt. Ltd.
- http://www.rehabcouncil.nic.in
- *The Right of Children to Free and Compulsory Education Act, 2009* [Internet]. New Delhi: Ministry of Law and Justice (IN), Legislative Department; 2009 Aug. 27. Available from: http://education.nic.in/Elementary/ free%20and%20 compulsory.pdf. Accessed on February 5, 2016.

# Chapter - 2

# Identification of Learning Disability

***— Dr Chhaya Soni***

**Abstract**

*Each child takes birth with his or her infinite capacity. He makes existence with own and our society to do appropriate behaviour through these capacities. But there are some children who have any type of disability and abnormal behaviour. It is well known that children with disabilities, like- learning disabilities (specific types of learning problems which is related to using their certain skills, like—reading, writing, listening, perceptual, personal and social behaviour, reasoning, mathematics etc.), as a group, feel difficulty to understand for minute difference among various letters, words, numbers and other facts. Also incapables to understand of relationship with others and community living outcomes as they transition to compared to their peers without these disabilities. These children are weaker than normal children by birth or after birth due to different conditions and also tend to have fewer opportunities for self-determination than their nondisabled peers. Such children are not less in number, if these children are not found out earliest then their learning capacity can become more less. It is seen, generally, people could not find out their problems on time or they try ignoring these problems, while to understand incapability of these children is extreme necessity. Through which could solve their problems. With this they will take education and understand precious facts of life. In this chapter it is tried different aspects and strategies for identifying learning disabled children/ students and to determination the same facts.*

***Keyword—****Assessment, Identification, Instructional Planning, Norm-referenced and Criterion- referenced Measure, Formal and Informal, Skill and Ability Model.*

## Introduction

***"Nobody asked me how I am learning,***
***Everybody just told me what to Learnt"***

In this world, every being has own existence through own characteristics. Similarly, every human being expresses his characteristics, works etc. and tries to prove his existence. A person works in different conditions or areas (favourable or unfavourable) according to his different capabilities. But if a person looks capability or he got this incapability by birth than he feels himself out of the society. If a person is not eligible to learn something then it may be hurdle in his personality development. In the context it is seen in special needs of children that they are good in physical appearance but their perception, motor co-ordination matter is incapable and they found themselves incapable in learning.

The act of teaching, re-teaching and working with struggling students is not a new concept for classroom teachers. Even in the 1900's students who attended school did not always work on the same assignments or subjects at the same time. Teachers would after assignment or order of instruction to help individual students (Ellis, 2005; Gwaltney, 2001). Interventions, formal and informal have been common in schools for many years. More recently Response to Intervention (RTI) has been implemented to ensure that all students receive any needed instruction and interventions to achieve academic success. RTI is a formal process implemented by schools to provide direct intervention for all students experiencing academic and behavioural difficulties (Gerzel Short and Wilkins, 2009). The primary goal of RTI is to provide the interventions a struggling student would need to become successful in the general education curriculum. If the interventions are successful, that student would continue in the general education setting. If interventions are not successful, the school district may decide to implement different interventions or may initiate a referral for special education eligibility testing.

Because students of today are the citizens of tomorrow and they are going to be the pillars of the country. Hence it is essential to ensure that each pillar is as strong as the other. Moreover, we cannot think of bringing about optimum human resource development without uplifting all categories of backward students. This can possible that each classroom has some learning disabled students. These students come to school regularly but they are likely to become dropouts if their educational needs are not adequately met. The nature and severity of a student's learning disorders will depend on the interaction between each-other personal characteristics (cognitive abilities, information-processing strengths/ weaknesses, personality, motivation, social-emotional maturity, achievement, cognitive style, knowledge), the characteristics of required tasks (how well tasks match the person's abilities and style) and the characteristics of the settings in which the individual lives, studies and plays (attitudes, interaction patterns, quality of learning through home and school experiences). These characteristic is like a mirror which indicates direction of ending and level and areas of learning disabilities.

Also it is seen, that the learning disabled students have near normal, normal and above normal intelligence envisages that these students should be identified as early as possible so that required intervention strategies can be planned at the earliest.

So that, now diagnosis includes description of behaviours that do not necessarily pinpoint a condition. For example, it may refer to a description of reading behaviour is not viewed as caused by some dysfunction within the child. This latter use of diagnosis is often used interchangeably with the terms assessment and evaluation. A multidimensional assessment framework is essential to discover how the strengths of the student can best be matched with task under setting attributes that are most likely to promote academic and social growth. The multiple perspectives that must be taken into account, together with technical and conceptual concerns about many of the assessment devices currently in use, make assessment far from a simple matter.

In the last decade, the term diagnosis has changed or expanded markedly. Often it has been interpreted within a medical orientation as the determination of a condition (e.g., pneumonia or trainable mental retardation) that either requires a specific treatment or implies that no treatment exist to correct the problem. Moreover, the condition is viewed as a problem within the child and uses the educational programme for understand to right way of problem and condition.

Educational programme for learning disabled students comprises at various steps. They are assessment, identification and planning instructional interventions.

## Assessment

Assessment is the process of gathering data for the purpose of clarifying strengths and weaknesses and making decisions that will facilitate the individual's growth educationally and psychologically. It is to popular opinion, assessment is not the same as testing; testing is just one part of the assessment process. Many other means of data collection are involved in assessment: observing interactions among the students, parents, teachers and peers; interviewing the student and significant others in his or her life; examining school records and past evaluation results; evaluating developmental and medical histories; using information from checklists completed by parents, teachers and the student; evaluating curriculum requirements and options; evaluating the student's style and rate of learning during trial teaching periods; using task analysis to identify which criteria still have to be mastered; and collecting data on peer acceptance, classroom climate, 'and teacher attitudes toward a student with disabilities, Prerequisites for appropriate assessment include being. Aware of multiple assessment purposes, models and methods, as well as securing sufficient training to evaluate and plan in a team context and across multiple domains.

## Identification (Way Need for Early Identification)

Early identification and prevention are very necessary for any category of challenging children. Early identification leads to prevention before complication. It is not only better but also cheaper to intervene before the disabilities become acute or complicated. If the learning disabled student has voice disorders which may be caused by any number of physical problems, it can be diagnosed by speech pathologists or other professionals and required remedial programmes can be devised at primary level itself. Similarly language disorders may result from such physical problems as hearing or speech impairment, example— if it is identified at early stage the teacher can employ preschool programmes rich in verbal experience and direct instruction in the fundamentals of language which have been found to be effective in overcoming the language problems of learning disabled students.

Learning disabilities caused by physical attributes like poor general motor co-ordination; poor manual dexterity etc. can be easily overcome if the problem is identified at early stage before it becomes worse or leads to complication. There are some students who stand out as being obviously extremely backward due to poor physical co-ordination, their clumsy manipulation and their very retarded speech. When these physical attributes are set right, learning disability can be tackled by providing physiotherapy and proper training. Identifying and intervening at early stage will be more feasible, fruitful, economical and also the operating causative factors so identifying learning disabled Students that required intervention strategies can be planned not only to alleviate the causative factor but also to ameliorate their learning process. The earlier, the better is the golden rule here.

Also it is seen past several years, more and more school districts have been moving to enrollment-wide screening programmes that have as one major function the early recognition of children who are displaying signs of development or impending learning disabilities. Although there are no universally accepted strategies for such screenings, there is nearly total agreement that screening does serve several functions in any organised attack on learning disabilities. The most obvious and easily recognised function of screening is various types of tests and teacher related activities. Problems diagnosed earlier are more likely to be less firmly entrenched and thus are more easily treated. Since many learning disabled children learn quite well, but unfortunately, learn the wrong things (like learning incorrect phonic strategies in reading). Identifying such misdirected learning early leads to easier extinction of bad habits and to the formulation of more productive behaviours. Early diagnosis can lead to the removal of blocks to normally paced learning experiences for these children.

## Initial Procedures for Identification

At initial stage we can facilitate different kinds of decisions, each of which may require different sets of information, (Salvia and Ysseldyke) identify a number of types of decisions that call for different types of assessment: like—**referral, screening and student progress** etc.

**Referral**

Each year three to five per cent of students are referred for psychological and educational assessment (Salvia and Ysseldyke). When students referred for reading and learning disabilities are tested, anywhere from half to three quarters are identified as requiring special attention. Unfortunately, the assessment process is so time consuming that it significantly cuts into the time that remains for school personnel to invest in remediating students' difficulties.

In order to address the issue of too much time and money being borrowed from intervention for the sake of testing, some school systems have developed pre-referral or teacher assistance teams, these teams consist of experienced general and special education teachers and other specialists, who consult with classroom teachers regarding a student differential in the classroom. In group or one-on-one consultation, team members clarify questions, suggest interventions and assess the need for more in-depth assessment after monitoring the outcome of recommended programme modifications. Therefore, the first priority of assessment needs to be consultation regarding how one might modify regular classroom tasks and settings to best meet the needs of the student who demonstrates academic weaknesses.

**Screening**

Screening, a quick process, detects individuals who may be learning disabled. For this standardised tests are frequently used. Screening also uses observations of teachers and parents, checklists, behaviour rating scales and information in the child's/student's history.

**Student Progress**

Student progress must be evaluated to determine any necessary programme modifications. Children with disabilities Teacher-constructed measures, standardised tests, classroom observation and behaviour checklists often are used to assess students' academic and social progress. Systematic monitoring of progress in the classroom, as often as once or twice weekly, has been associated with significantly higher rates of student learning. Clearly, analyses of student progress provide not only specific, programmatically useful information on student skills, strategies and behaviours, but also information on important curriculum and setting modifications.

## Instructional Planning

Assessment data are collected to assist educational, personnel ill planning programmes that will enhance the psychological adjustment and educational achievement of students with learning disabilities. Within this assessment goal, emphasis is placed on determining precisely which skills students have and have not mastered and how they approach learning tasks. Assessment issues are involved in identifying students as learning disabled. Our primary concern is with psycho-educational planning. Assessment practices that merely lead to identification are not sufficient for designing instructional programmes and for planning day-to-day teaching modifications.

In brief, assessment is an integral part of the educational process. Educational assessment can be defined as the process of collecting data for the purpose of specifying and verifying problems and for making educational decisions about students.

## Ways to Identify the Learning Disability

Assessment can involve tasks conducted with students or strategies that focus on the students' interactions with a variety of tasks and settings. Tests used in assessment have been categorised as **norm-referenced and criterion-referenced.**

## Norm-Referenced

Norm-referenced tests are most useful for screening and identification purposes. Test that have been standardised on a normative group, in order to compare an individual's performance to that of his or her peers, are called standardised or norm-referenced tests. These tests to be useful in the decision-making process, they must meet several criteria: (1) reliability- consistency of scores from one testing time to another (2) validity- the test measures what it is supposed to measure; (3) standardised administration procedures (if all examiners use similar procedures, a more accurate estimate of the student's performance relative to the normative group is possible) (4) norms based on an appropriate comparison group (similar socio-cultural and educational background).

An important function of well-constructed norm-referenced measures is screening children who might be at risk for psychological and educational problems. However, assessment teams cannot limit themselves to the use of norm referenced tests alone because these measures sample too few skills to be of much help in planning specifically what and how to teach students. Additional assessment approaches, such as criterion referenced and informal evaluation strategies are necessary.

## Criterion-Referenced

Criterion-referenced measures are most useful for identifying what to teach. This tests are intended to measure whether a person has mastered very specific skills and it's provide information on what to teach. Only a few norm-referenced tests are detailed enough to allow for interpretation in a criterion-referenced way. This test can be normed, although norms are not critical to its purpose.

Students' scores on criterion-referenced achievement measures can be affected by the amount of overlap that exists between their curriculum and the test items. More often than not, test items do not correspond with what has been taught in the classroom example— On math tests, more than half the content may be derived from topics never covered by the text. On reading tests, only in first and second grades does a large percentage of the content overlap with the vocabulary taught in the students' readers.

**Example:** A test that shows Amit to have mastered math better than 15 per cent of children at his grade level nationally is norm-based. A test that indicates he can add two-digit numbers, but not when regrouping is required, is criterion-referenced. The norm-referenced test will judge Amit's knowledge of letter sounds by sampling a few letters and comparing his percentage correct with that of the standardisation sample. In contrast, the criterion-referenced test is likely to ask Amit to give all twenty-six letter sounds.

In other way, Assessment procedures can be classified into two categories as:

1. Formal assessment
2. Informal assessment

### *1. Formal assessment*

Most formal assessment (using standardised tests) is conducted outside the classroom by school psychologists, social workers, language clinicians, physical therapists or medical personnel. On occasion a teacher who has extensive assessment training may evaluate students in this manner. Standardised tests gives reliability and validity data, which means that they compare a student's score with normative data collected on a regional or national level.

**Formal Instrument or Test and Batteries**

- **Basic School Skills Inventory (Valett, 1968).** This instrument is used to identify a number of different academic areas where a child may be experiencing difficulty.
- **Bender Gestalt Test for Young Children (Koppitz, 1964) or Bender Visual-Motor Gestalt Test (Bender, 1938).** An older instrument originally developed for clinical use with organic pathology, this test is used by many to check on or to predict academic achievement. There are severe disagreements about its efficacy for this purpose.
- **Boehm Test of Basic Concepts (Boehm, 1967).** Administered to small groups, this instrument measures the mastery of concepts required for school achievement during the first few years.
- **Detroit Tests of Learning Aptitude (Baker and Leland, 1935).** This test includes nineteen subtests measuring the basic elements of the learning process, such as visual and auditory attention span.
- **Developmental Test of Visual-Motor Integration (Beery and Buktenica, 1967).** This instrument measures developmental status in the areas of visual perception and fine motor integration.
- **Developmental Test of Visual Perception (Frostig, Lefever and Whittlesey, 1964).** Frequently included in screening and diagnostic batteries, this instrument is designed to assess five different areas of visual perception. This instrument has been the focus of considerable debate and some doubt has been

raised as to factor validity and the generalisation of results from remedial programmes based on DTVP data.

- **First Grade Screening Test (Pate and Webb, 1966).** This instrument screens groups for potential early learning problems. Sometimes used for general "tracking" guidance.
- **Illinois Test of Psycholinguistic Abilities (Kirk, McCarthy and Kirk, 1968).** This instrument, probably the most frequently used evaluative instrument in learning disabilities, measures language skills in a variety of ways. Its stated age norms run from about two years to about ten years. In practice it is used most often with children in the five to eight years-old range. The test is individually administered and quite time-consuming if administered in its entirety to a large number of children.
- **Kindergarten Teacher's Handbook (Meyers, Ball and Crutchfield, 1973).** This publication is actually a small booklet outlining a testing sequence for screening that includes a sub-portion of a number of different instruments, directions for interpretation and some remedial recommendations. Of particular use may be the year-end evaluation form that allows quick and simplified rating of a wide variety of behaviours, including such items as body concept, expressive and receptive language and math concepts. A number of individual behaviours are listed under each of the above and similar concept headings.
- **Lincoln-Oseretsky Motor Development Scale (Sloan, 1954).** This instrument invidually measures a number of different motor skill areas. Being somewhat time-consuming and complicated, this instrument is not typically used in large group screening.
- **Meeting Street School Screening Test (Hainsworth and Siqueland, 1969).** This instrument is really a small battery of subtests yielding scores dealing primarily with reasoning ability, discrimination and motor response and prior learning in academic areas (e.g., number concepts).
- **Peabody Picture Vocabulary Test (Dunn, 1965)**. Often used as a rough measure of intelligence in the young child, this older test also appraises receptive language vocabulary.

- **Preschool Inventory (Caldwell, 1970).** Suitable for children three to six years old, this inventory measures achievement in areas prerequisite for school success.
- **Pupil Rating Scale (Myklebust, 1971).** This 1 small booklet and easily used by the classroom teacher, this scale rates young children in the areas of auditory comprehension, spoken language, orientation, motor co-ordination and personal-social behaviour. Some question has been raised as to whether or not these areas represent five independent factors, but the instrument's validity in rough screening seems to be fairly well demonstrated.
- **Purdue Perceptual-Motor Survey (Roach and Kephart, 1966).** This survey (the authors carefully note that it is a survey and not a test) scores the children's performance in five general areas congruent with Kephart's general approach to evaluating and helping the slow learner. The areas include balance and posture, body image and differentiation, perceptual-motor match, ocular control and form perception. The transfer of motor training to school-subject related behaviour has recently become a controversial subject.
- **Screening Tests for Identifying Children with Specific Language Disability-Slingerland (Slingerland, 1964).** Three sets of group screening tests for early primary ages. School personnel tend to feel comfortable with this instrument since its parts resemble typical schoolroom activities.
- **Spache Diagnostic Reading Scales (Spache, 1972).** This individual test battery diagnoses reading difficulties in elementary-school-age children.
- **Stanford Diagnostic Reading Test (Karlsen, Madden and Cardner, 1968).** This group test measures a number of reading difficulty sub-areas for children in grades two to eight.
- **Test of Articulation (Goldman and Fristoe, 1969).** Similar to the following instrument, this test focuses on speech problems. These two instruments are often used together in screening for speech and hearing problems.
- **Test of Auditory Discrimination (Goldman, Fristoe, Woodcock, 1970).** Individually administered items check

children's ability to discriminate important sounds relatively unconfounded by other factors. This test may be used for children as young as four years old.

- **Test of Language Development (Newcomer and Hammill, 1977).** A prescriptive-diagnostic instrument incorporating measurement of a number of different spoken language sub-areas.
- **Test of Reading Comprehension (Brown, Hammill and Wiederholt, 1978).** This instrument appraises several different areas of reading comprehension with diagnostic supplements relative to the vocabulary of specific academic areas (e.g., mathematics).
- **Test of Written Language (Hammill and Larsen, 1978).** A comprehensive measure of written expression in the elementary school child.
- **Valett Developmental Survey of Basic Learning Abilities (Valett, 1966b).** This survey looks at skill development in the preschool and early elementary child in several different areas.
- **Vane Kindergarten Test (Vane, 1968).** Administered in part to individuals and in part to small groups, this instrument assesses four-to-six-years-old children's intellectual and academic behaviour and potential.
- **Vineland Social Maturity Scale (Doll, 1953).** A measurement of social development in the form of a social quotient is provided by this easily administered checklist of common behaviours for children up to age seven.
- **Wepman Test of Auditory Discrimination (Wepman, 1958).** Using the task of discriminating like and unlike words in the auditory mode, this quick and very easily administered instrument screens (in a somewhat rougher fashion) for the same behaviours as the previously mentioned Test of Auditory Discrimination (Goldman *et al.,* 1970). In many cases this simpler instrument is rough screening and the more sophisticated test for those cases needing more careful attention.

- **The Peabody Individual Achievement Test (PIAT)-** It includes five subtests: mathematics, spelling, general information and two tests of reading, recognition and comprehension.
- **The Brigance Diagnostic Inventories-**It is a series of measures used in a number of learning disabilities programmes and may be used for diagnostic as well as identification purpose.
- **Anton Brenner Development Gestalt Test of School Readiness (Brenner, 1964)-** Designed to assess school readiness in children five to six years of age, this individually administered instrument discriminates varying rates of maturation on a gifted to retarded continuum.
- **Developmental Indicators for the Assessment of Learning (DIAL)-** This report covers the results of an attempt by the Illinois office of public instruction (1972) to develop a preschool screening instrument.
- **Pre-Kindergarten Descriptive Inventory-**The Fairfield, Connecticut public schools (1972) have compiled a series of quick, individually administered items that are used to help identify needs of children before school entry.
- **The Wide Range Achievement Test (WRAT)-** It is widely used and provides scores in reading, spelling and arithmetic.
- Besides above mentioned tool, tester can use some others tools like— **Terman-meril scale, Wechsler-intelligence scale, Slosson intelligence test for children and adults, Kaufman assessment battery for children** etc.

### 2. *Informal Assessment*

Some of the information on which critical educational intervention is based may be the result of informal assessment. A variety of non-standardised assessment strategies can provide information about both what and how to teach. In the ongoing process of programme evaluation it is necessary to undertake a great deal of informal assessment to assure maximum benefit from the programmes. Informal assessment devices are procedures without rigid administration, scoring and interpretation rules. This assessment includes information gathered through observations of everyday student behaviour, examination of students' products such as papers, tests and presentations through discussion with students. They continue to note that informal assessment is the collecting, evaluating and use of information to establish goals, select strategies and measure outcomes.

There are various types of informal assessments devices, these are:

- **Curriculum-based Assessment:**

  Curriculum-based assessment (CBA) is the process of determining instructional needs by directly assessing specific curriculum skills. The term CBA can be used to describe a variety of assessment techniques that measure student achievement in the curriculum. That uses direct observation and recording of a student's performance in a local school curriculum as a basis for gathering information to make instructional decisions.

  In CBA, uses the actual classroom content to assess how students are progressing relative to their classmates, all of whom have been exposed to similar educational programming. Several investigators have found that decoding and reading comprehension progress can be reliably and validly reflected in the number of words a child reads accurately from a classroom reader in one minute. Spelling progress can be reliably assessed by measuring the number of correct letter pairs in a two-minute spelling list drawn from the curriculum and math progress can be assessed by the number of correct digits in a two minute sample of curriculum problems. Progress in written language can be ascertained from the number of words written in three minutes in response to a story starter or topic sentence.

- **Task Analysis**

  Another informal evaluation procedure assesses mastery of sub-skills by breaking down complex instructional goals into their component skills. In this way, a student's current knowledge can be pinpointed and the next skill to be taught is identified. It can be described as the process of identifying, breaking down and sequencing sub-components of a target behaviour and subsequently evaluating student progress toward the attainment of those sub-component skills. In designing and administering task assessment, the teacher must pinpoint a target behaviour or task and write a terminal objective's. The teacher then must isolate the behaviour selected and analyse it, breaking it down into teachable subtasks described in measurable terms. Once the essential sub-tasks have been determined, an assessment tool is developed containing questions at each level of the sub-task. The task analysis is of great value to the teacher to identify the skill or subskill in which the learning disabled students are experiencing difficulties.

- **Systematic Observation**

  Of the student in the classroom also can provide information about what and how to teach both academic and behavioural goals. In Classroom systematic observation has the advantage of assessing the problem in the setting where it occurs rather than generalising from a strange testing situation.

- **Trial Teaching**

  It is an assessments strategy that gets directly at the how-to-teach question. A variety of instructional techniques are systematically tried and evaluated, including varying materials, methods of presentation or response and types of feedback. In trial teaching, the focus of assessment becomes the responsiveness of the student's perceptions, problem solving, memory to instruction and how well the student applies this learning to novel tasks. The goal is to shed light on the extent and type of supports that will contribute best to a student's learning, as well as obstacles to avoid.

- Besides above **Interview, Questionnaires, Checklists, Case-history, rating scale etc.** also can be used for identification of learning disabled student under informal assessment.

## Model of Rating Scale for Identifying Learning Disabled Children/Students

| | *Above Average* | *Below Average* | *Average Remarks* |
|---|---|---|---|
| **1. READING AND WRITING** | | | |
| ***1. READING*** | | | |
| **(i) Kind of error** | | | |
| • Mispronunciation (example- **miser** pronunciations as **mister**) | | | |
| • Substitution (example-The **horse** was big. The **house** was big. | | | |
| • Refusal (Example) • This parrot is **very beautiful.** • The parrot is. | | | |
| • Addition (Example) • The cat ran after the rat. • The cat **fast** ran after the rat. | | | |
| • Omission (Example) • This is **my** scale. • This is scale. | | | |
| • Reversal (Example) • was—**saw**, no—**on**, oh—**ho** | | | |
| • Distortion (Example) • Rakesh • **Rahhes** | | | |
| • Accuracy | | | |
| • Speed | | | |
| • Spelling (incorrect) | | | |
| • Punctuation | | | |
| • Mature vocabulary | | | |
| • Attention on important word and letter | | | |
| • Verbal expression of precise and elaborate way | | | |

- Letter identification
  - Example—**U V, b d, p q**
- Word identification
  - Example—except—**accept**

**(ii) Writing**

- Neatness
- Legibility
- Speed
- Correct spelling
- Appropriate use of vocabulary
- Write word and sentence according to topic
- Precise and elaborate writing

**(iii) Others**

- Sequencing and organisation of thoughts
- Relevance of answers
- Conceptualisation of answer
- Elaboration of answer
- Difficulty in relating ideas in logical sequence
- Articulation problem

**2. *MATHEMATICS***

- Accuracy of additions
- Accuracy of subtraction
- Accuracy of multiplications
- Accuracy of division
- Accuracy of sequencing/order of numbering
- Example—**31, 32, 33, 34, 35, 63, 64.....**
- Recognise of number
- Example—**69, 36, 63, 45, 54.......**

**3. *PERSONAL AND SOCIAL BEHAVIOUR***

- Understanding of verbal instructions
- Understanding class-room discussions
- Retaining and recalling information
- Word recall
- Expression and confusion of facts and ideas
- Obeying classroom rules
- Staying in seat feel restless
- Unable to complete assigned work

- Recognise one's surroundings
  - time
  - place
  - direction
  - relationship
- Get along with peers
- Attending and listening to the teacher
- Co-operation
- Attention
- Organising ability
- Social acceptance (owns and other's)
- Responsibility
- Tactfulness

4. ***MOTOR CO-ORDINATION***
   - General co-ordination
     - (example—hands and feet at the same time and for same task)
   - Balance
     - (example—using their body of different way)
   - Manual dexterity
   - Awkword movements and are restless

- ***COGNITIVE***
  - Focusing on things
  - Memory process
  - Disparity between area of functioning
  - Experience considerable difficulty

NOTE —- *In above mentioned tool (rating scale), items related to different areas of identification learning disabled children are given. This will respond in form of above average, average, below average and remarks. There are some items whose response a tester/ researcher/teacher/identifier could get above average, average, below average but for some items tester…. Will have to write details in remark section through observation.*

## One more type of Assessment, i.e. Authentic Assessment

In recent years there has been a shift away from traditional standardised and paper-pencil classroom tests, toward strategies that are believed to better reflect learning outcomes that are "worthwhile, significant and meaningful-in short, authentic". These include exhibits, demonstrations, performances (art, music, play), experiments, debates, oral reports, written reaction papers to readings, portfolios of work samples and more. Portfolios can include seminal works that demonstrate motivation and mastery, multiple examples of concrete progress toward a goal, or evolving perceptions, strategies and thoughts as one progresses toward completion. These techniques refocus attention onto student-selected work that students value as important and reflective of their learning, rather than assessing only final outcomes of the teacher's choosing."

Authentic assessment encourages students to self-evaluate and offers a form of feedback that makes much more sense and is more instructionally useful than that garnered from rests. Authentic assessment approaches have been received with much excitement among educators and there is recognition that reliability and validity considerations are just as important here as with other types of assessment approaches.

## Diagnostic Approaches

The ability training model and skill model represent two fundamentally different approaches to the diagnostic prescriptive teaching process.

## Major Models Helpful in Assessment

### Ability Model

In the ability model the psycho-educational focus is on identifying strengths and weakness in ability or process areas and in assessing levels of performance in academic areas. This model is based on the premise that the cause of the learning problem is within the individual. Stresses the position that Learning disabled students suffer from impairment or dysfunctions in processes that are essential to learning. Perceptual –motor, visual perception, short attention span and auditory perception are some of the process areas that are highlighted. The basic tenets includes—

1. The basis of the learning problem is within the child (e.g. in information procession).
2. These processes underlie academic functioning.
3. These processes can be identified and strength and weaknesses can be assessed.

4. Valid and reliable instruments exist that assess the specified processes.
5. These processes can be remediated.
6. The student can benefit from teaching methods that are based on strengths and weaknesses identified in the process areas.

Some of the most commonly used tests for assessment of process or ability areas are:

1. Illinois test of psycholinguistic abilities.
2. Wepman auditory discrimination test.
3. Detroit tests of learning aptitude.
4. Frosting developmental test of visual perception.
5. Developmental test of visual-motor integration.
6. Subtests of the Wechsler intelligence scales for children and adults.
7. Slingerland screening tests for identifying children with specific language disability.

**Skill Model**

In the skill model—representing a behavioural viewpoint, features assessment of specific academic skills and task analysis (analysing the behaviour component and perquisite skill of a task), this model emphasises direct instruction in either the terminal academic behaviour or its immediate antecedents. Frequently a skill hierarchy is used in assessment and instruction. The basic tenets include

1. The locus of the handicap is primarily outside the child (i.e. an experience deficit exists).
2. Behaviour assessed is directly observable.
3. Test items should be similar to tasks demanded of the child in the classroom.
4. There is a hierarchy of skill and learners must sequentially pass through the steps.
5. There is a criterion of acceptable performance.
6. Direct skill instruction corrects inadequate responses.
7. Students can learn to generalise specific responses across condition.

While the skill approach uses standardised academic achievement tests, the major assessment procedures are non-standardised, consisting primarily of teacher-devised measures (informal) direct observations and criterion-referenced tests. After the initial assessment, the teacher measures pupil's progress on daily or continuously basis on the student's present level of functioning within a skill hierarchy.

## Conclusion

In brief, it is clear through above statements that learning disabled students can learn and educate all types of letter and words such as normal child. For this, firstly recognition of all those students is very necessary. Because we have to find in which area and type of learning problem those student are having. Besides it, diagnostic model- skill and ability is also helpful for screening of learning disabled student.

## References


- *A Guide of Informal Assessment*, www.brighthubeducation.com, retrieved on 04/09/15.
- *Advantages and Disadvantages of Formal and Informal Assessment*, www.termpaperwarehouse.com, retrieved on 04/09/15.
- Anastasi, A. and Urbani, S. (2006). *Psychological Testing.* New Delhi: Dorling Kindersley Pvt. Ltd.
- Bender, W.N. (2002). *Differentiating instruction for students with learning disabilities, Best Teaching Practices for General and Special Educators, A Joint Publication Council for Exceptional Children.* California: A Sage Publication Company Thousand Oaks, Corwin Press, INC.
- *Comprehensive Assessment and Evaluation of Students with Learning Disabled,* www.nasponline.org, retrieved on 04/09/15.
- Ellis, N. (2005). *One-room Schools holding on in Rural America,* Morning Education.
- *Forms of Assessment: Informal, Formal, Paper-Pencil, Study.Com,* retrieved on 04/09/15.
- Friend, M. and Bursuck, W.D. (2nd Edition). *Including Students with Special Needs A Practical Guide for Classroom Teachers.* London: Allyn and Bacon.
- Gerzel-short, L. and Wilkins, E.A. (2009). *Response to Intervention: Helping all Students Learn.* Kappa Delta pi Record. 45(3).
- Guerin, G. and Maier, A. (1983). Informal Assessment in Education. Mayfield, Palo Alto, CA.
- Gupta, S. P. and Gupta, A. (2006). *Modern Measurement and Evaluation (With Statistics).* Allahabad: Sharda Pustak Bhawan.

- Gwattney, T. (2001). *The Era of the Rural School.* Childhood Education, 78 (2).
- Jenkins, J. and Pany, D. (1978). *Standardised Achievement Tests: How Useful for Special Education?* Exceptional Children.
- Joeseph, R.A. (2004). *Vikas Shiksha Avam Punarvas.* Varanasi: Samakalan Publishers.
- Kerlinger, F.N. (2011). *Foundation of Behavioural Research.* Delhi: Surgeet Publication.
- Kirk, S.A. and Kirk, W.D. (1971). *Psycholinguistic Learning Disabilities: Diagnosis and Remediation.* Urbana: University of Illinois Press.
- Johnson, S.W. and Morasky, R.L. (1980). *Learning Disabilities.* London: Allyn and Bacon, INC.
- Mercer, C.D. (1979). *Children and Adolescents with Learning Disabilities.* London: Charles E. Merrill Publishing Co.
- Overton, T. (3rd Edition). *Assessment in special education an applied approach.* New Jersy: Prentice Hall, Upper Saddle River.
- Panda, K.C. (1997). *Education of Exceptional Children.* New Delhi: Vikas Publishing House.
- Prakash, P. (2008). *Education of Exceptional Children, Challenges and Strategies.* New Delhi: Kanishka Publication.
- Rachel Martinez and Andria Young (2011). *Response to Intervention: How is it Practiced and Perceived?* University of Houston, Victoria In International Journal of Special Education, issn-0827 3383, Vol. 26, No.1, p. 44.
- Reddy, G.L., Raman, R. and Kusuma, A. (2003*). Learning Disabilities, A practical Guide to Practitioner.* New Delhi: Discovery Publishing House.
- Reddy, G.L. and Sujathamalini, J. (2006). *Children with disabilities: Awareness, attitude and competencies of teachers.* New Delhi: Discovery Publishing House.
- Singh, M. (2010). *Education of Children with Special Needs.* New Delhi: Kanishka Publishers.
- Smead, V.S. (1977). *Ability Training and Task Analysis in Diagnostic/ Prescriptive Teaching.* The Journal of Special Education, 11(1).
- Smith, C.R. (1998). *Learning Disabilities the Interaction of Learner, Task and Setting.* London: Allyn and Bacon.
- Spreen, O. (1988). *Learning Disabled Children Growing Up, A Follow-up into Adulthood, Modern Approaches to the Diagnosis and Instruction of Multi Handicapped Children.* New York: Oxford University Press.
- Tahilians, H. (2004). *Learning Disability; A Remedial Programme.* Delhi: Gagan Deep Publications.
- Thorndike, R.A. and Christ, T.T. (2010). *Measurement and Evaluation in Psychology and Education.* New Delhi: PHI Learning Private Limited.

- Tucker, J. (1985). *Curriculum-Based assessment: An introduction, Exceptional Children.*
- Tucker, J. (1987). *Curriculum-Based assessment is no fad.* The Collaborative Educator, 1 (14).
- Werts, M.G., Culatta, R.A. and Tompkins, J.R. (2007). *Fundamentals of Special Education what Every Teachers Needs to know*. New Delhi: PHI Learning Private Limited.
- Ysseldyke, J.E. and Salvia, J. (1974). *Diagnostic Prescriptive Teaching: Two model*, Exceptional Children, 41.
- Ysseldyke, J.E., Algozzine, B. and Thurlow, M. (1998). *Critical issues in special education.* New Delhi: Kanishka Publishers.

# Chapter - 3

# Learning Disability: Challenges in Identification and Assessment

*— Dr Arvind Sharma*

**Abstract**

*Learning Disability lacks recognition as a disability in India. The acute lack of teacher awareness, assessment procedures or indigenous tools for assessment of processing deficits, intelligence testing and testing for proficiency in reading and writing further complicates the inherent complexities of the notion of Learning Disability (Karanth, 2002). While planning to make a diagnosis of LD one has to be considered that LD significantly interferes with academic and daily living that requires reading, mathematical and writing skills of children who affected with it. The issues that in particular make identification and assessment of children with Learning Disabilities in India difficult and challenging and that need to be addressed for timely treatment and remediation of the children are identification criteria, identification of reasons for the occurrence of a particular Learning Disability, identification of co-occurrence of other deficits along with Learning Disabilities in an individual, the implications of Learning Disabilities on the educational, personal and social life and intellectual functioning of an individual. Therefore present paper will through light upon few challenges regarding identification and assessment of Learning Disabilities.*

***Key words:*** *Learning Disability, Diagnosis, Assessment.*

## Introduction

The term 'Learning Disability' was first coined in 1963 by Dr Samuel Kirk, a psychologist, while delivering a speech at an education conference held in Chicago (Hammill, 1990). Learning Disability (LD) is a group of neurodevelopment disorders manifesting as persistent difficulties in learning to efficiently read (dyslexia), write (dysgraphia) or perform mathematical calculations (dyscalculia) despite normal intelligence, conventional schooling, intact hearing and vision, adequate motivation and socio-cultural opportunity (Lagae, 2008). Children with LD present with academic problems such as reading slowly and incorrectly, skipping lines while reading aloud, making repeated spelling mistakes, untidy/illegible hand-writing with poor sequencing and inability to perform even simple mathematics. They invariably fail to achieve school grades at a level that is matching with their intellectual abilities (Sharma, A, 2005). L Dafflicts almost 5-15 per cent of school-going children (Katusic, 2001).This invisible neurological handicap is believed to be a result of functional disruption in neural systems rather than an anatomic problem and is genetically inherited.

Depending on the type of difficulty and the related symptoms evident in a learner with Learning Disability, the disability may be classified into Dyslexia ('Word Blindness' or 'Reading disorder' leading to difficulty in reading, writing and spelling), Dyscalculia (difficulty in computation, Math, concepts of time and money), Dysgraphia (difficulty in written expression leading to illegible handwriting, spelling and composition), Dyspraxia (difficulty in fine motor skills and co-ordination), Auditory Processing disorder (difficulty in Interpreting auditory information affecting language development and reading), Visual Processing disorder (difficulty in interpreting visual information affecting reading, writing and math). When accompanied with other related disorders like Attention Deficit Hyperactivity Disorder (ADHD), the level of concentration and focus in learners as well gets affected, who as a result exhibit over-activity, get easily distracted and tend to be impulsive. Difficulty in sitting still, losing interest quickly, handling complexity, adaption and flexibility, attending to and remembering differentiation, judgement, symbolic thought perception of the patterns and rhythms of forms in knowledge and reflection are areas affected that probably define the abilities of individuals with Learning Disabilities (Crealock, *et. al.,* 1993).

## Diagnosing Learning Disabilities

While planning to make a diagnosis of LD one has to be considered that LD significantly interferes with academic and daily living that requires reading, mathematical and writing skills of children who affected with it. The classroom teacher plays the pivotal role in suspecting this condition early as he/she is the first to get an opportunity to closely observe a child's academic functioning in the school. A history of language delay, not attending to the sounds of words (trouble playing rhyming games with words, or confusing words that sound alike), along with a family history, are important red flags for dyslexia in preschool children (Shaywitz, 1998). An evaluation for Learning Disability should be considered for all children presenting with learning problems in preschool/school or those who get poor marks or grades in examinations in spite of having seemingly normal intelligence (Karande and Kulkarni, 2005). A conclusive diagnosis of Learning Disability cannot be made until the child is in the third grade, or about seven-eight years old, as some children are "normal late developers" and they outgrow their learning problems, unlike Learning Disability, which is a life-long disorder. However, children in the age group of five-seven years who have academic difficulties should also be assessed and if they display signs of Learning Disability on educational assessment should be considered as "at risk for Learning Disability" and remedial education started. These children need to be retested at eight years of age to either confirm or rule out the diagnosis of Learning Disability.

A multidisciplinary team comprising of pediatrician, counsellor, clinical psychologist and special educator is required for diagnosing Learning Disability. If Learning Disability goes undetected, the child's academic problems have an adverse impact on his or her quality of life, viz. self-image, peer and family relationships and social interactions (Karande *et. al.,* 2009). Unfortunately, in our country, many children with Learning Disability often remain undiagnosed because of a general lack of awareness leading to chronic poor school performance, class detention and even dropping out of school.

## Challenges in Identification and Assessment

The primary issues in the identification and assessment of Learning Disability appear to be the construction and validation of identification tools, identification criteria, identification of reasons for the occurrence of a particular Learning Disability, identification of co-occurrence of other deficits along with Learning Disabilities in an individual, the implications of Learning Disabilities on the educational, personal and social life and intellectual functioning of an individual, the probable causes of the deficit and the need and relevance of specific interventions and effect of remediation on an individual with Learning Disabilities. The issues that in particular make identification and assessment of children with Learning Disabilities in India difficult and challenging and that need to be addressed for timely treatment and remediation of the children are:

## Multidisciplinary Nature of the Field

Opinions about what constitutes a learning disability vary in (Moats,1993), part because LD is the concern of many disciplines and professions, including education, psychology, neurology, neuropsychology, optometry, psychiatry and speech and language pathology, to name a few. Each of these disciplines has traditionally focused on different aspects of the child or adult with learning disability, so divergent ideas and contentious disagreements exist about the importance of etiology, diagnostic methods, intervention methods and professional roles and responsibilities (Torgesen, 1991). It is not surprising that so many children are identified because each professional may view the child through his or her own idiosyncratic clinical lens. For example, optometrists may identify a child as having a learning disability if the youngster displays difficulties in visual tracking. Speech and language pathologists, on the other hand, become concerned if the child's vocabulary and syntactic development are not commensurate with expectations. Educators become concerned primarily when development in reading, writing and mathematics is deficient.

## Lack of Specific Identification Criteria

Probably the most significant and persistent problem in the field is the lack of a precise definition and a theoretically based classification system that would allow (1) the identification of different types of learning disabilities and (2) a means of recognising distinctions and interrelationships between types of learning disabilities and other learning disorders such as mental retardation, attention deficit disorder, speech and language difficulties and general academic underachievement (Fletcher *et. al,* 1991). At present, the field continues to construct and use vague and ambiguous definitions that rely heavily on the exclusion of alternative diagnoses. Lack of adherence to a consistent definition of Learning Disabilities to emphasise on the intrinsic and life-long nature of the condition; the understanding, acceptance and willingness to accommodate normal variations in learning and behaviour; sufficient competent personnel and appropriate programmes to support the efforts of teachers to accommodate the needs of children who do not have Learning Disabilities but who require alternative instructional methods; insufficient supply of competently prepared professionals to diagnose and manage exceptional individuals; false belief that underachievement is synonymous with Specific Learning Disability; the incorrect assumption that quantitative formulas alone can be used to diagnose Learning Disabilities; failure of multidisciplinary teams to consider and integrate findings related to the presenting problems; comprehensive assessment practices, procedures and instruments necessary to differentiate Learning Disabilities from other types of learning problems and preference for the label "Learning Disability" over "mental retardation" or "emotional disturbance," which leads to the misclassification of some individuals, are the primary issues in the identification of Learning Disabilities (NJCLD).

Epidemiological studies of Learning Disability are also fraught with difficulties ranging from the very definition of Learning Disability, identification and assessment, to socio-cultural factors unique to India and its implications in a pluralistic society being immense and cannot be easily dealt with (Karanth, 2002); where each type of Learning Disability needs to be individually addressed instead of being addressed under the broader umbrella term 'Learning Disability'.

## Issue of Stigma and Labelling

Stanovich (1993) observers argue that the term "learning disability" is too broad to be of any diagnostic value. He proposes that the general term learning disabilities be abandoned and that definitional and research efforts focus on the specific types of disabilities that are now identified in ambiguous terms. As noted earlier, the generic term learning disabilities encompasses disabilities in seven categories. Given the complexity and heterogeneity of each of these disabilities, it seems unrealistic to expect that any definitional clarity can be achieved by grouping them together under one label. To do so only obscures the critical features of each disability and makes research findings difficult to interpret. Definitions of specific learning disabilities can be more easily and successfully operationalised than generic definitions, as there search on disability in basic reading skills shows (Lyon, 1991). To establish valid prevalence estimates for the number of individuals with learning disabilities, the first step should be to establish explicit diagnostic criteria for each of the seven specific disability domains. At present, the greatest progress toward this goal has been in the area of disability in basic reading skills.

A major barrier which the children with disabilities experienced at school is often the attitude of the regular teachers (Agbenyega, 2007; Wall, 2002; Yu *et. al.,* 2011), who often considering children with disabilities as the responsibility of the resource teachers, hold them to be a 'disturbance' to the class causing distractions which delay course completion, hence, ignoring their presence and concentrating on execution of their lesson plans (Das and Kattumuri, 2014). While the intentions of the teachers generally appear to be noble and accommodating, they are found to lack the tendency to effectively engage students with special needs in the classroom (Gerber, 1992 and Soni, 2004). Also, the lack of sufficient knowledge and understanding about their students is another hindrance, though there seems to be the willingness to learn (Sengupta and Biswas, 2003). However there is no evidence of acceptance of a total inclusion (Avranides and Norwitch, 2002). The beliefs, attitudes and perceptions of regular teachers about students with disabilities and inclusive education play a significant role in the acceptance of these students and also the commitment of regular teachers in implementing and promoting inclusion (Opdal and Wormnaes, 2001).

The attitude of the parents of non-disabled children also poses hindrance for inclusion in regular schools when they resist accepting children with disabilities to study in the same class as their non-disabled child. Sometimes, parents of the children with disabilities themselves prefer 'alternative schooling' for their 'disabled' child in hope for some vocational gains, relaxations or to gain the benefit of medical rehabilitation, or in an attempt to escape bullying of their child by the non-disabled peers in regular schools.

Parents of children with Learning Disabilities usually are also not comfortable accepting their child's 'Learning Disability' and often lack the knowledge to use appropriate remedial education for learning difficulties. The lack of awareness in the community, parents and teachers, about Learning Disabilities and also regarding the provisions available for them, is yet another issue. While some teachers, administrators, professionals and parents, do seem to be aware of the concept of inclusive education, but are often not aware as to how it can be implemented in ordinary settings (Shahazadi, 2000; Crabtree and Williams, 2011). 'Parents often resort to concealing the fact lest the school would reject admission, pretending to be ignorant of the fact and waiting for the school to discover the child's special needs' (Sundaram, 2006). The expectations and anguish of the parents is in some ways justified for want of empathy from the schools for a typically developing children.

## Scarcity of Standardised Tools

Most of the tools used in India are either Western tools or adaption of Western tools. These tools used in India are a one-time-task, lacking revision, owing to the lack of credential body of experts and sufficient financial resources for periodic revisions with respect to their usability, reliability, validity and norms across different states in the country. Also ready-made standardised assessment tools are not available in the different languages to suit the multilingual social context of the country hence frequently criticised for being insensitive to the reader's linguistic environment and the characteristics of their writing system. Indigenous, language based reading assessment tests should be used that are sensitive to the characteristics of each language and its script specific features since reading processes depend on the nature of language and its script-specific features (Prema and Karanth, 2003).

## Lack of Teacher Awareness and Competency

In India, Learning Disability unfortunately lacks recognition as a disability. The acute lack of teacher awareness, assessment procedures or indigenous tools for assessment of processing deficits, intelligence testing and testing for proficiency in reading and writing further complicates the inherent complexities of the notion of Learning Disability (Karanth, 2002). The teacher certification programmes in India are short of sufficient courses in special education to prepare general education teachers for inclusive classrooms. Owing to the lack of proper training in the area, lack of familiarity with reading process and areas of reading skills which require assessment, creativity and 'trial and error' is what guides the course of remediation (Mirchandani and Sundaram, 2006). The role of speech language pathologists who are required to work in close co-ordination with teachers to set appropriate goals and activities for children in their classrooms and design intervention programmes for targeted children, is undermined in being determined by the clinical setting in which they work and in most cases the most important factor influencing their involvement with reading disability is their own interest, limiting successful intervention (Nirupama and Karanth, 2003).

## Lack of Proper Research in the Area

Learning Disabilities in India is relatively a new and less explored area, with only selected centres and departments being interested and involved in researching this field. The educational system in the country lays particular emphasis on 'knowing' rather than 'learning' and 'theory' in place of 'application' and is therefore inappropriate for students with Learning Disabilities. It is imperative to examine the issues pertaining to assessment and remediation in the Indian context since there is lack of indigenous research and the preference and dominance of Western adaptations in absence of an appropriate need-based assessment.

Most of the researches and intervention in the area of Learning Disabilities in India is being undertaken by the non-government and private organisations, with little substantial communication and participation between them and the state educational authorities. Further a divide exists also between the personnel in the health and educational fields in both the private and government sector hindering in effective medical interventions, though early identification and prevention programmes and provision of early intervention in basic reading skills in primary-grade general education classrooms can reduce the number of students with reading problems by upto70 per cent (Lyon, *et. al.*, 2001). In the researches done on Dyscalculia, the deficits are found to point towards two patterns of brain dysfunction; one where there are impairments of auditory perception, semantic memory and phonemic discrimination, whereas no deficits being in visuo- spatial skills, showing such children to be more deficient in reading and spelling than in arithmetic. These deficits have been interpreted as indicative of left hemisphere damage. In the other group of Dyscalculia, impairments of visuo-spatial perception, visuo-spatial analysis, tactual discrimination and finger agnosia are found while their auditory abilities remaining intact. This group is more impaired in arithmetic than in reading and writing and the deficits in neuropsychological functions indicative of right hemisphere damage (Rao, 2003). Studies done across several countries prove that the typologies have clinical significance from the viewpoint of diagnosis and warn against the improper clubbing of all children with Dyscalculia into one group, stressing on the rehabilitation programmes for these children to be planned carefully keeping in mind the nature of dysfunction. Within the multi-factorial framework, the gene-gene and gene-environment interactions may be a reason for the different symptoms in the Dyslexia spectrum resulting in other conditions like ADHD (Attention Deficit Hyperactivity Disorder) and CAPD (Central Auditory Processing Disorder) which surface in future implying that 'Specific Learning Difficulty' is more than just a difficulty with learning involved and one of the symptoms (McGrath *et. al.,* 2006).

Researches need to be conducted to understand the speech perception mechanisms in children with CAPD (Central Auditory Processing Deficits in Children with Learning Disability) to design comprehensive rehabilitation strategies, as no single test can provide complete information and may fail to detect the deficit at a particular level (Shivshankar, 2003).

## Indian Scenario

In India, learning disability is relatively a new and less explored area. Only selected centres and University's' departments has been interested and involved in researching in this field. Since 1st April 2010, the Government of India has implemented the Right of Children to Free and Compulsory Education 2009 (RTE Act) which makes education free and compulsory to all children, including those with disabilities, in the 6-14 years age group. A recent Parliamentary

Committee has suggested that LD be included in the definition of "child with disability" in the Right of Children to Free and Compulsory Education (Amendment) Bill 2010 (Dhar, 2010). Once LD is recognised as a disability, ample funds from the Sarva Shiksha Abhiyan, which is the flagship program for implementation of the RTE Act, would become available for the benefit of children with LD (Karande, 2010). These funds can be utilised to train classroom teachers, set up resource rooms in schools and employ remedial teachers. At present many children with LD studying in non-English (vernacular) medium schools and especially in rural areas, are going undetected for non-availability of standardised psychological and educational tests. Funds from this programme could be utilised by educational institutes to develop standardised psychological and educational tests in all Indian languages. Funds could also be utilised to start the undergraduate and postgraduate degree courses for people wanting to become remedial teachers and special educators.

## Conclusion

In a nutshell, the issues in identification and assessment are pivotal. Most authorities have expressed alarm at the rapid growth of students being identified as having learning disabilities. Critics of the field have used this expansion as evidence that this is an ill-defined category consisting of many students who need nothing more than better instruction from general education teachers. Defenders of the field are also concerned that much of this growth is unwarranted and indicative of confusion over definition and diagnostic criteria. They fear many children are being misdiagnosed and that the increase has provided ammunition for critics, there by jeopardising services for students who truly have learning disabilities.

Some have noted that increase in the number of students identified as learning disabled has occurred in direct proportion to the decrease in number of students identified as mentally retarded. They have identified that greater reluctance of parents to identify children as mentally retarded resulted in over identification of children as learning disabled. Another reason for increase in prevalence of learning disabled may be because is relatively new. It may take few years to decide how to identify children in this category. Teachers in countries like India where LD is not widely understood have the onus of explaining the nature of the problem to the parents and helping them to, both, understand and accept it. Given the complexities of the situation, the only children with LD in India who have managed are those, whose parents are sensitive to the needs of their child and managed to provide extensive and at times alternate support during their school years. A few changes that have come about in terms of educational and legal provisions have also been the result of parental activism. Parental understanding and support will continue to be the most crucial factor in the successful education of children with LD. Nevertheless, with greater sensitivity on the part of the teacher and the society at large, the parental burdens can be ameliorated at least to some extent.

Summarily, it is to acknowledge the complexity of LD and move towards more comprehensive diagnostic procedures that incorporate the complexity. The goal should be complete description of LD.

## References


- Francis, D.J., Fletcher, J.M., Shaywitz, B.A., Shaywitz, S.E. and Rourke, B. (1996). *De_ning learning and language disabilities: Conceptual and psychometric issues with the use of IQ tests*, Language, Speech and Hearing Services in Schools, Vol. 27, pp.132-143.
- Jha, Madan, M. (2010). *From Special to Inclusive Education in India: Case Studies of Three Schools in Delhi.* Pearson Education India.
- Kaniel, Shlomo and Feuerstein, Reuven. (2006). Special Needs of Children with Learning Difficulties. Oxford Review of Education, Vol. 15, No. 2, pp. 165-179.
- Karanth, P. *Learning disabilities in the Indian context.* [Online]. 2002; Available at:http://www.nalandainstitute.org/asp_les/ learning.asp
- Karanth, P. (2003). 'Introduction'. In Karanth and Joe Rozario (eds), *Learning Dis-abilities in India: Willing the Mind to Learn* (pp.17-29). New Delhi: Sage Publications.
- Kirk, S.A. (1963). *Behavioral diagnosis and remediation of learning disabilities. In Conference on the Exploration of the Perceptually Handicapped Child.* Evanston, IL: Fund for Perceptually Handicapped Children, pp.1–7.
- Kulkarni M, Karande, S, Thadhani, A, Maru, H, Sholapurwala, R. (2006). *Educational provisions and learning disability.* Indian J Pediatr.; 73: 789-93.
- Karande, S. (2008). Current challenges in managing specific learning disability in Indian children. J Postgrad Med.; 54:75-7.

- Karande, S, Bhosrekar, K, Kulkarni, M, Thakker, A. (2009). *Health-related quality of life of children with newly diagnosed specific learning disability.* J Trop Pediatr.; 55:160-9.
- Kyleigh Schubert (2011). *Teaching students with Learning Disabilities and Attention Deficit Hyperactivity Disorder.*
- Lagae L. (2008). *Learning disabilities: definitions, epidemiology, diagnosis and intervention strategies.*Pediatr Clin North Am.; 55:1259-68.
- Lyon, G.R., Gray, D.B., Kavanagh, J.F. and Krasnegor, N.A., eds. (1993. *Better understanding learning disabilities: New views from research and their implications for education and public policies.* Baltimore:Paul H. Brookes.
- Mirchandani, P. (2006*). Dyslexia. India Parenting: An On-line Newsletter.* Available at: www. indiaparenting.com/articles/data/artl0 007.shtml
- Mishna, F. (2003). *Learning disabilities and bullying: Double jeopardy,* Journal of Learning Disabilities, Vol. 36, pp. 336-347.
- Mukhopadhyay, S. and Mani, M.N.G. *Education for All, Year 2000 Assessment: Education of Children with Special Needs* (2002) in Govinda, R. (Ed.), Education India 2000. New Delhi: Oxford Press.
- Prema, K.S. and Karanth, P. (2003). *Assessment of Learning Disability: Language Based Tests.*P.Karanth and J. Rozario (Ed). Learning Disability in India: Willing the Mind to Learn. Sage: New Delhi.
- Ramaa, S. (2000), *Two Decades of Research on Learning Disabilities in India.* Dyslexia News Worldwide. John Wiley and Sons, pp. 268-283.
- Sharma, Arvind (2011). *Diagnosis and Remediation of Language Disabilities*, Lambert Academic Publishing, Germany.
- Shaywitz, B.A. and Shaywitz, S.E. (1994). *Measuring and analysing change.* In *Frames of reference for the assessment of learning disabilities: New views on measurement issues*. G.R. Lyon, ed. Baltimore: Paul H. Brookes, pp. 29-58.
- Shaywitz, S.E., Fletcher, J.M. and Shaywitz, B.A. (1994). *Issues in the definition and classification of attention deficit disorder.* Topics in Language Disorders 14:1-25.
- Torgesen, J.K. (1991). *Learning disabilities: Historical and conceptual issues. In Learning about learning disabilities.* B.Y.L. Wong, ed. New York: Academic Press, pp. 3-39.
- Yu, L., Su, X. and Liu, C. (2011): *Issues of teacher education and inclusion in China.* PROSPECTS, Vol. 1, No. 41, pp. 355-369.
- Zigmond, N. (1993). *Learning disabilities from an educational perspective. In Better understanding learning disabilities: New views from research and their implications for education and public policies*. G.R. Lyon, D.B. Gray, J.F. Kavanagh and N.A. Krasnegor, eds. Baltimore: Paul H. Brookes, pp. 251-72.

# Chapter - 4

# Learning Disabled: Understanding the Misunderstood

— *Dr Rashmi Singh*

## Abstract

*The history of learning disability is relatively young. Prior to 1940s there was no clear cut definition and concept of learning disability. Learning disabled students were regarded as lazy, dumb and mentally retarded. Gradually with the advent of technological innovation and the pioneering work of many educators, psychologists and neuro-pathologists, the picture of learning disability became somewhat concretized. But the problem is that still there are many myths prevalent in general class regarding characteristics of learning disabled students. They are still considered in general as mentally retarded by parents and some class room teachers also. But now it is becoming very clear that the I.Q. of a learning disabled student is either average or above the average. So there is lot of awareness required in this direction, i.e. learning disability is a neurological disorder. It is the result of a nervous system that has been wired a little differently. The brain is not retarded but it processes information in a certain different way than the usual. There are other clear cut causal factors for being learning disabled. This paper will try to uncover several myths regarding learning disability and try to present this concept in totality. So that one can diagnose learning disabled students correctly and provide them special education accordingly. Eventually then learning disabled students can overcome their weaknesses and work on their strengths resulting in their academic and social excellence.*

***Key words:*** *Learning disability, Mental-retardness, Neurological disorder, Information processing, Special education, Academic and Social excellence.*

## Introduction

Article 26 of the Universal Declaration of human rights has stated that everyone has the right to education. India has taken sixty two more years for commencement of right to education in April 2010. This means every individual has a basic right to education whether he or she is a special child or the normal one. Special children demand special type of education in accordance with their special needs. It should be the joint responsibility of centre and state to provide such type of education to the needy ones. Prior to this, it is necessary that first of all there is clear cut diagnosis of children's specialties in each side of continuum, i.e., both on the positive and negative sides. It is sad to acknowledge that there are many myths prevalent in society regarding various types of special children in which learning disabled students top the list. It is the call of the hour that there must be awareness regarding clear understanding of peculiarities of learning disabled students, then only one can talk about their special education programme.

1. **Understanding Learning Disability:** A learning disability is a neurological based processing problem. In such cases, brain of an individual has wired differently, hence it processes information in a different or in a faulty manner that's why individual has behaved differently. Such as cortex of the brain has four main functions: language skills, motor skills, thinking skills and organisation skills, if any or all of these areas have been wired in a different manner, the individual has shown disability in the respective field.

So we can say learning disability or LD is an umbrella term which includes various disorders related to listening, speaking, reading, reasoning and mathematical calculations. Gradually with the expansion of knowledge related to the phenomenon of LD, it has become clear that LD may also include an attention deficit component whereas ADHD (Attention Deficit Hyperactivity Disorder) is a different thing. LD has no correlation with lower intelligence, instead for being learning disabled, a person must has average or above average intelligence.

The discrepancy between his capability and achievement is an indication of LD. Hence LD is also termed as hidden handicap or hidden disabilities. Because the person looks perfectly normal but behaves differently when compared with the person of the same age. It could be happen that learning disabled children remain unnoticed by parents and teachers and may be tagged as "underachievers", "dumb" and "lazy".

Many special educators such as Richard Lavoie and Janet Z. Giller has advocated that learning disability has a social component also. These children feel out of step with their peers and being ridiculed most often because they fail to understand non-verbal communication and gestures, misperceive the meaning of a tone, interrupt with other one's space and unable to respond empathetically. Hence training in social skills is utmost important for inclusion in their special education programme. After all a successful social life is the first requirement for a child's happiness and overall growth.

**2. History of Learning Disability:** Before we move further about in-depth knowledge of LD, we have to look back in the history of evolution of LD. The field of learning disability is relatively newer. It has its recent past. Prior to 1937, LD has not found its recognition in literature. Till 1940 to 1960, students with learning disabilities were thought to be slow learners. First time in 1960, it was found that many children who had been classified as mentally retarded were having normal intelligence when tested. William Cruickshank has suggested that their progress was being hindered by deficits in perception and deficit in attention (Harwell, 2008).

The term learning disabilities has been attributed to Samuel Kirk, who used it in public during a presentation to a group of parents at the first conference of the Association for Children with Learning Disabilities in 1963. The most significant event of the 1970s was the passage of public law 94-142 (the Education of All Handicapped Children Act) by congress of USA in 1975. This law became known as the "mainstreaming" law. In the late 1980s the Regular Education Initiative (REI) encouraged special education and regular education to join the resources. "Inclusion" was the buzzword then. It was assumed that special children would be better served by their general education teachers in regular classrooms; if their teachers had help from special education personnel. In 1990, Public law 94-142 was retitled and expanded. It is now called the Individuals with Disabilities Education Act (IDEA) (Harwell, 2008).

Now the situation of learning disability is very much clear. The 2002 LD roundtable produced the following latest definition of learning disability as: SLD are specific in the sense that these disorders each significantly affect a relatively narrow range of academic and performance outcomes.

SLD may occur in combination with other disability conditions but they are not primarily to other conditions such as intellectual disability, behavioural disturbance, lack of opportunities to learn or primary sensory deficits (Bradley *et. al.,* 2002).

**3. Types of Learning Disability**: As it has been proved now that mis-wiring of brain in certain areas given rise to the phenomenon of learning disability. Hence which type of wiring is disaffected in the brain that type of disability has been produced? Sometimes these problems may co-occur with other disorders of attention and execution but they are significantly distinct. Calculation and each type has specific name for it which are as follows (Cortiella, 2014):

**3.1. Dyslexia:** It is a specific learning disability (SLD) that affects an individual's reading and related language based processing skills. Its common characteristics are:

- Difficulty with phonemic awareness (the ability to break up words into their component sounds and difficulty with matching letter combinations to specific sounds).
- Difficulty with accurate or fluent word recognition or both, word decoding, reading rate, reading comprehension and written expression.

**3.2. Dysgraphia:** It is a SLD that affects an individual' handwriting ability and fine motor skills. Its common characteristics include:

- Illegible handwriting, inconsistent spacing between letters or words.
- Poor spatial planning on paper.
- Multiple spelling errors.

- Difficulty with syntax structure and grammar.
- Difficulty with composing writing as well as thinking and writing at the same time.

**3.3. Dyscalculia:** A specific learning disability that affects an individual's ability to learn math facts. Common characteristics of this type are:

- Difficulty with counting, learning number facts and doing math calculations.
- Difficulty with telling time, estimating number quantities.
- Trouble with problem solving strategies.

**3.4. Associated disorders:** The above said are three main types of SLD, which are usually accompanied by certain information processing disorders that can be classified as areas affected such as:

**3.4.1. Auditory Processing Disorder:** Also known as Central Auditory Processing Disorder, this is a condition that adversely affects how sound that travels through the ear is processed by the brain. Individuals with this type of disorder have trouble with:

- Auditory discrimination (the ability to notice, compare and distinguish the distinct and separate sounds in words).
- Auditory figure-ground discrimination (the ability to pick out important sounds from a noisy background).
- Auditory sequencing (the ability to understand and recall the order of sounds and words).

**3.4.2. Visual Processing Disorder:** It is the term used to describe a weakness in the ability to understand and use visual information. Individuals with this type of disorder have trouble with:

- Visual discrimination (the ability to notice and compare the features of different items and to distinguish one item from another).
- Visual figure-ground discrimination (the ability to distinguish a shape or printed character from its background).

- Visual sequencing (the ability to see and distinguish the order of symbols, words or images).
- Visual closure (the ability to know what an object is when only parts of it are visible).
- Spatial relationships (the ability to understand how objects are positioned in space).

**3.4.3. Non Verbal Learning Disorder:** A disorder which is usually characterised by a significant discrepancy between higher verbal skills and weaker motor, visual, spatial and social skills. Typically an individual with NVLD has trouble interpreting non-verbal cues like facial expressions or body language and may have poor co-ordination.

**3.4.4. Executive Functioning Disorder:** This is a disorder which has an in-efficiency in the cognitive management system of the brain that affects a variety of processes such as planning, organisation, strategising, paying attention to, remembering details and managing time and space. This is not a learning disability but these characteristics are often seen in those with LD and ADHD.

Insignificant inattention, hyperactivity, distractibility or a combination of these are the characteristics. Although not a learning disability, one-third of those with LD, also have ADHD. Unlike LD, features of this disorder can be attributed to neuro-chemical imbalances that can be effectively treated with a combination of behavioural and medicinal therapies.

**4. Causal Factors of Learning Disability:** Inspite of so much research on the learning disability, we do not know about its clear cut causal factors. But it is clear now that it is the resultant of mis-wiring in the brain of the affected individual. Studies have suggested about the indication of its causal factors which are as follows (Silver, 2006):

**4.1. Genetic Pattern:** Almost as many as 50 per cent of learning disabled children have inherited this brain pattern. It is the genetic code which directs the brain to wire itself differently. If this defective genetic code is in familial pattern, then it is very much probable that the child may born with this disability.

**4.2. Fetal Development:** Although it has not been proved but there is a probability that use of improper medication during the pregnancy by mother may result in a learning disabled child. Proper nutrition and avoidance of smoke and liquor is very much stressed for better results.

**4.3. Metabolites and Toxins:** Toxins in the blood and brain during pregnancy can result in brain dysfunction or brain damage of the born child. Lead and mercury has proved to be fatal.

**4.4. Substance Abuse:** Substance abuse also has played its part in the occurrence of LD. Studies suggest as many as 50 per cent of the babies of mothers who used crack cocaine during pregnancy especially during the first trimester show evidence as they grow with learning disability. Not only this if father has used certain drugs, he could also produce disorders by unsuitable sperm production.

**4.5. Problems at Delivery:** Fetal distress at delivery could suggest a higher probability to produce learning disability in later life.

**4.6. Factors in Childhood:** Infections such as encephalitis may cause changes in the brain, possibly resulting in learning disability. Head trauma may also cause structural changes in the brain and possibly result in academic difficulties.

In last it can be concluded that although we know a lot but still we do not reach at a conclusion. We can talk only in terms of probabilities hence we cannot discuss in terms of preventive measures but only of hope for preventive efforts for better results. In terms of learning disabled students there is concept of "habilitation" instead of rehabilitation because here a function has not lost which has to be regained but the individual has born with certain neurological disorder. This habilitation involves special education programme which covers many therapies including training in social skills.

**5. Special Education Programme:** Prior to provide special education to learning disabled students it is necessary to first diagnose them in a right manner. LD can be identified by psychiatrists, school psychologists, clinical psychologists and neuropsychologists through a series of intelligence and academic testing. Now-a-days much current research has focused on a treatment oriented diagnostic process known as Response to Intervention (RTI). This model includes early screening for all students, placing those students who have difficulty into research based early intervention programme rather than waiting until they meet diagnostic criteria. Those who respond will not require further intervention and non-responders referred to further assistance through special education.

Although learning disability cannot be overcome in the sense of being cured, learning disabled students can learn strategies that minimise their disabilities' negative impact. Special education for students with learning disabilities has to have certain features in it. As Zigmond (1997) described it, "*is a first and foremost instruction an individual need. It is carefully planned. It is intensive, relentless and goal directed. It is empirically supported practice, drawn from research. To provide special education means to set priorities and select carefully what needs to be taught. It means teaching something special and teaching it in special way.*" There is no "one size fits all" approach to the instruction of students with LD. Each individual is different, has some uniqueness of his disability and has different level of severity thus required a unique approach. But one thing which is common for all that learning disabled students required least restrictive environment for them. Many researchers have suggested different components and strategies for the intervention programme of learning disability, which has presented here in a summarised way. (Price, 2009) has advocated about the nine key components of special education for learning disabled students, which are:

**5.1.1. Identification and Assessment:** Success of any initiative venture for learning disabled students depends upon the early and correct identification of them. It has been discussed earlier that there is so much confusion prevalent regarding the concept of learning disability. In practice, the emphasis on identifying LD students who are eligible for special education services has resulted in reliance on a discrepancy between intelligence test scores and achievement as the criteria. However, at the 2002 LD summit in the U.S., there was consensus that the ability achievement discrepancy was "neither necessary nor sufficient" for LD identification. In the U.S., federal policy, namely the Individuals with Disabilities Education Act (IDEA), was amended in 2004 to reflect a more current understanding of the concept of LD. The requirement of an intellectual achievement discrepancy was removed and the Act allowed the use of "Response to Intervention" (RTI) data as part of the evaluation for special education to assist in the identification and determination of eligibility of students with LD.

**5.1.2. Individualised Programme Plans:** It is referred to as IPP or IEP, Individual Education Plan suiting to the unique needs of students with learning disability. Each student is unique hence education for him has developed in accordance to his needs not for the students with learning disability in general.

**5.1.3. Collaboration:** It is the key word. Collaboration of different personnel such as student, teacher, parent, special education teacher and other professional is required to meet the complexities of learning disability. Only this team can facilitate the ongoing pressing needs of the individual.

**5.1.4. Meaningful Parent Involvement:** Parent involvement and student achievement has a direct correlation. Role of parents has also shifted from passive viewer to an active member in the recent years, who can participate in the decision-making process. As learning disability has a genetic connection, it is possible that parents may also have this problem. In this case their involvement must become more meaningful.

**5.1.5. Ongoing Assessment:** Ongoing monitoring of students' progress has proved to be very beneficial. Formative assessment is the key word. Direct and frequent measures of reading, writing and math can provide information to improve instruction and increase the achievement of students. The immediate and corrective feedback is particularly helpful to students (Ysseldyke, 2001).

**5.1.6. Accommodations:** "An accommodation is a change or alteration to the regular way a student is expected to learn, complete assignments or participate in the classroom" (Alberta Education, 2002, p. 47). Accommodations include: classroom or physical changes, such as alternative seating; instructional changes such as providing notes for a student with difficulty in writing; and changes in testing such as providing extended time. Accommodations do not provide the student with LD an advantage over their peers but make them at par with their peers by providing same opportunities from their angle.

**5.1.7. Assistive technology as an accommodation:** This is the era of technology; technology means something which makes our efforts easier. Assistive technology enhances learning for students with LD and can range for "low-tech" tools such as raised or highlighted lines on paper, to "mid-tech" tools such as talking calculator, to more complex "high-tech" tools such as screen reading software. Appropriateness of AT must be specifically chosen with the help of an occupational therapist. Use of AT has proved very efficient in creating differentiated learning environment.

**5.1.8. Self-Advocacy:** Self-advocacy means taking action on one's behalf. This would be possible only when one can identify his own likes, dislikes, capabilities, strengths and weaknesses and take part in the decision-making process for the planning. But this is not the easy move because generally students with LD have low self-confidence and vague in terms of understanding. Research has shown that the component of self-advocacy skill has also helped in the execution of individualised education programme.

**5.1.9. Transition Planning:** A transition is when something changes in the student's world such as routines, relationships, settings and roles. Educational transition means changes in grade, moving from regular classroom to a special classroom or moving towards higher education. Transition planning involves identifying the skills and strategies that a student will need for a future change early on and planning instruction to develop them.

A meta-analysis of intervention studies by Swanson, Hoskyn and Lee (1999) supported a combined model for students with LD with the following elements:

**5.2.1. Sequencing:** It means breaking down the task, sequencing short activities, giving step by step prompts to the students with LD for their ease.

**5.2.2. Drill Repetition and Practice Review:** More practice works in a better way for the students.

**5.2.3. Segmentation:** It involves breaking down into smaller units and then synthesising the facts into a whole.

**5.2.4. Directed Questioning and Response:** Making the student active learner in the dialogue between teacher and student by engaging them in a series of questions and answers.

**5.2.5. Controlled Difficulty:** Difficulty must be provided in a controlled way, i.e., tasks are sequenced from easy to difficult progressively.

**5.2.6. Use of Technology:** Use of computers or graphics to facilitate presentation and feedback.

**5.2.7. Instruction in Small Groups:** Group dynamics played its part in the facilitation of better learning.

In addition to these very strategies and components required for the special education programme for learning disabled students, some other ones which need space in the present discussion are:

**5.3.1. Direct Instruction:** It involves careful sequences of instruction, rapid and frequent responding and immediate feedback and correction of errors.

**5.3.2. Strategy Instruction:** It involves teaching students "how to learn". Students are taught how to approach tasks and to use knowledge to solve problems.

**5.3.3. Scaffold Instruction:** It means gradual reduction of assistance and reciprocal teaching.

**5.3.4. Cognitive Training:** It is meant to self monitoring or self instruction by students with LD.

**5.3.5. Meta-comprehension Training:** It provides students with strategies for thinking about remembering the major points in the material being read.

**5.3.6. Mnemonics:** It is memory enhancing instruction, involves the use of key words and other ways of assisting memory.

The discussion of special education programme for learning disabled students would definitely be incomplete without the remembrance of training in social skills. As it has been said earlier that learning disabled students also have nonverbal learning disorder, due to which they have failed to understand the social conventions in the same way as others do. They misinterpret body language, misperceive jokes and have inaccurate awareness of self and others. In totality they have poor social skills. Hence training in social skills enables them to be successful in their social interactions. The above said components are the essential ones suggested by the renowned figures, in addition to this other factors can be incorporated as the situation demands.

## Conclusion

The present literature about learning disability is mainly U.S. in origin. Indian situation is far behind from the satisfactory level. We have still could not achieve the dream of universalisation of primary education. Even the resources available for those schools which are running have in very bad conditions. In these conditions providing the least restrictive environment for learning before the learning disabled students is like day dreaming. Not only for learning disabled students but for the special children as a whole, the situation is in neglected condition. There is lot of insensitivity prevalent in the society about the capabilities of these special individuals. There are a very few special schools where the top class education has been provided by the trained, sensitive and efficient personnel. Career of special education is not seemed as lucrative and not popular so that various talented ones grab this field as their profession.

There is lack of serious efforts by media as well in this direction so that this field can become the medium of discussion among the so called educated and the laymen. Very few literature is available, whatever available is in scanty and incoherent way. Actor, director Aamir Khan has made a film on this topic named as '*Tare Zameen Par*', which has gained box office success as well as critical acclaim. It denotes that this is the subject which is very touchy, people can correlate themselves to this very sensitive issue. But even the success of this film could not encash those opportunities which can make something remarkable and big in this direction. A lot has to be done in this field so that these very individuals can also taste the sweetness of academic and social success and not assumed them as burden for family as well as society. Then only we can achieve the mission of providing education to all in accordance with their unique demands.

## References


- Cortiella, Candace and Horowitz, Sheldon H. (2014). *The State of Learning Disabilities: Facts, Trends and Emerging Issues*. 3rd Edition. New York: National Centre For Learning Disabilities.

- Giler, Janet Z. (2011). *Socially ADDEPT: Teaching Social Skills to Children with ADHD and LD and Asperger's*. 2nd Edition. Jossey Bass: San Fransisco.
- Hallahan, Daniel P. *et. al.*, (2005). Learning Disabilities: Foundations, Characteristics and Effective Teaching. Pearson/ Allyn and Bacon.
- Harwell, Joan M. and Jackson Rebecca Williams. (2008). *The Complete Learning Disabilities Handbook: Ready to Use Strategies and Activities for Teaching Students with Learning Disabilities.* 3rd Edition. Jossey Bass: Amazon.com.
- Lavoie, Richard *et. al.*, (2006). *Its So Much Work to be Your Friend: Helping the Child with Learning Disabilities find Social Success*. Simon and Schuster: New York.
- Price, Anne (2009). *Best Practices in Teaching Students with Learning Disabilities.* Calgary Learning Centre.
- Silver, Larry B. (2006). *The Misunderstood Child: Understanding and Coping with Your Child's Learning Disabilities.* 4th Edition. New York McGraw Hill: Three Rivers Press.
- http://idaamerica.org/types-of-learning-disability (accessed on October 18, 2015)
- https://en.wikipedia.org/wiki/learning-disability (accessed on October 18, 2015)

# Chapter - 5

# 3 R of Learning and Learning Disability: Challenges and Possibilities

— *Dr Deepa Awasthi*

**Abstract**

*Learning disability is a wide area includes a number of issues related to challenges faced by students during learning. It also includes various ways of learning. The term Learning disability was first coined by Samuel Kirk in 1963. Concept of three R was given by Sir William Curtis in 1795. Reading, writing and arithmetic are the core skills which are needed by any student during his/her education. But there are some students who are not able to read or write or do mathematical operations as conveniently as other students. These people come under the umbrella of learning disability. Particular disorder for reading disability is known as dyslexia, for writing disability dysgraphia and for disability in mathematical operations it is known as dyscalculia. This chapter will focus on types of learning disability with special reference to dyslexia, dysgraphia and dyscalculia. Role of teachers and parents has been emphasised to tackle these disabilities.*

***Keywords:*** *Learning, Disability, Teacher, Parents.*

## What is Learning Disability?

Learning disability includes a wide range of areas of functioning in which an individual feel difficulty in working in typical manner. It also includes learning in different manner. Learning disabilities are neurologically based processing problems which can interfere with learning basic skills such as reading, writing and arithmetic or/and with higher level skills such as organisation, time planning, abstract reasoning, long-or short-term memory etc. These learning disabilities affect an individual's life academically as well as his/her relationship with family and peers.

The term Learning disability was first coined by Samuel Kirk in 1963. He used this term to express the difficulties faced by children in understanding school-related basic skills such as speech, language, reading, spelling, writing and mathematics.

**Definitions of Learning Disability**

Learning disability can be defined in various ways:

According to National **Advisory Committee of Handicapped Children**, headed by S. A. Kirk (1968): "Children with special learning disabilities exhibit a disorder in one or more of the basic psychological processes involved in understanding or in using spoken or written language. These may be manifested in disorders of listening, thinking, talking, reading, writing, spelling, or arithmetic. They include conditions which have been referred to as perceptual handicaps, brain injury, minimal brain dysfunction, dyslexia, developmental aphasia, etc. They do not include learning problems which are primarily due to visual, hearing, or motor handicaps, to mental retardation, emotional disturbance or to environmental deprivation."

**National Joint Committee on Learning Disabilities NJCLD** defined the term learning disability in 1980s as: "a heterogeneous group of disorders manifested by significant difficulties in the acquisition and use of listening, speaking, reading, writing, reasoning or mathematical abilities."

According to **National Joint Committee on Learning Disabilities** (1989): "Learning disability is a generic term that refers to a heterogeneous group of disorders manifested by significant difficulties in the acquisition and use of listening, speaking, reading, writing, reasoning, or mathematical abilities. These disorders are intrinsic to the individual, presumed to be due to central nervous system dysfunction and may occur across the life span. Problems in self-regulatory behaviours, social perception and social interaction may exist with learning disabilities but do not by themselves constitute a learning disability. Although a learning disability may occur concomitantly with other handicapping conditions (for example, sensory impairment, mental retardation, serious emotional disturbance) or with extrinsic factors (such as cultural differences, insufficient or inappropriate instruction), they are not the result of those conditions or influences."

**U.S. Office of Special Education Programmes** (2002) defined Learning Disability in following manner- "The central concept of SLD (Specific Learning Disability) involves disorders of learning and cognition that are intrinsic to the individual. SLD are specific in the sense that these disorders each significantly affect a relatively narrow range of academic and performance outcomes. SLD may occur in combination with other disabling conditions, but they are not due primarily to other conditions, such as mental retardation, behavioural disturbance, lack of opportunities to learn, or primary sensory deficits.

**Learning Disability Roundtable (2002)**, has defined Learning Disability as disorders of learning and cognition that are intrinsic to the individual. These are specific in the sense that these disorders each significantly affect a relatively narrow range of academic and performance outcomes.

## Types of Learning Disability

On the basis of processing issues Learning Disability can be divided in the following types:-

- **General Processing Issues:**
  1. **Attention:** The ability to stay on task in a sustained, selective, or divided way.
  2. **Working Memory:** The ability to retain and process information for short time periods.
  3. **Processing Speed:** The rate at which the brain handles information.
  4. **Long-term Memory:** The ability to both store and recall information for later use.
  5. **Visual Processing:** The ability to perceive, analyse and think in visual images.
  6. **Auditory Processing:** The ability to perceive and conceptualise what is heard.

7. **Logic and Reasoning:** The ability to reason, prioritise and plan.

- **Specific Learning Disorders:**
  1. **Dyslexia:** A reading disability (the student has trouble reading written words fluently, out loud).
  2. **Dysgraphia:** A writing disability (the student has difficulty with forming letters and legibility).
  3. **Dyscalculia:** A math disability (the student struggles with math problems and concepts).
  4. **Dyspraxia:** A motor coordination disability (also known as Sensory Integration Disorder).
  5. **Dysphasia:** A language disability (the student has difficulty with reading comprehension).
  6. **Aphasia:** A language disability (the student has difficulty understanding spoken language).
  7. **Central Auditory Processing Disorder:** A sensory disability related to processing sounds.
  8. **Visual Processing Disorder:** A sensory disability related to processing images.
  9. **Non-verbal Learning Disorder:** A visual-spatial disability related to body control.

## 3 R and Learning Disability

Three R are the significant basic skills required at elementary level. These 3 R explains reading, writing and arithmetic abilities. The original three Rs are identified by Sir William Curtis in 1795. Reading, writing and arithmetic are the skills which are foundations of future life. Reading is a cognitive process of decoding symbols in order to derive meaning. It is means of language acquisition, of communication and of sharing ideas. Writing is a medium of communication that represents language through inscription or recording of signs. Arithmetic reflects operations related with numbers. These skills are the basic component of an individual's learning. Any individual starts his/her learning by acquiring these skills. But learning of these basic skills is very difficult task for the persons with learning disability. Types of learning disability associated with these 3 R are:

- Dyslexia
- Dysgraphia, and
- Dyscalculia

These learning disabilities hinder an individual's learning at very basic level.

## Dyslexia

Dyslexia is a language-based learning disability. Dyslexia refers to a cluster of symptoms, which result in people having difficulties with specific language skills, particularly reading. Students with dyslexia usually experience difficulties with other language skills, such as spelling, writing and pronouncing words. Dyslexia affects individuals throughout their lives; however, its impact can change at different stages in a person's life. Dyslexia is referred to as a learning disability because it can make it very difficult for a student to succeed academically in the typical instructional environment and in its more severe forms, will qualify a student for special education, special accommodations, and/or extra support services.

### Causes

People with dyslexia have been found to have problems with identifying the separate speech sounds within a word and/or learning how letters represent those sounds, a key factor in their reading difficulties. Dyslexia is not due to either lack of intelligence or desire to learn; with appropriate teaching methods, students with dyslexia can learn successfully.

Dyslexia occurs in people of all backgrounds and intellectual levels. People with dyslexia can be very bright. They are often capable or even gifted in areas such as art, computer science, design, drama, electronics, math, mechanics, music, physics, sales and sports. In addition, dyslexia runs in families; having a parent or sibling with dyslexia increases the probability that one may also have dyslexia. For some people, their dyslexia is identified early in their lives, but for others, their dyslexia goes unidentified for their life time.

### Symptoms of Dyslexia

There are some common symptoms of Dyslexia. Such as-

- Learning to speak.
- Learning letters and their sounds.
- Organising written and spoken language.
- Memorising number facts.
- Reading quickly enough to comprehend.
- Keeping up with and comprehending longer reading assignments.
- Spelling.
- Learning a foreign language.
- Difficulty with remembering simple sequences.
- Difficulty understanding the rhyming of words.
- Pronunciation difficulties.

## Dysgraphia

The word dysgraphia comes from the Greek words *dys* meaning "impaired" and *graphia* meaning "writing by hand".Dysgraphia is a deficiency in the ability to write. It is a type of transcription disability, means that it is writing disorder associated with impaired hand writing. It is characterised when one's writing skills are below those expected given a person's age.

### Types of Dysgraphia

According to International Dyslexia Association, Dysgraphia can be broadly categorised in three categories:

- ***Dyslexic dysgraphia:*** In Dyslexic dysgraphia spontaneously written text is illegible, especially when the text is complex. Oral spelling is poor, but drawing and copying of written text are relatively normal. Finger tapping speed is normal.
- ***Motor dysgraphia:*** Both spontaneously written and copied text may be illegible, oral spelling is normal and drawing is usually problematic. Finger tapping speed is abnormal.
- ***Spatial Dysgraphia:*** Persons with spatial dysgraphia display illegible writing, whether spontaneously produced or copied.

Oral spelling is normal. Finger tapping speed is normal, but drawing is very problematic.

**Symptoms**

Some of the common symptoms of dysgraphia are-

- Cramping of fingers while writing short entries.
- Odd wrist, arm, body, or paper orientations such as bending an arm into an L shape.
- Excessive erasures.
- Mixed upper case and lower case letters.
- Inconsistent form and size of letters, or unfinished letters.
- Misuse of lines and margins.
- Inefficient speed of copying.
- Inattentiveness over details when writing.
- Frequent need of verbal cues.
- Referring heavily on vision to write.
- Poor legibility.
- Handwriting abilities that may interfere with spelling and written composition.
- Having a hard time translating ideas to writing, sometimes using the wrong words altogether.
- May feel pain while writing.

## Dyscalculia

Dyscalculia may be understood as difficulty in learning arithmetic like difficulty in understanding and manipulating of numbers and numerical facts. It is a kind of specific developmental disorder. According to American Psychiatric Association (2013), It is a specific learning disorder and characterised by impairments in learning basic arithmetic facts, processing numerical magnitude and performing accurate and fluent calculations. These difficulties must be quantifiably below what is expected for an individual's chronological age and must not be cused by poor educational or daily activities or by intellectual impairments.

**Symptoms of Dyscalculia**

Dyscalculia involves frequent difficulties with everyday arithmetic tasks like the following:

- Difficulty when counting backwards.
- Poor sense of number and estimation.
- Difficulty in remembering 'basic' facts, despite many hours of practice/rote learning.
- No strategies to compensate for lack of recall, other than to use counting.
- Difficulty in understanding place value and the role of zero in the Arabic/Hindi number system.
- No sense of whether any answers that are obtained are right or nearly right.
- Tendency to be slower to perform calculations.
- Forgetting mathematical procedures, especially as they become more complex, for example 'long' division.
- Addition is often the default operation. The other operations are usually very poorly executed (or avoided altogether).
- Avoiding tasks that are perceived as difficult and likely to result in a wrong answer.
- Weak mental arithmetic skills.
- High levels of mathematics anxiety.
- Difficulty reading analog clocks.
- Difficulty stating which of two numbers is larger.
- Inability to comprehend financial planning or budgeting, sometimes even at a basic level; for example, estimating the cost of the items in a shopping basket or balancing a check book.
- Difficulty with multiplication-tables and subtraction-tables, addition tables, division tables, mental arithmetic, etc.
- Difficulty with conceptualising time and judging the passing of time.
- Problems with differentiating between left and right.

- Inability to visualise mentally.
- Difficulty reading musical notation.
- Difficulty with choreographed dance steps.
- Difficulty comprehending things relating to occurrences in different time zones.
- Inability to grasp and remember mathematical concepts, rules, formulae and sequences.
- Inability to concentrate on mentally intensive tasks.

## How to help them?

Learning disabled children can also learn in better way with proper support of their parents and teachers. They can help them in organising their work and study and can suggest different ways to overcome their weaknesses.

### Role of Teacher in Dyslexia

- Teacher should help the student to identify his/her specific learning style like visual or auditory.
- Books with large print can be used.
- Teaching in whole is the best way to teach them. As dyslexic students easily understand any word, sentence or concept as whole. So teacher has to focus on this whole concept while teaching.
- Teacher should try to complete a unit in single sitting to avoid short-term memory loss.
- Teacher should concentrate on ideas of these students and avoid some grammatical errors. Teacher should value their ideas.
- These students ask a lot of questions and without their answers they cannot concentrate in class so teacher should try to answer their queries as often as possible.
- Teacher should not criticise these students.
- Teacher should use diagrams to describe concepts as it is helpful in preparation of mind maps.

- Teacher should present materials in small units in form of whole (each unit must be complete in it).
- As dyslexic students feel difficulty in taking notes they can be given pre-printed notes.

**Role of Parents in Dyslexia**

Role of parents in learning of dyslexic students is very important. They can motivate the child to perform better and to overcome the challenges of the life due to dyslexia.

- Parents can adopt paired learning to assist child in reading. Through their proper recitation students can easily grasp the pronunciation.
- Parents can watch TV shows with their children and help them in understanding the concept.
- Parents can use small trip as an effective mean to provide practical experiences.
- Parents should keep in touch with teachers of their child to understand and solve their problems.
- Grand parents can also play an important role in dyslexic student's learning by chatting frequently because this will be helpful in enhancing vocabulary of these students.

**Role of Teacher in Dysgraphia**

- Teacher should be patient and react positive while a dysgraphic student practise handwriting.
- Teacher should encourage proper grip and posture while writing.
- Teacher can permit them to use word processor.
- Teacher can use oral exam and allow them to take help of a scribe.
- Teacher should avoid criticism for illegibility.
- Teacher should provide extra time for writing tasks.
- Teacher should reduce the amount of copying needed to complete a task.
- Notes outline can be provided by the teacher to minimise the time required for writing.

- Teacher can allow audio or video form of report submission in any project.
- Teacher can also suggest some hand exercises to the students when fatigued.

**Role of Parents in Dysgraphia**

- Parents should provide emotional support to these students to release their stress.
- Parents should arrange writing material with proper grip which helps in writing.
- Parents should not criticise them for illegible hand writing.
- Parents should admire conceptual knowledge of their child and motivate them for practise proper hand writing.
- Parents can suggest some specific exercises and mediation to their children for physical development as well as increase in concentration.

**Role of Teacher in Dyscalculia**

- Teacher should focus on understanding the mathematical concepts.
- Teacher should provide extra time to solve numeric problems.
- Teacher can give easier assignments to the dyscalculic students as compared to other students.
- Teacher should help students by using concrete material to link mathematical symbols and concepts to quantity.
- Teacher should try to draw pictures of word problems.
- Teacher can allow use of coloured pencils to differentiate problems.
- Teacher should proceed from simple to complex to discuss mathematical concepts.
- Teacher should provide a lot of practice for any new skill.
- Teacher should reduce emphasis on memorisation and encourage practise.
- Teacher can use mnemonic devices to learn steps of a math concept.
- Teacher should make learning an active process.

**Role of Parents in Dyscalculia**

- Parents should get information about signs, causes and treatment of dyscalculia as knowing a problem is the first step to solve it.
- Through use of household things like utensils, clothes or toys, parents can help in understanding concept of numbers. But this should be in form of game and should not become a burden for child.
- Parents should provide peaceful space for doing homework with least disturbance. They can frame a break time schedule for their child means they can give ten minutes rest or a glass of juice etc. to their child after five numerical.
- Mathematics is the subject which inculcates reasoning and problem solving in the child. So the parents can also provide a calculator to tackle number phobia and help them in concentrating the basic skills of reasoning and problem solving.
- Praise and love of parents is the ultimate way of tackling emotional aspects of child suffering from dyscalculia.

## Conclusion

Dyslexia, dysgraphia and dyscalculia are the learning disabilities which affects individual's basic learning skills of reading, writing and doing arithmetic operations respectively. There could be many students suffering with these disabilities in some or the other way. Role of teachers and parents is of great importance in this context. With little effort a big change can be planned in these students. Through proper guidance and emotional support they can also perform like other students.

## References

- About dyscalculia. www.aboutdyscalculia.org
- Bcon, A.M. and Benett, S. (2013). *Dyslexia in higher education: a decision to study art.* European Journal of Special Needs Education. Vol. 28, Issue 1, pp. 19-32.
- *Dealing with Dysgraphia- a dyslexic disorder.* www.indiaparenting.com
- *Dyscalculia. British Dyslexia Association.* www.bdadyslexia.org.uk

- *Dysgraphia.International Dyslexia Association.* www.dyslexiasd.org
- *How parents can help?*www.dyslexia.ie
- Knobelauch, L. How to assist a student with Dysgraphia in the classroom. www.superduperinc.com
- *Learning Disability.* www.en.wikipedia.org
- Morin, A. At A glance: Classroom accommodation for Dysgraphia. www.understood.org
- *Some types of learning.*www.learninggrx.com
- *Types of learning disabilities.* www.ldaamerica.org

# Chapter - 6

# Dyslexia: A Reading Disorder

— *Dr Vandana Singh and Sunil Kumar Bhagat*

**Abstract**

*A reading disorder is when one has difficulty in reading or understanding material within a reading. Most people with reading disorders have problems with their phonemic (sound/symbol relationships) awareness development. This means they have a difficult time putting together letters to make a sound. In reading disorder, there is a significant gap between the expected level of performance and actual achievement. Difficulties in reading can occur on many levels and reading disorder may have several causes that manifest in different ways. There are many different symptoms and types of reading disorders and not everyone with reading disorder has every symptom. Children with reading difficulties stop and start frequently mispronounce word and skip others entirely. These types of children soon grow ashamed as they struggle with a skill their classmates master easily. There is no known way to prevent reading disorder. Early intervention is a key to prevent the problems associated with reading disability. The present article aims at describing the symptoms, causes, types and remedies of reading disorders and also some approaches to improve reading skills in students.*

***Keywords:*** *Reading disorder, Symptoms, Causes, Types, Remedies.*

## Reading Disorder

Reading disorder was first recognised in the late nineteenth century, when it was called pure word blindness, then developmental alexia. Starting in the 1960, educators commonly referred to reading disorder as dyslexia, from the Greek work 'dys', meaning 'poor' or 'inadequate' and word 'lexis' meaning words or languages. Reading disorder is a condition in which reading ability is significantly below the norm in relation to chronological age and overall intellectual potential. It is also referred as reading disability. Reading disorder occurs when a person has trouble with any part of the reading process.

A reading disorder is when one has difficulty in reading or understanding material within a reading. Most people with reading disorders have problems with their phonemic (sound/symbol relationships) awareness development. This means they have a difficult time putting together letters to make a sound. Reading disability is a condition in which a sufferer displays difficulty reading resulting primarily from neurological factors. These disorders are present from a young age and usually result from specific difference in the way the brain processes language. Children with reading difficulties stop and start frequently mispronounce word and skip others entirely. These types of children soon grow ashamed as they struggle with a skill their classmates master easily.

People with mild reading impairment do not read for fun. For them, reading requires so much efforts that they have little energy left for understanding what they have just read. Contrary to what many people believe, National Institute of Child Health and Human Development (NICHD) Research has shown that reading disability affects boys and girls at roughly the same rate. Reading disabled boys however are more likely to be referred for treatment as they are more likely to get the teacher's attention by misbehaving. Reading disabled girls may escape the teacher's attention, as they may withdraw into quiet day dreaming. Another common misconception is that reading disabled people reverse letters and write in mirror image. In fact, such reversals are common among all beginning writers - reading impaired and non-reading impaired alike.

Reading disorder can cause severe problems in reading and consequently in academic work, even in people with normal intelligence, educational opportunities, motivation to learn, to read and emotional self control. Reading disorder is different from slowness in learning or mental retardation. In reading disorder, there is a significant gap between the expected level of performance and actual achievement. Difficulties in reading can occurs on many levels and reading disorder may have several causes that manifest in different ways. Common problems in people with reading disorder include:

- Slow reading speed.
- Poor comprehension in aloud, or silent reading.
- Omission of words while reading.
- Reversal of words or letters while reading.
- Difficulty decoding syllables or single words and associating them with specific sounds (phonics).
- Limited sight word vocabulary.

## Symptoms

There are many different symptoms and types of reading disorders and not everyone with reading disorder has every symptom. People with reading disorder may have problems recognising words that they already know and may also be poor spellers. Other symptoms may include the following:

- Trouble with handwriting.
- Difficulty reading quickly.
- Problems reading with correct expression.
- Problems understanding the written word.
- Difficulty in identifying single words.
- Problems understanding the sound in words, sound order or rhymes.
- Problems with spelling.
- Transposing letters in words.
- Omitting or substituting words.
- Poor reading comprehension.
- Slow reading speed (oral or silent).

In addition of these symptoms, children with reading disorder often have other delays or learning problems. These include:

- Delays in spoken language.
- Confusion with directions, or right/left handedness.

- Confusion with opposites (up/down, early/late).
- Mathematics disorder.
- Disorder of written expression.
- Faulty pencil grip and letter formation.
- Task avoidance.
- Anxiety.
- Weak impulse control.
- Distractibility.
- Problems with comprehension of spoken language.
- Confusion of mathematical signs and computation processes.

## Types of Reading Disability

Reading disability have been classified as either dyseidetic, dysphonetic or mixed. Children with the ***dyseidetic*** types are able to sound out individual letters phonetically but have trouble identifying patterns of letters when they are grouped together. By comparison, ***dysphonic*** readers have difficulty relating letters to sounds, so their spelling is totally chaotic. Children with ***mixed*** reading disability have both the dyseidetic and dysphonic types of reading disorder.

This may be presented diagrammatically as follows:

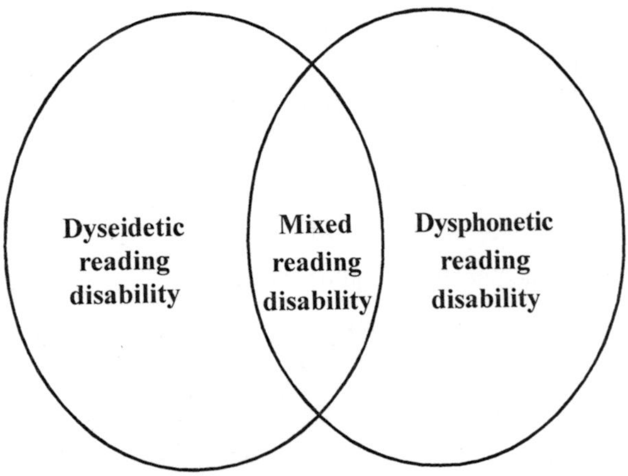

Few researchers currently propose that there are three kinds of developmental reading disabilities that are often overlap but that can be separate and distinct.

**Phonological Deficit**, implicating a core problem in the phonological processing system of oral language. **Processing speed / Orthographic Processing Deficit** affecting speed and accuracy of printed word recognition (also called naming speed problem or fluency problem.

**Comprehension deficit**, often conceding with the first two types of problems, but specifically found in children with social-linguistic disabilities (e.g., Autism spectrum), vocabulary weaknesses, generalised language learning disorders and learning difficulties that affect abstract reasoning and logical thinking.

These subtypes of reading disability may be presented diagrammatically as follows:-

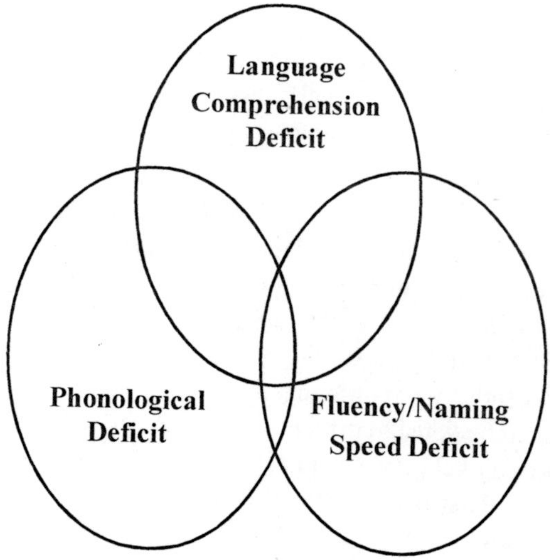


If a student has a prominent and specific weakness in either phonological or orthographic processing, they are said to have a single deficit in word recognition. If they have a combination of phonological and orthographic processing deficits, they are said to have double deficit. Double deficit children are more common than single deficit and are also the most challenging to remediate.

**Causes**

Learning to read is a complex task. It requires condition of the eye muscles to follow a line of print, spatial orientation to interpret letters and words, visual memory to retain the meaning of letters and sight words, sequencing ability, a grasp of sentence structure and grammar and the ability to categorise and analyse. In addition, the brain must integrate visual cues with memory and associate them with specific sounds. The sounds must then be associated with specific meanings. For comprehension, the meaning must be retained while a sentence or passage is read. Reading disorder occurs when any of these processes are disrupted. For that reason, the roots of reading disorder have proved difficult to isolate and may be different in different individuals.

Despite the complexity of reading disorder, researchers have found that the condition is at least partially inherited. In 1999, the *Centre for Reading Research, Norway* studied a large family with reading problems. By evaluating the reading and writing abilities of about 60 family members across four generations, the researchers were able to pin-point mutations in specific genes that are associated with reading and writing deficits.

It appears that reading disorder may also have causes other than genetic inheritance, as about half the people do not come from families with a history of the problem. Many theories suggest that functional problems in specific areas of the brain underlie reading disorder. Given the complicated demands on the human nervous system involved in reading, it is entirely possible that there are several different problems in brain function related to difficulty in learning to read. What is known that 90 per cent of children diagnosed with reading disorder have other language deficits still other research suggests a possible link with a subtle visual problem that affects the speed with which affected people can read.

**Diagnosis**

Reading abilities in children must be evaluated on individual basis in order to make a diagnosis of reading disorder and distinguish it from slow learning or low intelligence. The examiner must take into account the child's age, intelligence, educational opportunities and such cultural factors as whether the language spoken at home is different from the language taught and used at school. Reading disorder is diagnosed when a child's reading achievement is substantially below what would be expected after taking these factors into account. In addition, the reading problems must interfere in significant ways with the person's school work or daily life. If a physical condition is present (e.g., Mental retardation, poor eyesight or hearing loss), the reading deficit must be in excess of what one would normally associate with the physical handicap.

Diagnosis is complicated by the fact that 20 per cent - 55 per cent of children with reading disorder have attention-deficit / hyperactivity disorder (ADHD), a behavioural disorder that aggravates learning difficulties. In addition, about one-quarter of children with reading disorder have conduct disorder. Oppositional defiant disorder and depression also occur in higher than-average rates in children with reading disorder. Almost all people with reading disorder have difficulties spelling and about 80 per cent of them have other language problems. Anyone who is suspected of having reading disorder or any other learning disability should have a comprehensive evaluation, including hearing, vision and intelligence testing. The test should include all areas of learning and learning processes, not just reading. In school age children this evaluation often involves a team of educators, educational psychologists and child psychiatrist.

## Treatments for Reading Disorder

Any child, who has a diagnosed learning disability, including reading disorder or dyslexia, should be eligible for an individual Education Programme (IEP) that provides customised instruction at school, designed to address the disability.

Treatment approaches vary from visual stimulation to special diets to enhanced reading instruction. However, it is generally agreed that customised education is the only successful remedy. The American Academy of Ophthalmology, the American Academy of Pediatrics and the American Association for Pediatric Ophthalmology and Strabismus have issued a policy statement warning against visual treatments and recommending a cross-disciplinary educational approach. In general, all good progress are:-

- **Sound Symbol (Phonics) based.** They break words down into their smallest visual components: letters and the sounds associated with them.
- **Multisensory.** Good programmes attempts to form and strengthen mental associations among visual, auditory and kinesthetic channels of stimulation. The student simultaneously sees, feels and says the sound-symbol association. For example, a student may trace the letter or letter combination with his or her finger while pronouncing a word out loud.
- **Highly structured.** Remediation begins at the level of the single letter-sound; works up to digraphs (a pair of letters representing a single speech sound); then in words and sentences in a systematic fashion. Repetitive drill and practice serve to form necessary associations between sounds and written symbols.

## Prognosis and Prevention

Many famous and successful people have suffered from reading disorders, including at least two Presidents of the U.S. How well a person compensates for this disorder depends on the severity of the impairment and the type of educational remediation that he or she receives. Generally, people who are identified as having a reading disorder before grade three and who receive intensive reading education can do well. There is however a great deal of variation among people in intelligence, educational opportunities and the will to overcome a reading disorder, as well as in the type and severity of the problem. All these factors combine to determine the ultimate outcome of this disorder. The prognosis is usually good if the condition is diagnosed early and the person is enrolled in a good remedial programme. Strong self-esteem, together with supportive family, friends and teachers also improve a person's chances of overcoming this disorder.

There is no known way to prevent reading disorder. Early intervention is the key to prevent the associated symptoms of low self-esteem, lack of interest in school and poor behaviour that often accompany low academic achievement.

How to improve reading outcomes of students with or at risk for reading disorders (Some studies):

**Adams (1990) and Torgesen (1999)** focused on the act of decoding and identified phonological awareness and grasp of the alphabetic principle as malleable sources of influence on young students' foundational reading skills. Research has also focused on the more complex skills required for reading comprehension including oral language skills, vocabulary, background and academic knowledge among others (Snow, 2001)

**Glenberg and Colleagues (2004)** conducted three different experiments with first and second graders. Across these experiments, these researchers discovered that manipulating toys, watching toys being manipulated and the imagining the toys generally increased children's comprehension of the story when compared to the students in the control conditions. That is they were better able to remember what they had read, even after some time had passed.

The researchers then explored that children who had the opportunity to enact the stories and watch their group members enact stories were better able to recall the stories after time had passed than did the children in the re-reading condition.

Next the researchers examined whether enacting stories with toys or watching someone enact stories would improve the listening comprehension skills of Native American students who were struggling readers. Native American students are at high risk for developing reading disabilities because they frequently are learning English as second language and are disproportionately more likely to live in poverty. It was found that enacting the stories and enacting complex language by creating concrete representations helped Native American students with reading difficulties better understand complex stories.

Thus, the results of these researchers' studies suggest that reading comprehension interventions that make abstract and complex stories more concrete by enacting them with toys or other visual imagery should support all student' reading and listening comprehension skills including students with or at risk for reading disabilities.

**Denton and Collegues (2010)** scaled up a supplementary reading intervention designed to increase the intensity of intervention for first graders with or at risk of reading disabilities. Their supplemental reading intervention, *Responsive Reading Instruction,* was used with first graders for whom whole-class instruction was ineffective. These students assigned randomly to Responsive Reading Instructions or to typical school-designed interventions. Responsive reading instruction included word work, scaflolded reading and rereading of decodable books. This was along with supported writing, in which students took turns generating a sentence for all students in the group to write with teacher assistance. There were significant positive effects of Responsive Reading Instruction compared to typical school designed interventions on students' reading achievement in addition to generally better reading outcomes, 91 per cent of students who received Responsive Reading Instruction achieved grade level expectations compared to only 79 per cent of control students (grade level expectations were defined as within half a standard deviation of the national norms). The area that remained weakest for Responsive Reading Instruction and control students was oral reading fluency. Moreover, students in Responsive Reading Instruction and control interventions received similar amounts of time in small groups, suggesting that intensity may be as much about the content of instruction as simply increasing intervention time.

**Hagan-Burke, Zou, Johnson Simmons and Coyne (2010)** examined the impact of instruction that takes advantage of current understandings on best practice for literacy instruction in Kindergarten and how these practices might affect reading development for students with and without behaviour problems. They defined these best practices as instruction that integrates phonemic awareness, the alphabetic principle and decoding and is explicit, systematic and code based. They found that explicit, systematic and code-based instruction was more effective than was the business-as-usual control instruction for children with externalising behaviour (e.g., fighting, talking back to teachers, tantrums) and children who were hyperactive and easily distracted.

Thus, researches shows that providing intensive intervention to students with low reading skills in kindergarten and first grade generally improves reading outcomes later on. Students who were English learners and students with behavioural problems also improved reading skills more than students in control groups when the interventions were systematic and included a focus on phonics.

**Vadasy and Sanders 2008a, 2008b, 2009** conducted a study to investigate whether fluency interventions that focus on repeated reading or reading a range of text, along with opportunities to practice reading in the classroom generally improve students' fluency and comprehension. They found that two intervention practices, repeated reading and wide reading, are associated with gains in reading fluency. In addition, improving students' reading rates takes considerable practice. Moreover, whereas gains in fluency generally improve comprehension, fluency gains do not appear to influence decoding or vocabulary. These results suggest that for students with slow reading rate, specific instruction to teach decoding and vocabulary should likely continue into the intermediate grades.

**Saenz, McMaster, Fuchs and Fuchs (2007)** reviewed nearly 20 years of research on Peer Assisted Learning Strategies (PALS), which was designed to improve the reading development of students in Kindergarten through six grade and in high school. They found that, across studies, PALS was generally effective in improving reading outcomes, including in high poverty schools. In grade 2-6 and high school, PALS practice activities include reading aloud to develop reading rate and accuracy and also comprehension task such as recall and summarisation. Results again were positive, with students in PALS classes improving in reading rate and comprehension on average, when compared to students in control classes. A test of high school implementation also found that students who participated in PALS developed stronger reading comprehension than did students in control classrooms.

Another form of peer assisted learning that has been tested across multiple studies is Collaborative Strategic Reading (CSR), which was designed to be used for students beyond the primary grades. It was found that after 18 weeks of intervention of CSR, students in the CSR group scored higher, on average, than did students in the control group on all aspects of reading comprehension arrested.

Interventions that are differentiated to targets an individual student's profile of component skills can improve reading development. **Corner, Morrison, Al Otaiba, Fisherman, Schatschnierder and**

**Collegues (2004)** have found in their study that students in the ISI (Individualised Student Instruction) classroom demonstrated generally stronger word reading and comprehension gains than did students in control classrooms.

## Conclusion

So many causes are responsible for reading disorder including genetic and other than genetic. Therefore, a comprehensive evaluation is needed to diagnose this problem. Children with reading disorder overcome their difficulties if they receive appropriate treatment at early age. Using visual imagery to make passage or stories more concrete, supplemental reading intervention, fluency intervention, peer-assisted learning strategies, individualised student instructions etc. can improve reading skills of children.

## References


- Adams, M.J. (1990). *Beginning to Read: Thinking and Learning about Print.* Cambridge, MA: The MIT Press.
- Arunachalam, N. (2010). *Educating Children with Special Needs.* A.P.H. Publishing Corporation, New Delhi.
- Bock, Robert (1998). *Why children succeed or fail at Reading: Research from NICHD's Programme in Learning Disabilities.* Health Publication. National Institute of Child Health and Human Development. Retrieved from www.ldonline.org/article/223
- Connor, C.M. Morrison, F.J. and Others (2004). *Beyond the Reading Wars: Exploring the effect of child-Instruction Interactions on Growth in Early Reading. Scientific Studies of Reading,* 8(4), 305-336. As reported in improving Reading Outcomes for students with or at Risk for Reading Disabilities NCSER 2014-3000, U.S. Department of Education. Retrieved from http://ies.ed.gov>pdf>20143000.
- Denton, C.A., (Mathes, P.G., Swanson, E., Nimon, K. and Kethley C. (2010). *Effectiveness of a supplemental Early Reading Intervention Scaledup in Multiple Schools. Exceptional children,* 76(4), 394-416. As reported in improving Reading Outcomes for students with or at Risk for Reading Disabilities NCSER 2014-3000, U.S. Department of Education. Retrieved from http://ies.ed.gov>pdf>20143000.
- Glenberg, A.M. and Colleague (2004). *Activity and Imagined Activity can Enhance Young Children's Reading comprehension.* Journal of Educational Research, 96(3), 424-436. As reported in improving Reading Outcomes for students with or at Risk for Reading Disabilities NCSER 2014-3000,

U.S. Department of Education. Retrieved from http://ies.ed.gov>pdf>20143000.

- Hagan-Burke, S. Kwok, O. Zau, Y., Johnson, C. Simmons, D. and Coyne, M.D. (2010). *An Examination of Problem Behaviours and Reading Outcomes in Kindergarten Students.* The Journal of Special Education, 20, 1-18. As reported in improving Reading Outcomes for students with or at Risk for Reading Disabilities NCSER 2014-3000, U.S. Department of Education. Retrieved from http://ies.ed.gov>pdf>20143000.
- Hallahan, Daniel P. and Kauffman, James M. (2000). *Exceptional Learners: Introduction to special Education,* 8th edition. Boston: Allyn and Bacon.
- http://en.m.wikipedia.org>wiki>Reading Disability.
- Karanth, Pratibha (2003). *Learning Disabilities in India*. Sage Publication, New Delhi.
- Saenz, L. Mc Master, K., Fuchs, D. and Fuchs, L.S. (2007). *Peer-Assisted Learning Strategies in Reading for students with Different Learning Needs.* Journal of Cognitive Education and Psychology, 6(13), 395-410.
- Snow, C.E. (2001). *Reading for understanding. Santa Monica, CA: RAND Education and the Science and Technology Policy Institute.*
- Vadasy, P.F. and Sanders, E.A. (2008b). *Repeated Reading Intervention: Outcomes and Interactions with readers' skills and classroom Instruction.* Journal of Educational Psychology, 100, 272-290. As reported in improving Reading Outcomes for students with or at Risk for Reading Disabilities NCSER 2014-3000, U.S. Department of Education. Retrieved from http://ies. ed.gov>pdf>20143000.
- Vadasy, P.F. and Sanders, E.A. (2009). *Supplemental Fluency Intervention and Determinants of Reading Outcomes. Scientific Studies of Reading*, 13(15), 383-425.
- Vadasy, P.F. and Sanders, E.A. (2008a). *Benefits of Repeated Reading Intervention for Low Achieving Fourth and Fifth-Grade Students.* Remedial and Special Education, 29, 235-249.
- www.minddisorders.com
- www.readingrockets.org/article/types-reading-disability.

# Chapter - 7

# Education for Learners with Dyslexia

— ***Professor AmitaBajpai***


### Abstract

*Specific learning disability Dyslexia afflicts 5-15 per cent of school-going children. Over the last decade; awareness about this invisible handicap has grown in India. However, much needs to be done to ensure that each afflicted child gets an opportunity to achieve his or her full academic potential in regular mainstream schools. In order to achieve this ideal scenario, all 'regular' classroom teachers should be sensitised to suspect and trained to screen for this disability when the child is in primary school. This chapter mainly deals with the educational problems of the dyslexic children and suggests the learning styles and teaching strategies to ensure that these children may receive regular education with affordable remedial education.*


***Key words:*** *Dyslexia, Education, Learning styles, Teaching strategies.*

## Dyslexia

Dyslexia is a language-based learning disability. Dyslexia refers to a cluster of symptoms, which result in people having difficulties with specific language skills, particularly reading. Students with dyslexia usually experience difficulties with other language skills, such as spelling, writing and pronouncing words. Dyslexia affects individuals throughout their lives; however, its impact can change at different stages in a person's life. It is referred to as a learning disability because dyslexia can make it very difficult for a student to succeed academically in the typical instructional environment and in its more severe forms, will qualify a student for special education, special accommodations, and/ or extra support services.

***The formal definition of Dyslexia***

*Dyslexia is a specific learning disability that is neurological in origin. It is characterised by difficulties with accurate and/or fluent word recognition and by poor spelling and decoding abilities. These difficulties typically result from a deficit in the phonological component of language that is often unexpected in relation to other cognitive abilities and the provision of effective classroom instruction. Secondary consequences may include problems in reading comprehension and reduced reading experience that can impede the growth of vocabulary and background knowledge.*

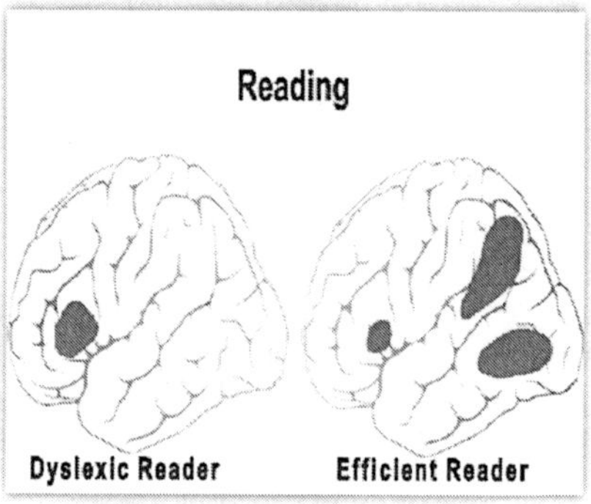


***Comparison of the brains of Dyslexia Reader and Efficient Reader***

Dyslexics use the brain regions that process written language differently than those without the disorder. Some scientists speculate that dyslexics use the specific area inadequately and may compensate by using other brain areas, such as the inferior frontal gyrus, which is located in the front of the brain and is associated with spoken language.

## Causes of Dyslexia

The exact causes of dyslexia are still not completely clear, but anatomical and brain imagery studies show differences in the way the brain of a person with dyslexia develops and functions. Moreover, most people with dyslexia have been found to have problems with identifying the separate speech sounds within a word and/or learning how letters represent those sounds, a key factor in their reading difficulties. The main areas where the dyslexic feels difficulty are:

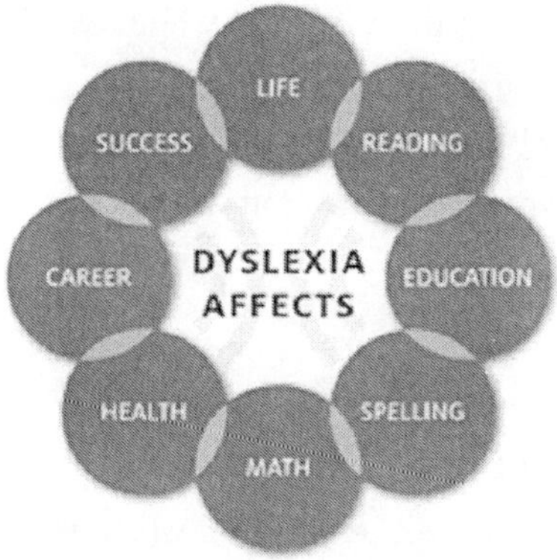


***Areas which Dyslexia affects***

Dyslexia is not due to either lack of intelligence or desire to learn; with appropriate teaching methods, students with dyslexia can learn successfully. Dyslexia occurs in people of all backgrounds and intellectual levels. People with dyslexia can be very bright. They are often capable or even gifted in areas such as art, computer science, design, drama, electronics, math, mechanics, music, physics, sales and sports. In addition, dyslexia runs in families; having a parent or sibling with dyslexia increases the probability that you will also have dyslexia. For some people, their dyslexia is identified early in their lives, but for others, their dyslexia goes unidentified until they get older.

## Main Educational Effects of Dyslexia

***Reading and perceptual difficulties which can include:***

- Early difficulties in acquiring phonic skills.
- A high proportion of errors in oral reading.
- Difficulty in extracting the sense from written material without substantial re-reading.

- Slow reading speed.
- Inaccurate reading, omission of words.
- Frequent loss of the place when reading.
- An inability to skim through or scan over reading matter.
- A high degree of distractibility while reading.
- Perceived distortion of text (words may seem to float off the page or run together).
- A visually irritating glare from white paper or white-boards.

*Writing problems*

These can include:

- An intractable spelling problem.
- Confusion of small words such as which/with.
- Omission of words, especially when the writer is under pressure.
- Awkward handwriting and/or slow writing speed.
- An unexpected difference between oral and written expression, with oral contributions being typically of a much higher quality than written accounts of the same subject matter in terms of structure, self-expression and correct use of words.

*Other Difficulties:*

Further important factors in dyslexia include the following:

- **Early Speech and Language Problems.** Many dyslexic children have received speech therapy, usually for phonological difficulties, especially between the ages of three and seven.
- **Glue Ear** (Otitis media). It is common in children with dyslexia and usually affects the acquisition of auditory discrimination skills, which in turn impacts on development of phonics in reading.
- **Immune System Disorders**. There is a high incidence of immune system disorders (e.g., asthma, eczema) amongst children with dyslexia. The reason for this is not understood at present.

- **Oral Skills**. Although many dyslexic children are fairly articulate, others demonstrate a lack of logical structure in speech as well as in writing. Oral skills can be further compromised by difficulties in word retrieval or by mispronunciation and spoonerisms. A delay in producing a response may actually be due to a slight lapse between hearing what is said and understanding it – inefficiency in aural processing possibly connected with the working memory system.
- **Numeracy**. In about 60 per cent of cases, dyslexia affects numeracy skills. This can take the form of unexpected inaccuracy in calculation or copying of digits, failure to remember calculation procedures, difficulties with remembering multiplication tables. Gifted dyslexic mathematicians and scientists are sometimes found to have unusually weak computational skills.
- **Co-morbidity with other Developmental Disorders, e.g. ADHD or Dyspraxia**. A range of characteristics, under the general heading of attention dysfunction like ADD and ADHD, can have a significant overlap with dyslexia. A short attention span or a high level of distractibility can undermine the whole educational process. Associated characteristics are an inability to get started when faced with certain mental activities and also trouble switching from one type of activity to another. Additionally, or alternatively, dyslexic problems can overlap with dyspraxia which is sometimes referred to as the 'clumsy child syndrome' or 'developmental co-ordination disorder'.

**Social and Emotional Factors.** High levels of anxiety and stress have been identified as the most indicative behavioural correlates of dyslexia. These are bound to affect performance. A 'panic' reaction is experienced by some dyslexic people when placed in situations where they cannot cope. The cumulative effect of tiredness, necessitated by additional effort at every educational level, should not be underestimated.

- **Organisation.** Disorganisation, a poor sense of clock time (often associated with underlying memory problems) and a poor awareness of space (often associated with dyspraxia) tend to make effective time management very difficult for many people with dyslexia.

- **The Secondary Effects of Dyslexia.** Although significant discrepancies between obvious ability and unexpectedly poor academic performance should alert teachers to the presence of dyslexia at an early age, the problem may go unnoticed for several years. Under-achievement in literacy despite normal schooling and satisfactory oral and intellectual skills may persist through childhood. This gives rise to the secondary effects of dyslexia, which include loss of confidence, low self-esteem and frustration. Older students find that years of humiliation in the classroom and constant fear of being 'shown up' take their toll.
- **Compensatory Strategies**. Because of the development of compensatory strategies, by adulthood, literacy skills of many dyslexics can appear superficially adequate, especially if the person is very bright. However, these strategies are likely to break down when the individual is confronted with tasks that are more challenging than previously experienced (e.g., when going to college). This has been referred to as the **'Dyslexia Fuse Effect'**: i.e. the dyslexia 'fuse' blowing as a function of the educational or information processing load placed upon it.

## Classroom Strategies for Students with Dyslexia

Schools can implement academic accommodations and modifications to help students with dyslexia succeed. For example, a student with dyslexia can be given extra time to complete tasks, help with taking notes and work assignments that are modified appropriately. Teachers can give taped tests or allow students with dyslexia to use alternative means of assessment. Students can benefit from listening to books on tape and using text reading and word processing computer programmes.

Teaching students with dyslexia across settings is challenging. Both general education and special education teachers seek accommodations that foster the learning and management of a class of heterogeneous learners. It is important to identify accommodations that are reasonable to ask of teachers in all classroom settings. The following accommodations provide a framework for helping students with learning problems achieve in general education and special education classrooms. They are organised according to accommodations involving materials, interactive instruction and student performance.

## Accommodations Involving Materials

Students spend a large portion of the school day interacting with materials. Most instructional materials give teachers few activities or directions for teaching a large class of students who learn at different rates and in various ways. This section provides material accommodations that enhance the learning of diverse students. Frequently, paraprofessionals, volunteers and students can help develop and implement various accommodations. Material accommodations include the following:

- ***Clarify or simplify written directions.*** Some directions are written in paragraph form and contain many units of information. These can be overwhelming to some students. The teacher can help by underlining or highlighting the significant parts of the directions. Rewriting the directions is often helpful.
- ***Present a small amount of work***. The teacher can tear pages from workbooks and materials to present small assignments to students who are anxious about the amount of work to be done. This technique prevents students from examining an entire workbook, text, or material and becoming discouraged by the amount of work.
- ***Block out extraneous stimuli.*** If a student is easily distracted by visual stimuli on a full worksheet or page, a blank sheet of paper can be used to cover sections of the page not being worked on at the time. Also, line markers can be used to aid reading and windows can be used to display individual math problems. Additionally, using larger font sizes and increasing spacing can help separate sections.
- ***Highlight essential information***. If an adolescent can read a regular textbook but has difficulty finding the essential

information, the teacher can mark this information with a highlight pen.

- ***Use a placeholder in consumable material.*** In consumable materials in which students progress sequentially (such as workbooks), the student can make a diagonal cut across the lower right-hand corner of the pages as they are completed. With all the completed pages cut, the student and teacher can readily locate the next page that needs to be corrected or completed.
- ***Provide additional practice activities.*** Some materials do not provide enough practice activities for students with learning problems to acquire mastery on selected skills. Teachers then must supplement the material with practice activities. Recommended practice exercises include instructional games, peer teaching activities, self-correcting materials, computer software programs and additional worksheets.
- ***Provide a glossary in content areas.*** Students often benefit from a glossary of content-related terms.
- ***Develop reading guides.*** A reading guide helps the reader understand the main ideas and sort out the numerous details related to the main ideas. A reading guide can be developed paragraph-by-paragraph, page-by-page, or section-by-section.
- ***Use an audio recording device.*** Directions, stories and specific lessons can be recorded. The student can replay the tape to clarify understanding of directions or concepts. Also, to improve reading skills, the student can read the printed words silently as they are presented on tape.
- ***Use of assistive technology.*** Assistive technology products such as tablets, electronic readers/dictionaries/spellers, text to speech programmes, audio books and more can be very useful tools.

## Accommodations Involving Interactive Instruction

The task of gaining students' attention and engaging them for a period of time requires many teaching and managing skills. Teaching and interactions should provide successful learning experiences for each student. Some accommodations to enhance successful interactive instructional activities are:

- ***Use explicit teaching procedures***. Many commercial materials do not cue teachers to use explicit teaching procedures; thus, the teacher often must adapt a material to include these procedures. Teachers can include explicit teaching steps within their lessons (i.e., present an advanced organiser, demonstrate the skill, provide guided practice, offer corrective feedback, set up independent practice, monitor practice and review).
- ***Repeat directions***. Students who have difficulty following directions are often helped by asking them to repeat the directions in their own words. The student can repeat the directions to a peer when the teacher is unavailable. If directions contain several steps, break down the directions into subsets. Simplify directions by presenting only one portion at a time and by writing each portion on the chalkboard as well as stating it orally. When using written directions, be sure that students are able to read and understand the words as well as comprehend the meaning of sentences.
- ***Maintain daily routines***. Many students with learning problems need the structure of daily routines to know and do what is expected.
- ***Provide a copy of lesson notes.*** The teacher can give a copy of lesson notes to students who have difficulty taking notes during presentations.
- ***Provide students with a graphic organiser***. An outline, chart, or blank web can be given to students to fill in during presentations. This helps students listen for key information and see the relationships among concepts and related information.
- ***Use step-by-step instruction***. New or difficult information can be presented in small sequential steps. This helps learners with limited prior knowledge who need explicit or part-to-whole instruction.

- ***Simultaneously combine verbal and visual information.*** Verbal information can be provided with visual displays (e.g., on an overhead or handout).
- ***Write key points or words on the chalkboard/whiteboard.*** Prior to a presentation, the teacher can write new vocabulary words and key points on the chalkboard/whiteboard.
- ***Use balanced presentations and activities.*** An effort should be made to balance oral presentations with visual information and participatory activities. Also, there should be a balance between large group, small group and individual activities.
- ***Use mnemonic instruction.*** Mnemonic devices can be used to help students remember key information or steps in a learning strategy.
- ***Emphasise daily review.*** Daily review of previous learning or lessons can help students connect new information with prior knowledge.

## Accommodations Involving Student Performance

Students vary significantly in their ability to respond in different modes. For example, students vary in their ability to give oral presentations; participate in discussions; write letters and numbers; write paragraphs; draw objects; spell; work in noisy or cluttered settings; and read, write, or speak at a fast pace. Moreover, students vary in their ability to process information presented in visual or auditory formats. The following accommodation involving mode of reception and expression can be used to enhance students' performance:

- ***Change response mode.*** For students who have difficulty with fine motor responses (such as handwriting), the response mode can be changed to underlining, selecting from multiple choices, sorting, or marking. Students with fine motor problems can be given extra space for writing answers on worksheets or can be allowed to respond on individual chalkboards/whiteboards.
- ***Provide an outline of the lesson.*** An outline enables some students to follow the lesson successfully and make appropriate notes. Moreover, an outline helps students to see the organisation of the material and ask timely questions.

- ***Encourage use of graphic organisers.*** A graphic organiser involves organising material into a visual format. To develop a graphic organiser, the student can list the topic on the first line, collect and divide information into major headings, list all information relating to major headings on index cards, organise information into major areas, place information under appropriate subheadings and place information into the organiser format.
- ***Place students close to the teacher.*** Students with attention problems can be seated close to the teacher, chalkboard/ whiteboard, or work area and away from distracting sounds, materials, or objects.
- ***Encourage use of assignment books or calendars.*** Students can use calendars to record assignment due dates, list school related activities, record test dates and schedule timelines for schoolwork. Students should set aside a special section in an assignment book or calendar for recording homework assignments.
- ***Have students turn lined paper vertically for math.*** Lined paper can be turned vertically to help students keep numbers in appropriate columns while computing math problems.
- ***Use cues to denote important items.*** Asterisks or bullets can denote questions or activities that count heavily in evaluation. This helps students spend time appropriately during tests or assignments.
- ***Design hierarchical worksheets.*** The teacher can design worksheets with problems arranged from easiest to hardest. Early success helps students begin to work.
- ***Allow use of instructional aids.*** Students can be provided with letter and number strips to help them write correctly. Number lines, counters, calculators and other assistive technology can help students compute once they understand the mathematical operations.
- ***Display work samples.*** Samples of completed assignments can be displayed to help students realise expectations and plan accordingly.

- ***Use peer-mediated learning***. The teacher can pair peers of different ability levels to review their notes, study for a test, read aloud to each other, write stories, or conduct laboratory experiments. Also, a partner can read math problems for students with reading problems to solve.
- ***Use flexible work times***. Students who work slowly can be given additional time to complete written assignments.
- ***Provide additional practice.*** Students require different amounts of practice to master skills or content. Many students with learning problems need additional practice to learn at a fluency level.
- ***Use assignment substitutions or adjustments***. Students can be allowed to complete projects instead of oral reports or vice versa. Also, tests can be given in oral or written format.

## Computers and Literacy Skills

Word processing is really helpful for the dyslexic child for many reasons:

- It is easier and quicker to press a key than to form a letter.
- Typing looks good throughout the text and the child ends up with a piece of work he/she can be proud of.
- Print on the screen or on paper looks more like the printed form in which we usually see words, so dyslexics are more likely to see mistakes.
- Dyslexics won't mind having a go on a word processor because it is easier to edit mistakes using the spell check.
- Random thoughts, words or paragraphs can be moved and put into order.
- Word processed work is easier to read for children and teachers.

## Conclusion

***'If a child does not learn the way you teach then teach him the way he learns.'***

Students with dyslexia can reach both academic and personal goals provided that their needs are recognised and they are appropriately supported. It is not the sole responsibility of the dyslexia specialist to teach these students; it should be the responsibility of the whole school. Arguably, all children learn best when their strengths and difficulties are recognised by their teachers, when they are taught to their preferred learning styles and when they have some control over their own learning. If we can give students more choice in the ways in which they learn and explore with them the reasons why they are learning, then, perhaps, we can improve their motivation and enable them to achieve greater success. Motivation is therefore very important to effective learning. Once students are achieving success, then they will begin to feel good about themselves. Students with dyslexia can improve their performance, attainment and the way they feel about themselves if they are encouraged to use their preferred learning styles. When students with dyslexia are taught to their strengths and given more ownership over their learning, then their whole school experience may be improved.

Since dyslexics often have good intelligence and even may be gifted in some areas. ***Albert Einstein*** was a genius and a dyslexic. ***Alexander Graham Bell*** the inventor and scientist, ***Pierre Curie*** the scientist, ***Tom Cruise*** the actor grew up and succeeded despite poverty, frequent relocations, inadequate schooling and dyslexia. ***Pablo Picasso*** became a famous, trendsetting art icon despite and no doubt because of, his apparent dyslexia. Famous Athletes like Olympians ***Bruce Jenner*** and ***Greg Louganis*** as well as auto racing star ***Jackie Stewart*** are self-acknowledged dyslexics. Dyslexics may be exceptional, versatile and creative. It is believed that a little motivation can get them on the right track.

## References


- Simmons, F. R. and Singleton, C.H. (2000). *Reading comprehension abilities of dyslexic students in higher education.Dyslexia*: An International Journal of Research and Practice, 6, 178-192.
- Griffiths, Y.M. and Snowling, M.J. (2002). *Predictors of exception word and nonword reading in dyslexic children: The severity hypothesis.* Journal of Educational Psychology, 94(1), 34-43.
- Lyon, G.R. (1995). *Towards a definition of dyslexia.* Annals of Dyslexia, 45, 3-27.
- Torgesen, J.K. (2002). *The prevention of reading difficulties.* Journal of School Psychology, 40, 7-26.
- Thomson, M. (1990). *Developmental Dyslexia (3rd edition*). London: Whurr.
- Rao, L. G. (2008). *Education of Persons with Intellectual Disabilities in India.* Salud Publica de Mex, 50 (suppl. 2), 205-212.
- International Dyslexia Association (2000). *Dyslexia Basics, Just the Facts,* The International Dyslexia Association website, http://www.interdys.org/fact%20sheets/Basics%20FS%20N.doc, Accessed Oct 29 2015.
- Karanth and Rozario (Eds.). *Learning Disabilities in India: Willing the Mind to Learn* (pp. 30- 43). New Delhi: Sage Publications.
- Rashmi Agrawal (2010). *Learning Disabilities; Teaching Learning Strategies.* Shipra Publication, New Delhi.
- http://www.lucidresearch.com
- https://en.wikipedia.org
- https://www.vub.ac.be/downloads/dyslexia.pdf

# Chapter - 8

# Supporting Learners with Dyslexia

*— Dr Preeti Jaiswar*

## Abstract

*Disability refers to sensory, physical and intellectual impairments, communication, emotional and behaviour disorders mental health problems and multiple disabilities, but all the disabilities is not means the social or economic obstacle of child growth. Some children do not seem to struggle with reading and writing. They have trouble with complex language skills, such as grammar, reading comprehension and more in-depth writing. Dyslexia can also make it difficult for people to express themselves clearly. It can be hard for them to stable their thoughts during conversation. They may have trouble finding right words to say and others struggle to understand what they are hearing. This is especially true when someone uses nonliteral language such as jokes and idiom. Dyslexia is a reading disorder; it is characterised by trouble with reading, despite normal intelligence. Different people are affected to varying degrees. Problems may include difficulties in spell words, reading quickly, writing, sounding words in the head, pronouncing words when reading loud and understanding what one reads. Often these difficulties are first noticed at school, when someone who previously could read loses their ability, it is known as alexia. The difficulties are involuntary and people with this disorder have normal desire to learn. Child with dyslexia can stir up a lot of emotions. You may look ahead if this learning issue will affect your child. But dyslexia is not a prediction of depression and failure. Dyslexia is very common and many successful people have dyslexia. After diagnosis of the dyslexia it is very important to take care of it as soon as possible. In this problem parent can help their child on basic level in treatment or removal of dyslexia condition, teachers, doctors and experts also play an important role to prevent dyslexia.*

***Keywords:*** *Dyslexia, Reading disorder, Learning issue, Diagnosis.*

## Dyslexia

In India, five to ten per cent of people have some impairment or disabling condition. This means that India has a huge population of disabled people at the policy level, progressive legislation, schemes and provisions exist for them. But at ground level, the disabled continue to be neglected and marginalised, with the onus of care on the family rather than the community. India needs to mark a shift from the medical model of intervention to community based rehabilitation of the disabled. The concept of disability differs from society to society. Because attitudes towards disability are deeply rooted in socio-cultural values, the term disability has been defined in many ways besides, other terms, such as 'impairment' and 'handicap' have been synonymously used for disability. Disability may be many types like physical, vocal, visionary, locomotors and mental but a different type of disability is also discovered in which child looking healthy in all ways but he have collective problems like writing, reading, learning, this problem or disability is called Dyslexia. In 1881, dyslexia was identified by Oswald Berkhan, but Rudolf Berlin firstly stated the term dyslexia in 1887. In 1896, he used the term to refer to the case of a young boy who had a problem in learning, read and write, despite showing typical intelligence and physical abilities in all other respects. A British physician named W. Pringle Morgan published a description of a reading and learning disorder in a report to the British medical journal titled "Congenital Word Blindness". The distinction between phonological and surface types of dyslexia is only descriptive and without any etiological assumption as to the underlying brain mechanisms. Dyslexia is a reading disorder; it is characterised by trouble with reading, despite normal intelligence. Different people are affected to varying degrees. Problems may include difficulties in spell words, reading quickly, writing, sounding words in the head, pronouncing words when reading loud and understanding what one reads. Often these difficulties are first noticed at school, when someone who previously could read loses their ability, it is known as alexia. The difficulties are involuntary and people with this disorder have normal desire to learn. Child with dyslexia can stir up a lot of emotions. You may look ahead if this learning issue will affect your child. But dyslexia is not a prediction of depression and failure. Dyslexia is very common and many successful people have dyslexia. In research it has been proved that there are different ways of teaching that can help people with dyslexia succeed. There's a lot you can do as a parent too. If you just start, there is no need to tackle everything at once. You can start helping your child simply by learning more about the symptoms, causes and strategies that can be used at home and in school. The best way to understand dyslexia is to understand what it is not. It is not a sign of low intelligence or laziness. It is also not due to weak vision. It is a common condition that affects the brain processes written and spoken language.

Dyslexia is primarily related with trouble reading. Some specialists and educators may refer it as a reading disorder or reading disability. But it can also affect writing, spelling and even speaking. People with dyslexia may be too intelligent and they can still understand complex ideas. Sometimes they need more time to work through the information. They can understand the things in a different way to process the information, such as listening to an audiobook in place of reading it.

If your child is suffered with dyslexia, he would not outgrow it. It is a lifelong condition. But that does not mean your child cannot be happy and successful. There are many teaching techniques and tools that can help your child. In fact, many people with dyslexia have successful careers in business, science and the arts. There are lots of famous people with dyslexia. This list includes director Steven Spielberg, investor Charles Schwab and actress Whoopi Goldberg. People suffering with dyslexia are often very creative. It is not clear that this type of creativity comes from thinking outside or from having a brain that's "wired" a bit differently. It is important to keep in mind, that struggles with reading and other issues can lead to de-motivation and frustration. The stress of dealing with schoolwork can make kids with dyslexia lose the motivation to keep trying.There are lots of tools and strategies that can help. It might take some trial and error for you to figure out which work best for your child. But finding the right strategies and seeing improvement can boost your child's confidence.

**Skills for Reading Comprehension:** It is very hard to read single word for kids with dyslexia. Dyslexia also makes it hard to understand and remember what they read. In elementary school, students are expected to read a passage of text and answer the questions about it. This is known as reading comprehension and it is important for building a strong base for success in school. Students suffering with dyslexia have reading comprehension problems because they need to develop many underlying skills, such as:-

- **Connecting letters to sounds:** Children have to learn that each letter of the alphabet is associated with a particular sound or sounds. It is known as "phonics." Once your child can make these connections, he will be able to speak words correctly.
- **Decoding text:** Decoding is the process of sounding out words. Once dyslexia suffered child can decode individual words, he/she can start to make sense of entire sentences.
- **Recognising similar words:** The ability to read a familiar word without having to sound it out is called "word recognition." The more words kids can recognise by sight, the faster they will be able to read. Normally readers can recognise a word by sight after sounding it out a dozen or so times. Students with dyslexia may need to see it more than 40 times.
- **Reading fluently:** Fluent readers can recognise the words by sight and quickly sound out unfamiliar words. They also can read smoothly and easily at a good rate. Fluency is essential for good reading comprehension.
- **Understanding the text:** Strong readers can remember what they have just read. They can summarise it and recall specific details. Readers suffered with dyslexia can confuse sounding out individual words. This interrupts the flow of information and makes it harder to understand and relate the new material to what they already know.

Dyslexia does not affect only reading and writing ability. It may affect everyday skills and activities of your child.

- **Social skills:** There are many ways Dyslexia can affect your child's daily life, it can affect school life, struggling in school can make your child feel inferior to other kids. Your child may stop trying to make new friends or may avoid group activities. Child may feel lonely that nobody understands him. Child may also have trouble understanding jokes or sarcasm.

- **Listening ability:** People with dyslexia tend to be better listeners than readers. But dyslexia can make it hard to understand. This means your child could have trouble that what the teacher is saying in the classroom.
- **Memorising ability:** Kids with dyslexia takes more time to read a sentence that they may not remember the sentence that came before it. This makes it tough to grasp the meaning of the paragraph.
- **Navigation:** Children with dyslexia may have problem with directional concepts such as "left and right", "near and far". This can lead to fears about getting lost in school hallways and other familiar places.
- **Time management:** Dyslexia can make it hard to tell time or stick to a schedule.

If your child has been having trouble reading, it is a better idea to find out what's going on and get him some extra help. That's why kids who start out struggling with reading rarely catch their own. A lot of scientists, researchers, doctors have been studying dyslexia for decades. They know which teaching methods and tools can help children with dyslexia succeed. If dyslexia is diagnosed by third grade, it is easier to catch up.There is no way to know the exact number of people suffered with dyslexia. But we do know that features of dyslexia are very common. In fact, the term dyslexia is often used to mean disabilities with reading. That figure doesn't tell the whole story, however. It only covers students who are getting services under the special education.

Dyslexia is thought to have two types of cause; one may be related to speaking and another to visual. It is a cognitive disorder, not a problem of intelligence, due to dyslexia child may be highly emotional. Researchers actually tell the causes of dyslexia. But they do know that genes and brain differences might influence a child's chances of having dyslexia. Here are some of the possible causes of dyslexia.

- **Brain activity:** Our brains have to translate the symbols which we see on the page into sounds. Then those sounds have to be combined into meaningful words. Generally the areas of our brains responsible for language skills work in a predictable way. But if your child has dyslexia, those areas do not work together in the same way. Kids with reading problems using different areas of the brain to compensate.
- **Brain anatomy:** Suffering with dyslexia does not mean that your child is not intelligent. In fact, many people with dyslexia have above-average intelligence. But their brain may think or look different from the brain of people who do not have dyslexia.
- **Genes and heredity:** Dyslexia may be genetically and hereditary, it runs in families. So if your child has dyslexia, there is a chance that you or other family members may have it too. About 40 per cent of siblings of children with dyslexia may have the same reading issues. Scientists have also found several genes associated with reading and language processing issues.

Dyslexia affects some people more severely than others; your child's symptoms may be different from another child. Some kids with dyslexia have trouble with reading and spelling. Others may struggle to write or to tell left from right or direction problem some are not able to judge height and speed of objects.

Some children do not seem to struggle with reading and writing. They have trouble with complex language skills, such as grammar, reading comprehension and more in-depth writing. Dyslexia can also make it difficult for people to express themselves clearly. It can be hard for them to stable their thoughts during conversation. They may have trouble finding right words to say and others struggle to understand what they are hearing. This is especially true when someone uses nonliteral language such as jokes and idiom.The sign of dyslexia may also look different at various ages. Some of the warning signs for dyslexia, such as a speech delay, seems before a child reaches kindergarten. Though, dyslexia is identified in grade school. As schoolwork gets more demanding, trouble processing language becomes more apparent. Many children have one or two of these issues on occasion. But kids with dyslexia have several of these issues and they don't go away.

Here are some symptoms of dyslexia in children at different level:-

**Symptoms in Kindergarten Level**

- Trouble in recognising the letters of the alphabet.
- Difficulty in learning of new words.
- Has a smaller vocabulary than other kids the same age.
- Problem to match letters to sounds, such as not knowing what sounds *b* or *h* make.
- Has difficulty blending sounds into words.
- Struggles to pronounce words correctly.
- Trouble of learning to count or say the days of the week and other common word sequences.
- Trouble in rhyme.

**Symptoms in Middle School Level**

- Difficulty in gripping a pencil.
- Difficulty in using proper grammar.
- Trouble in learning new skills and memorising things.
- Struggles with reading and spelling.
- Confuses the order of letters, such as writing "cat" instead of "cut".
- Has trouble remembering facts and numbers.
- Gets tripped up by word problems in math.
- Trouble in following a sequence of directions.

**Symptoms in High School Level**

- Problem in reading loud.
- Problem in reading at the expected grade level.
- Problem in understanding jokes or idioms.
- Difficulty in organising and managing time.
- Problem to summarise a story.
- Difficulty in learning a foreign language.

There are some tests that can indicate the probability whether a person carry dyslexia. If diagnostic testing indicates that a person may be dyslexic, such tests are often followed up with a full diagnostic assessment to determine the nature of the disorder. Tests can be mentored by a teacher or computer.

To know what's causing your child's reading issues can help in a variety of ways. Your child's teachers can use the information to figure out which methods of reading instruction to use. A right diagnosis could also open the doors to more resources and support at school. These resources might include one-on-one tutoring sessions with a reading specialist and a computer or laptop your child can use at home and at school.

There is not only a single test for dyslexia and getting a formal identification, for this we requires involvement of a team of professionals. In evaluation process you may use questionnaires to fill about your child's strengths and weaknesses. Your child's teachers may be asked to do the same thing. Here are the steps involved:

***Examination by Doctor-*** Doctor may test your child's vision and hearing to see if these could be affecting her ability to read. He will also ask you about your child's development and whether other family members have reading problems or other learning related issues.

***Referral to a Specialist-*** Your child may be tested by a psychologist or other professional who specialises in learning issues. These specialists can provide insights into how your child thinks. They will do tests to zero in on which areas child is struggling with. Your child will be asked to read words and do some rhyming, spelling and writing, among other things.The specialists will discuss their findings and recommend ways to help your child. These may include a type of tutoring called phonological awareness training. This can help improve your child's understanding of how sounds and letters go together.

It is never too early to start asking questions and getting your child some extra help. As soon as your child starts getting the right kind of help, the better his chances are of catching up to other kids of her age and make child normal very soon.There are resources in place to help infants and toddlers develop the language skills needed to become good readers. It is not necessary that reading and writing problem may be sign of dyslexia. There are also conditions that can look like dyslexia because they have some of the same symptoms. Here are some conditions that can similar with dyslexia:

- **ADHD (Attention Deficit Hyperactivity Disorder)** is refers difficulties in numbers recognition, reading and remembering. Due to this disorder child also feels inferior to other normal children. It may begin in adulthood as the result of a brain injury, stroke or dementia. Dyslexia is separate from reading difficulties caused by insufficient teaching or either hearing or vision problems.
- **Auditory Processing Disorder** affects kids ability to sort through the sounds they hear. They may struggle to understand what people are saying. Reading can also be tough for them. That's because so much of reading involves connecting sounds with letters. Kids with this disorder often have trouble recognising the difference between letters like *b* and *d* and sounding out new words.
- **Visual Processing Issues** can make it hard to see the difference between letters or shapes. Child with this disorder may have of blurry vision or of letters "hopping around on the page." They may try to compensate by closing one eye. They often reverse letters when writing and struggle to stay within the lines.
- **Dysgraphia** can affect children's ability to write and spell. In this disorder child face a problem to make diagram and latters. It can also make it hard to organise their thoughts on paper. Many kids who suffered with dysgraphia also have dyslexia.
- **Dyscalculia** makes it hard to do math. In this disorder child struggles with numbers, he will not able to do mathematical calculation. Many kids have serious difficulties in both reading and math. Trouble learning to count is associated with both conditions.
- **Executive Functioning Issues** can affect child ability to organise, manage and stay on task. Kids with weak Executive functioning issue may struggle with reading comprehension.

There are many ways parents and teachers can help with each of these conditions. Some strategies may work better for some conditions than others. That's why it is a good idea to get professionals to help you identify which issues your child is struggling with. More information can lead you to more effective ways to help.

## Suggestions

### *Professional help in Dyslexia*

Many people can help your child improve him reading and writing skills. These people can be work at your child's school. Following people may help your child in improvement from dyslexia condition.

### *Teacher*

Schools have been working for decades to help students with reading issues. Your child's teacher may be familiar with many methods of reading instruction and try different approaches to help your child. These might include giving extra time on tests your child use high-tech tools like word-prediction. Software School also may help your child academically without a diagnosis. Teachers may use Informal support and strategies to help instruggling students. Set up a meeting to talk about your mutual concerns. Teachers use to help common skills strategies for child speaking, reading and writing and having child's repeat directions back to the teacher. Teacher may use special strategies for child development to come out of problems which he is facing in reading and writing, it is called special education techniques. Under special education programme, some experienced teacher firstly observes that which type of problem child is facing. After that teacher use solution strategies which is useful for child improvement.

### *Doctor*

Dyslexia can make your child physic, stressful, it also effect on your child's self-esteem. Doctors use effective tools to improve him and get rid of all above problems. Psychologist understood the exact problem from which child is suffering and then he use problem solving suggestions to avoid child stress.

### *Parent*

Every parent can also help their children to diagnose and treatment of dyslexia. Firstly parents should know the actual problem related to reading, writing and learning. After that they should take advice to the experts of this disability. They should be more careful regarding treatment and removal of dyslexia. Helping your child with dyslexia can be a challenge, particularly if you are not confident. But you donot have to be an expert to help work on certain skills or strengthen your child's self-esteem.

Keep in mind that kids and families are all different, so it is not essential that all options will work for you. Do not panic if the first strategies you try are not effective. You may need to try different approaches to find what works best for your child. Here are some things you can try at home:

- **Read out loud every day.** If your child is very young, read picture books together. For a teenager, consider reading magazine or newspaper articles or maybe a recipe. Billboards, store-discount signs and instruction manuals are also fair game. Hearing you read can let your child focus on understanding the material and expanding his overall knowledge base. Do it every chance you can get.
- **Check your child's interests.** Provide a variety of reading materials, such as comic books, mystery stories, recipes and articles on sports or pop stars. Look for good books that are at your child's reading level. Kids with dyslexia and reading problem are more likely to power through a book if the topic is of great interest to them.
- **Use audio-visual tools.** You can arrange some audio visual material, which can improve hearing and learning problem, some stores sell books for younger kids that come with a recording of the story on a CD that prompts them when it is time to turn the page. Listening to a book while looking at the words can help your child learn to connect the sounds she is hearing to the words she is seeing.
- **Observation.** Watching your child more closely and note his behaviour may reveal patterns and triggers that you can begin to work around. Your notes will also come in handy if you want to talk to teachers, doctors or anyone else you enlist to help your child.

- **Look for apps and other high-tech help**. Now it a time of technology many digital and soft apps have been arrived in market which can be used to help in Word processing and spell-check for kids who have trouble with reading and spelling. Voice-recognition software can help older students tackle writing assignments by letting them dictate their ideas instead of having to type them.
- **Focus on effort, not outcome.** Praise your child for trying hard and emphasise that everyone makes mistakes—you included! Help your child understand how important it is to keep practicing and give hugs, high-fives or other rewards for making even the smallest bits of progress. Your encouragement will help your child stay motivated.
- **Make your home reader-friendly.** Try to stock every room with at least a few books or magazines your child might be interested in reading. Take a book when you go out for pizza or on a trip and read it to your family so you can all discuss it. Look for other creative ways to encourage reading and writing at home.
- **Boost confidence.** Always prays your child for his small effort, your child should always think that his parent is always with him in all condition. This feeling will be beneficial for your child's self-esteem and confidence.

## References


- Brain, works (2009). *It's called Dyslexia,* Popular Prakashan, p.12.
- Das, J.P (2009). *Reading difficulties and dyslexia*, SAGE Publication Pvt. Ltd., Edition first, pp. 36-48.
- Godwin, J. (2012). *Studying with dyslexia*, Publisher: Palgrave Macmillan.
- Lapkin, E (2014). Reviewed by Elizabeth Bobbin, M.Ed.
- http//www.understood.org
- http//www.nature.org

# Chapter - 9

# Dysgraphia: When Writing Hurts

— *Dr Akanksha Singh*

**Abstract**

*Good and legible handwriting is prerequisite for written communication. At primary and preprimary level teachers pay special emphasis on good handwriting of the students. Poor handwriting affects most academic activities of the student. This poor handwriting may be sometimes due to Learning Disability. Learning Disability refers to a group of disorder that affects a broad range of academic and functional skills of an individual. Learning disorders are of many types. Dysgraphia is disorder of written expressions. There are many symptoms of Dysgraphia. It is very essential to identify the specific difficulty of the student and timely intervention can help them to improve their weakness. Proper intervention and individual mentoring may significantly help in overcoming these writing difficulties. In present paper it has been discussed that how to recognise the child with learning disability and various intervention techniques.*

***Key words***- *Learning disability, Dysgraphia, Intervention.*

## Learning Disorders

Humans communicate with each other by oral or written communication or through sign language. In written communication, handwriting plays an important role. It is one of the important skills for effective communication. It is believed that most people are lazy in writing and often prefer something that is free from the task of writing. It can be said that writing is the highest and most complex form of communication that is learned in the latest stage of language skills series. The listening, speaking and reading are in fact a prerequisite for writing. In practice, writing deals with a few very specific skills including the ability to keep the subject in mind, setting the issue as words, drawing the graphical form of each letter and word, using correct tool for writing and having enough visual-motor memory. Among the basic academic skills, writing has been called the most tangible skill. The difference between writing and other communication skills is the written document which remains.

Handwriting is generally the storage of information. The data are written objectively and everyone can use it in every time and place. From the benefits of handwriting we can refer to the limited amount of data that human memory can hold and the unlimited amount of data that can be stored in written form. Thus, humans are not only able to learn the knowledge of their ancestors, but also they can use them to achieve new discoveries and new conclusions. Good handwriting easily conveys what writer wants to communicate. Many times teachers find that handwriting of the students is not good or even illegible. Many times it is not only bad handwriting but it may be due to learning disability.

Learning disability refers to a group of disorder that affects a broad range of academic and functional skills of an individual. Here it is important to mention that it is not due to hearing or vision disorder but some genetic or neurological factors are responsible for it. Learning disorders are due to brain-based problems. Unexpected under-achievement may be the symptom of learning disability. Because of learning disability these children do not learn as fast as other children. These learning disabled children may be intellectually average or above average. It is important to diagnose learning disabled children and help them to overcome these disadvantages.

There are some misconceptions or myths related to learning disability (LD) which is essential to be clarified. These are as follows-

- LD is due to cultural or linguistic differences.
- LD is due to inadequate instructions.
- LD is due to low socio-economic status.
- LD is due to hearing or vision problem.
- LD is due to lack of motivation.

- LD is indicative of low intelligence.
- LD is mentally retardedness.

## Types of Learning Disorders

Learning disorders are of many types-

1. Learning Disorder of Oral Language.
2. Learning Disorder of Mathematics (Dyscalculia).
3. Learning Disorder of Reading (Dyslexia).
4. Learning Disorder of Writing (Dysgraphia).

**1.** ***Learning Disorder of Oral Language-*** It is disability related to listening, speaking and understanding.

**2.** ***Learning Disorder of Mathematics (Dyscalculia)***-It is child's disability in performing the mathematical calculations expected of his/her age, intellectual capacity and educational level.

**3.** ***Learning Disorder of Reading (Dyslexia)*** -Learning disorder of Reading is most common disorder. It affects child's school performance. Reading disability is also known as dyslexia. Reading includes number of sub skills. In Dyslexic child following problems may be present according to severity-

(a) Inability to name letters

(b) Inability to read words

(c) Inability to read sentences

## Types of Dyslexia

Hinshelwood (1971) gave the taxonomy of reading disorder (dyslexia) which is as follows (a) Attention Dyslexia (b) Neglect Dyslexia (c) Letter by letter reading (d) Deep Dyslexia (e) Phonological Dyslexia.

***Attention Dyslexia-*** This is a rare form of dyslexia which is caused by poor attention control, a disorder in which the subject may have considerable difficulty in reading when more than one letter or word is presented.

***Neglect Dyslexia-*** It usually occurs due to brain damage. The affected person misidentifies letters in certain spatial regions of either a word or a group of words. Person may misread the first half of the word or last half of the word.

***Letter by Letter reading***-This is also known as pure dyslexia in which subject reads words by spelling the constituent letters (e.g., 'pencil' as 'p'-'e'-'n'-'c'-'i'-'l'). Subjects take unusually long time while reading loudly as well as silently.

***Deep Dyslexia***-In this type of dyslexia semantic errors are most prominent. They substitute semantically related words for the words they are trying to read. They find it easier to read concrete words rather than abstract ones.

***Phonological Dyslexia***-People suffering from phonological dyslexia usually have difficulty in reading non-words aloud.

**4. Dysgraphia (Learning Disorder of Writing)**–*Dys* means difficulty and *graphia* means writing. Dysgraphia is disorder of written expressions. The shortcomings of writing are related to the visual - motor coordination and dysgraphia. Many children cannot take advantage of the skills of writing by hand, because they have not learned the pre-writing skills. These skills include understanding the relationship between the upper and lower of body, recognition a variety of sizes and shapes, correct pencil grip and correct paper position.

***A Second Grade Student with Dysgraphia***

**Symptoms of Dysgraphia**

- Mix of upper case and lower case.
- Reversal (reversing direction letter faces along a vertical axis).
- Inversion (flipping letters along a horizontal axis so that the letter is upside down).
- Transposition (sequence of letters in a word is out of order).
- Irregular letter size, shape and inconsistency in writing.
- Wrong grip of pencil/pen. Holding thumb over two fingers.
- Spelling mistakes, punctuation errors.
- Illegibility.
- Refusal to complete writing task/fatigue.
- Poor use of line and space. (Amount of space between letters and words).
- Slow copying and writing.
- Writing from wrist.
- Use of wrist, arm, body or paper in awkward position while writing.
- Wrong positioning of paper.
- Wrong posture.

Apart from these symptoms while diagnosing Dysgraphia advice of trained practitioner in this field is very necessary.

Teachers should be aware of the signs and symptoms of dysgraphia and not dismiss a child as simply having sloppy handwriting. If a teacher starts to see a trend of illegible writing, it is appropriate for them to question whether this child has dysgraphia. Teachers should note which parts of the writing process are most difficult for the child. While dysgraphia often occurs along with another disability, many students with dysgraphia can exhibit high academic achievements in other subjects (Richards, 1999). Figure 1 shows an example of the handwriting of a second grade student with dysgraphia and a typical second grader's handwriting. The characteristics of dysgraphia are varied and students can exhibit any one or more of these characteristics.

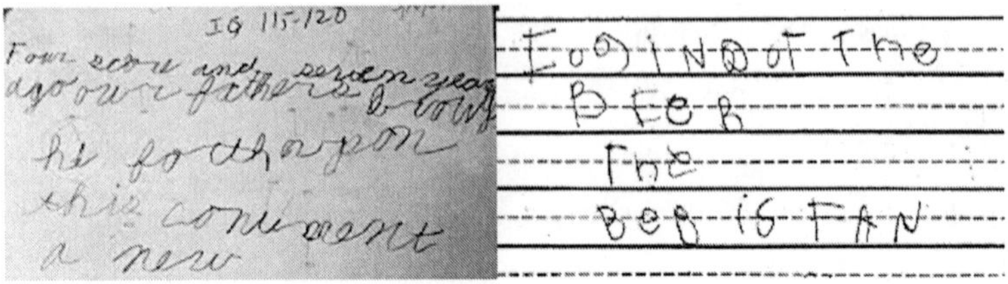

*Fig. 1: A second grade student's handwriting with Dysgraphia*

## Types of Dysgraphia

***Fine Motor***-It is due to deficient fine motor skill. Here written work of child is illegible. In this type of dyslexia child could not physically control /move pencil to replicate the given form.

***Visual Spatial***-It is due to defect in understanding of space. Students have problem in keeping their writing on line and difficulty with spacing between words and letters.

***Language Processing***- Trouble in writing down ideas on paper.

***Spelling***-Unable to understand spelling rules, trouble in telling that word is misspelt.

***Grammar***- It is due to poor understanding of the Grammar.

Writing itself is a very complex activity. The Determinants of good handwriting (Jena, S.P.K., 2013) are:

1. Letter formation and strokes of individual letter.
2. Uniformity of size and proportion of letter.
3. Space between words and letters.
4. Slant (consistency in direction of writing).

## Assessment of Dysgraphia

Dysgraphia can be assessed by formal and informal methods.

***Formal assessment*** tool are standardised tools for different grade students. Some of them are-

- Zaner-Bloser staff Scale,
- Basic school skill inventory Diagnostic etc.

In Zaner-Bloser staff Scale teacher judges student handwriting on the following elements –letter formation, vertical strokes in manuscript and start in cursive, spacing, alignment and proportion, line quality.

Basic school skill inventory Diagnostic by Hammill and Leigh (1983) assess writing skill such as writing from left to right, gripping a pencil, maintaining proper writing position, staying on the line etc.

***Informal assessment*** is based on close examination. Most of the psychologists, special education teacher and instructors use informal methods. It depends on teacher's observation of subject on attitude, habit, willingness, analysis of written work and knowledge of spelling rules. Problem of pronunciation, articulation and knowledge of dialect have to be also observed. In informal assessment teacher also tries to find out the spelling errors through various diagnostic tests.

## Dysgraphia Checklist

Dysgraphia may only recently been recognised and does not have the same stigma surrounding it as dyslexia, but it is very important that it is recognised as soon as possible. If these problems are not picked up at an early age, they impact on a child's self-esteem and take a long time to sort out. Here a sample checklist is provided for dysgraphia.

---

**DYSGRAPHIA CHECKLIST**

***Student's Name*** ________________ ***School*** ________________________

***Date*** ____________ ***Grade*** ____________ ***Student's DOB*** ________________

**Describe: Enter the number that best describes the child's writing behavior.**
**Never or rarely = 0 Sometimes = 1 Often = 2 Very Often = 3**

- Generally illegible writing (despite appropriate time and attention given the task).
- Mixture of printing and cursive writing on the same line.
- Writes in all directions, i.e. right slant then left slant.
- Unfinished words or letters, omitted words.
- Inconsistent position on page with respect to lines and margins.
- Cramped fingers on writing tool.
- Strange wrist, body or paper position.
- Talking to self while writing, or carefully watching the hand that is writing.

---

*(Cond...)*

- Poor organisation on the page.
- Inefficient speed in copying.
- Slow or laboured copying or writing-even if it is neat and legible.
- Poor spelling.
- Bizarre spelling.
- Frequently needs verbal cues and sub-vocalising.
- Slowly implements verbal directions that involve sequencing and planning.

**Note:-** *Eight items scored with a 2 or 3 indicate possible characteristics of Dysgraphia.*

## Intervention

When the writing task is the primary barrier to learning or demonstrating knowledge, then accommodations, modifications and remediation for these problems may be in order. How can a teacher determine when and what accommodations are merited? The teacher should meet with the student and parents, to express concern about the student's writing and listen to the student's perspective. It is important to stress that the issue is not that the student can't learn the material or do the work, but that the writing problems may be interfering with learning instead of helping. They should discuss how the student can make up for what writing doesn't seem to be providing. First of all it is important to seek help from the experts. Individual attention is very much essential. Motivation and supervised writing can help them.

For improvement there should be emphasis on the following practices:-

- Cutting with scissors.
- Finger painting.
- Tracing and colouring activities.
- For Eye-hand co-ordination drawing of geometrical forms.
- Chalk board activities.
- Dot to dot joining.
- Many apps are also available on which child can learn by moving their finger.
- More time for written tasks, including notetaking, copying and tests.

- Encourage keyboarding to increase the speed and legibility of written work.
- Provide a model of written work.
- Use of paper or writing instruments of different colours.
- Use of paper with raised lines to keep writing on the line.
- Shorten writing assignments.
- Extra time for writing activities.
- Remove neatness as grading criteria.

Four types of Educational Interventions can be used for eliminating the Dysgraphia:

***A-Self-learning:*** It includes speaking loudly at the time of writing and directing him/herself through speech. Children develop their behaviour by speech; they pass through four stages:

1. Directing behaviour by adults.
2. Directing behaviour by loudly speaking with him and connecting the words with action.
3. Directing behaviour by slow speaking and whisper.
4. Directing behaviour by speech therapy.

***B- Self-monitoring:*** In this case, children are asked to pause after each word to see if they have gripped the pen correctly. Otherwise, he should be corrected based on his/her evaluation. This is actually getting feedback from himself.

***C- Relaxation and Refreshment:*** The child will be asked to write five minutes, then play and engage in desired activities for ten minutes. Since the stress at the time of writing increases the fatigue of children, the rest intervals will help the child to calm and refresh him/herself.

***D- Mental - movement exercises:*** This exercise includes the way of gripping the pen and keeping the thumb half-open. The child tries to grip the pen correctly and in the best status.

## The Power of POWER

Students with dysgraphia, like many other students, often have a hard time getting started on a writing assignment. A helpful compensatory strategy for all such students would be to teach and encourage the use of pre-organisation strategies (Richards, 1999). These can include outlining, colour-coding main ideas, or writing main ideas on flash cards and rearranging them in the desired order. A strategy developed to assist students who have problems organising their writings into correct paragraph form is the mnemonic POWER:

**P** - Plan your paper;

**O** - Organise your thoughts and ideas;

**W** - Write your draft;

**E** - Edit your work; and

**R** - Revise your work before producing a final draft (Richards 1999).

## Cursive Writing Instead of Printing

For many children with dysgraphia, cursive writing has several advantages. It eliminates the necessity of picking up a pencil and deciding where to replace it after each letter. Each letter starts on the line, thus eliminating another potentially confusing decision for the writer. Cursive also has very few reversible letters, a typical source of trouble for people with dysgraphia. It eliminates word-spacing problems and gives words a flow and rhythm that enhances learning. For children who find it difficult to remember the motor patterns of letter forms, starting with cursive eliminates the traumatic transition from manuscript to cursive writing. Writers in cursive also have more opportunity to distinguish b, d, p and q because the cursive letter formations for writing each of these letters is so different. Orton (1937) found that children with dysgraphia tend not to advance as quickly as other children in school and their handwritten work suffers because of its illegibility. He found that incorrect paper position could lead to cramped fingers, which can directly lead to poor handwriting. He suggests that one correct the paper position and the slant of letters for better handwriting. Orton also found that some students focus on their hand rather than on the formation of letters. Orton blindfolded some students to see the effect on their handwriting. He found that for students who overly focused on their hand, being blindfolded helped them concentrate on the feel of formation and thus, on the legibility of the letters.

## Creative Writing with Computer Graphics

Students with learning differences who struggle with writing may be very frustrated because they have many creative ideas that they wish to express in a story format. Other students who struggle may have difficulty thinking of ideas. Both types of students benefit by using computer software that encourages them to add graphics, colour and other fun aspects to their story. If the student struggles with spelling, it will be important to provide enough assistance so that the spelling problems do not interfere with the student's ideation and creativity. The goal of the activity is to encourage the student to express ideas fluently using a written format. Word processing facilitates proofreading and editing activities because it eliminates the need for rewriting the paper. It is recommended as a strategy for older students when dealing with longer and/or more complex writing assignments. It is also valuable for younger students who struggle with writing and/ or who become fatigued with the process of writing using a pencil or pen.

Voice-activated software such as ***Dragon Naturally Speaking 13*** can be especially helpful within the writing process for students who have difficulty with the mechanical aspects of writing and written expression. However, there are several necessary prerequisites that must be in place before a student will be successful in using voice-activated software. Some of these are listed below:

- The student *must* reorganise the information in advance.
- The student must be able to state the phrases and sentences fairly fluently, without using filler words such as "um" or "uh".
- The student must speak clearly without excessive slurring of words.
- The student must have a basic understanding of word processing procedures.

Many dysgraphia students have difficulty with correct fingering in keyboarding skills. However, it is important to expose students to the correct fingering to develop quick visual locating skills for letters on the keyboard, ideally without having to look each time.

One important strategy is to have the student practice keyboarding skills approximately 10 minutes a day (this can be part of a homework assignment). The student should use a variety of child-oriented typing tutor programmes and work to develop appropriate skills to the best of his ability. At the same time, whenever the student types for ideas or content, whether a word, a sentence or a whole paragraph, he should be allowed to use whatever fingering he wants. Eventually, the goal is for the student to automatically incorporate at least some correct keyboard fingering when typing content.

Apart from these activities cognitive behavioural programme include mediation of functioning by cognitive process. They go beyond the stimulus response connection. This approach believes that writing is a cognitive activity that involves a number of skills, such as goal directedness, hierarchical organisations of goals, employing appropriate mental process as planning sentence generation and revision. Children with LD may have difficulties in these basic skills required for good writing. They find difficulty in generating the content, framing the text, transcription, planning text and revising the text.

It can be concluded that it is very essential to diagnose learning disability of the child. LD leads to negative impact on academic functioning of the child and further problems related to anxiety, depression and low level of self-esteem. Proper diagnosis and intervention can definitely improve a student's deficient skills. While diagnosis many areas like handwriting, spelling difficulty, language understanding needs to be considered.

Many schools do not have systematic instructional programmes in handwriting and spelling. Schools must include experts for these areas. Sensitively handling of these issues is very much essential. Healthy and supportive environment which is also the ethos of inclusive education is very much essential for the well-being of the learning disabled students.

## References


- Jena, S.P.K. (2013). *Learning Disability: Theory and practice,* Sage Publications India Pvt. Ltd., New Delhi.
- Hammill, D. D. and Leigh, J. E. (1983). *Basic school skills inventory-*diagnostic. Austin, Texas: pro-Ed.

- Hinshelwood, J. (1896). *Congenital Word Blindness*, H.K. Lewis, London.
- http://www.interdys.org/ewebeditpro5/upload/Understanding_Dysgraphia_Fact_Sheet_12-01-08.pdf
- http://psychology.wikia.com/agraphia.
- Orton, S. T. (1937). *Reading, writing and speech problems in children.* New York, NY: W.W. Norton & Company
- Richards, R. (1999). *The source for dyslexia and dysgraphia.* East Moline, IL: Lingui Systems.

# Chapter - 10

# Dyscalculia: Maths Learning Disabilities

—*Dr Meenakshi Dwivedi*


## Abstract

*For many children, mathematics is an inherently difficult subject to learn. Between five and eight per cent of children between the ages of 6 and 14 have a particular type of cognitive deficiency that limits their aptitude to acquire knowledge and understanding of fundamental ideas in numeracy (Geary, 2004). Increasingly, researchers in the cognitive sciences are studying this deficiency under the name dyscalculia, a disorder in which normally intelligent children demonstrate specific disabilities in learning mathematics. Teachers need to be informed about dyscalculia so that they can implement strategies that intentionally and explicitly accommodate students who have this disorder. The objectives of this paper, therefore, are to define dyscalculia, to consider the origins of dyscalculia in psychological, biological and pedagogical contexts, to describe the criteria required to diagnose students with dyscalculia and to delineate practical methods and instructional designs that can be implemented in the classroom to address the specific learning needs of dyscalculia learners.*


**Keywords:** *Dyscalculia, Numeracy, Mathematics, Instructional design.*

## Dyscalculia

In cognitive science and the pedagogical and neuropsychological fields, different views exist of mathematical learning disorders. Dyscalculia has been defined as a specific mathematical learning disorder (MLD), where the mathematical ability is far below expected for a person's age, intelligence and education.

The term Dyscalculia was coined in the 1940s but did not really become fully recognised until the 1974 work of Czechoslovakian researcher *LADISLAV KOSC*. He defined the disorder as "a structural disorder of mathematical abilities" caused by impairment to the parts of the brain used in mathematical calculations, without simultaneous impairment to one's general mental abilities. (In Layman's terms: You're bad at math because parts of your brain aren't working properly, but you're not otherwise mentally handicapped.) Today, some research communities also use the terms "math dyslexia" and "math learning disability" to refer to the condition.

Dyscalculia is a condition that affects the ability to acquire arithmetical skills. Dyscalculia learners may have difficulty understanding simple number concepts, lack an intuitive grasp of numbers and have problems learning number facts and procedures. Even if they produce a correct answer or use a correct method, they may do so mechanically and without confidence. Very little is known about the prevalence of dyscalculia, its causes, or treatment. Purely dyscalculia learners who have difficulties only with number will have cognitive and language abilities in the normal range and may excel in nonmathematical subjects. It is more likely that difficulties with numeracy accompany the language difficulties of dyslexia.

Dyscalculia affects the ability to acquire arithmetical skills. Dyscalculia learners may have difficulty understanding even very simple numerical ideas. They may find the daily math's lesson a source of enormous anxiety since they struggle to understand what is obvious to all their classmates. Unfortunately, dyscalculia is not widely recognised. For dyscalculics, the situation is rather like that for dyslexics 30 years ago. Teachers, parents, the world at large, think they must be stupid not to understand ideas and methods easily acquired by the rest of us. People may regard the label "dyscalculia" the kind of excuse middle-class parents make for their underachieving children, just as people used to regard the label "dyslexia".

It is a condition that affects the ability to acquire arithmetical skills. Dyscalculia learners may have difficulty understanding simple number concepts, lack an intuitive grasp of numbers and have problems learning number facts and procedures. Even if they produce a correct answer or use a correct method, they may do so mechanically and without confidence.

Dyscalculia is a big problem not just for individuals who suffer from it, but for the nation. The best current estimates suggest that about five-six per cent of children of average to superior intelligence will have a real specific learning deficit for maths. Individual with Dyscalculia are not unintelligent, but struggle to learn mathematics despite having an adequate learning environment at home and at school. Dyscalculia is assumed to be due to a difference in brain function.

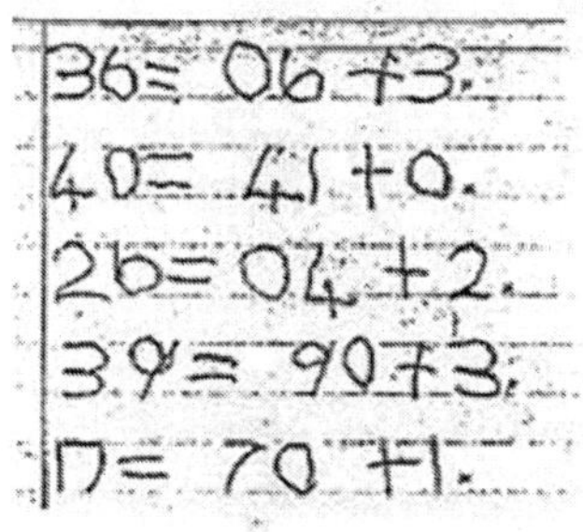

***Maths worksheet of a Dyscalculia Learner of Class Three***

## Definitions

Dyscalculia is a broad term that includes many different kinds of difficulties in learning mathematics. Dyscalculia is also used for naming general difficulties in learning basic mathematics. Some of the different definitions include:

- ***Developmental Dyscalculia*:** According to a number of researchers (Kosc, 1974, Shalev and Gross-Tsur, 1993, 2001, Wilson and Dehaene, 2007), this type of dyscalculia originates from a specific impairment in the brain function. However, this definition has not always been fully acknowledged by the research community. The neuroscience research field has though progressed, where studies are conducted concerning the brain (Wilson and Dehaene, 2007).
- ***Acalculia*:** Where a person has lost all sense of meaning of numbers or where the person still understands numbers but is

unable to perform basic calculations like addition and multiplication, due to a neurological damage.

- ***Pseudo-Dyscalculia***: Finding math difficult, based on emotional blockage or a confidence problem.

Someone living with Dyscalculia will have difficulty in the arenas of math reasoning, computation (addition, subtraction, multiplication and division), math memory, math writing, sequencing and math speaking, as well as visual-spatial orientation. A Dyscalculia learner will be challenged by both memory and retrieval difficulties, in addition to processing errors and will need to employ coping strategies his entire life. Those who suffer with the disability have been known to comment that Dyscalculia causes numbers to "slip their minds," that looking at large numbers is like trying to read an unknown language or even that it is as if their mathematics "memory banks" continually get erased after a lesson.

## Symptoms of Dyscalculia

- Difficulty working with numbers.
- Confused by math symbols.
- Difficulty with basic facts (adding, subtracting, multiplying and dividing).
- Often will reverse or transpose numbers (36: 63).
- Difficulty with mental math.
- Difficulty telling time.
- Difficulty with directions (as for playing a game).
- Difficulty grasping and remembering math concepts.
- Poor memory for layout of things (for example, numbers on a clock).
- Limited strategic planning skills (like used in chess).
- Relies on tangible supports such as fingers, tally marks.
- Slowness in given answers to math questions.
- Difficulty with estimation and approximation.
- Difficulty finding different approaches to one problem.

- Trouble with visualising patterns, different parts of a math problem, or identifying critical information needed in problem solving.
- History of academic failure contributing to the development of learned helplessness in mathematics.

## Methods for Diagnosing Dyscalculia

Currently, there are three well-documented methods for diagnosing dyscalculia. The following sections describe each of the three methods in detail.

### 1. Child's Attainment of Age-appropriate Mathematical Skills

The first method for determining whether or not a child is likely to have dyscalculia can be implemented easily in schools using existing student data and resources. Through the administration of a standardised assessment designed to measure the child's attainment of age-appropriate mathematical skills (Shalev and Gross-Tsur, 2001), educators might be able to form a diagnosis of dyscalculia if at least one of the following two circumstances is revealed:

- An inconsistency between the intellectual capability of the child and the results of the assessment (Geary, 2004; Reynolds, 1984); or,
- A significant disparity, usually of at least two-year levels, between the child's ordinal year of study and his or her arithmetic aptitude.

However, both circumstances are too general to assess accurately the specific extent to which a child may have dyscalculia. Therefore, some students might be incorrectly ascertained as dyscalculia when they might actually be affected by other more predominant learning difficulties.

### 2. Direct Observation of Dyscalculia Tendencies

Another way to detect the signs of dyscalculia involves the direct observation of a majority of the following behaviours:

- Undeveloped strategies for problem solving (Geary, 1990);
- Computational errors caused by a poor working memory span;

- Deficiencies in the long-term recall of arithmetic facts (Geary, Hamson and Hoard, 2000);
- Slow rate of processing of basic mathematical skills (Geary and Brown, 1991);
- Inability to recognise the commutativity of addition and multiplication.
- High rates of errors, particularly those that appear careless (Geary, 1993); and,
- Troubles with visual and spatial functioning (Rourke and Finlayson, 1978).

**3. The Dyscalculia Screener**

One solution could be the Dyscalculia Screener developed by Butterworth (2003). The Dyscalculia Screener consists of a series of item-timed tests that quickly and reliably identify dyscalculia without influences from other potential causes of an inadequate achievement in numeracy. Its primary objective is to measure the instinctive numerical proficiency of children between the ages of 6 and 14. Because human beings possess a biological inclination to gain a foundation level of understanding of numerical concepts, certain basic mathematical skills develop naturally without formalised education (Ginsburg, 1997). For example, a person can conceptualise size (that six is bigger than five), number (that a set of objects has a numerical value) and counting (that four comes after three). The Dyscalculia Screener, therefore, is designed to measure a child's level of inherent numeracy through simple tests involving counting dots and comparing numbers. Because the essential aspect of the tests is the speed with which the subject responds to the questions, Butterworth (2003) developed the Dyscalculia Screener as a software programme to administer the testing procedure. The programs will also collate the subject's responses, automatically analyse the aggregated results and finally calculate a standardised score.

However, any student who is struggling with mathematics would routinely demonstrate one or more of these performance indicators. Just like the assessment of a child's attainment of age-appropriate mathematical skills, this method may incorrectly assess non-dyscalculic children as dyscalculic. Therefore, a comprehensive and unambiguous approach is needed to correctly identify dyscalculia in students so that instructional designs can be modified to accommodate them in the classroom.

## Assistive Technology for Dyscalculia

Children with disabilities experience unique learning challenges in classroom environment, ones which often differ from their peers. It is important when using technology in a classroom that all students will benefit from its learning outcomes. Assistive technology can be used to help students with dyscalculia perform in the classroom. It enables students with learning disabilities to independently learn. Assistive technology can also provide the learning disabled students with remedial and compensatory support. Categories of dyscalculic learning disabilities that affect mathematics learning include spoken language, written language, arithmetic and reasoning. There is a variety of assistive technology that can help students with different types of dyscalculia overcome these difficulties. Software titles such as "Mighty Math," available for the classroom and at home, incorporates math learning into interactive video, using stories, music and visual cues to help students relate math concepts to everyday life. ***Electronic Math Worksheets, Math Software-Number Race, Adapted Measuring Devices*** like Talking measuring jugs, colour coded measuring cups, ***Reading books, Babakus, iPad, Kurzweil 3000*** etc. are the useful devices for the learners with dyscalculia.

## Difference between Dyscalculia and Dyslexia

One analysis discovered that approximately 17 per cent of dyscalculia children are also dyslexic and another 26 per cent experience the effects of attention deficit hyperactivity disorder (Shalev, Manor and Gross-Tsur, 1997).

A simple definition primarily identifies dyslexia with difficulties in reading written text fast and fluently. Dyscalculia, on the other hand, refers to difficulties with handling and carrying out specific mathematical tasks. Here the differences are very obvious. However, there are also some points of overlap. There is a variant of dyscalculia that could be called **Dyslexic Dyscalculia**. This problem manifests primarily in reading difficulties which then lead to mathematical problems for the child. These can be problems with reading numerical symbols and configurations in written tasks or difficulties with reading multi-digit numerals, so that 12 become 21. With an error like this in the reading of the task, then obviously the solution will be incorrect, even if the calculations are accurate.

There are in fact several similarities between difficulties with reading and counting. One of the more significant and most disabling, is the previously mentioned automatisation-difficulty. This can be recognised in the lack of "flow" or fluency in reading words such as and, that, to and as may not be "automatic", hindering the fluency of reading. Difficulties that correspond to this in mathematics concern the ability to quickly retrieve numerical facts such as the multiplication tables from the memory.

There are several other indirect similarities between difficulties with reading and mathematics. A poor working memory is one of the more obvious. In reading, the problem can be recognised when a child reads slowly but steadily, but then cannot remember the word or the text they just read. The professional term for this inability to recall the beginning of a task while you are completing the end of it is called the phonological loop. Mathematical problems caused by working memory are evident in tasks that must be solved mentally, in the head. The student may run into great difficulties keeping different numbers in the memory while he is doing the calculation. In other cases, the student may have problems remembering longer instructions or commands. Maybe she will only remember a part of what was supposed to be done. The rest is forgotten, because the information was never stored in her memory.

## Instructional Modifications Designed to Accommodate Dyscalculia Learners

Once a student has been ascertained as having dyscalculia, there are practical methods and instructional designs that can be incorporated into the classroom. Researchers have provided a list of strategies that have been proven to help students who suffer from dyscalculia. This list is categorised into strategies for improving reading skills, improving mathematical problem-solving skills and general instructional design:

***Improving Reading Skills-***

- Break up large sections of text with page breaks and bullet points.
- Use a sans serif font (i.e., without heads and tails, such as Arial or Tahoma) which is easier for dyscalculia students to read.
- Do not justify the text (as this paper does), because the extra spacing required for justification makes it more difficult to read.
- Use coloured overlays to reduce the glare from black type on white paper, which is often a problem for students who have difficulties with visual perception.

***Improving Mathematical Problem Solving Skills-***

- Photocopy mathematics books, which are generally difficult to read because of the interspersement of diagrams, tables and charts, with the relevant sections placed in a more sequential order.
- Separate multi-step problems into small, manageable steps.
- Use a line reader, if available, to highlight a line of work and fade the other lines into the background.
- Use coloured pens or markers to highlight various parts of a question.
- Use colour in spreadsheets to delineate the different columns and rows.
- Edit down the output tables of statistical analyses so that the student can focus on the relevant sections.

***General Instructional Design-***

- Supplement missing or incomplete notes.
- Put up large wall posters to remind students of various basic concepts that cannot be easily recalled in short-term memory.
- Use system cards to aid in memorisation.
- Provide flow diagrams or tree diagrams to clarify procedures.

- Provide mind map diagrams to help with the development of a long-term project.
- Employ typical strategies for engaging visual learners to a greater degree.
- Move through a lesson at the student's own pace so that he or she does not become bogged down by the material.
- Teach skills in organisation, studying and time management.
- Focus on revision prior to an examination.

This list is not exhaustive of all the ways in which to cater for a dyscalculia student. However, using these approaches in mathematics education would facilitate the learning of all students, regardless of whether or not they have been ascertained as having a learning disorder.

The latest work in mathematical learning disorders has revealed that dyscalculia learners are indeed affected by this condition in significant ways both academically and socially (Ackerman and Dykman, 1995). Because general life skills require a certain degree of numerical aptitude, dyscalculia children become adults who are severely impeded by their inabilities to reason quantitatively thereby affecting their fundamental understandings of time, money, direction and space. Poor numeracy skills have been proven to be more detrimental to a person's employability than poor literacy skills. Thus, it is vitally important that educators, particularly mathematics educators, take a genuine interest in the problems caused by dyscalculia.

## Conclusion

Dyscalculia is curable. If the child is getting the right treatment and help, the possibility of development in mathematical ability is greatly increased. However, often some parts of the difficulties remain in a milder form, for example, difficulties with recalling numerical facts. It is usual that the student will continue to have features of those difficulties, in a mild form, throughout adult life. Ability to concentrate, however, usually considerably improves and with that often comes the understanding of mathematical concepts and symbols. Many students with dyscalculia are able to complete mathematical tasks, but within a longer than average time frame. They are unable to retrieve numerical facts from their memory fast enough and must expend a lot of energy doing so.

Dyscalculia is not an illness so it cannot be cured. Dyscalculia is a special need and requires diagnosis and support. This support is designed to give children an understanding of their condition and equip them with coping strategies that they can use in the classroom and in their day-to-day encounters with numbers. Dyscalculia is a debilitating disorder that affects a person's ability to conceptualise the operations and processes of fundamental mathematics. Although its origins are still not entirely clear, there are strategies that have been proven to ascertain dyscalculia correctly as a discrete learning disorder. In all likelihood, the Dyscalculia Screener is the best tool currently available to accurately quantify the degree to which a child suffers from the learning disorder. Because numeracy is a significant part of daily life, it is vital that dyscalculia students be given special consideration to develop their own capacities of mathematical cognition. Instructional methods, such as those outlined earlier, can be integrated into a mainstream classroom to assist students with mathematical learning disabilities.

## References


- Ackerman, P. T. and Dykman, R. A. (1995). *Reading-disabled students with comorbid arithmetic disability. Developmental Neuropsychology*, 11, 351-371.
- Bird, R. (2011). *The Dyscalculia Resource Book*, Sage Publications, New Delhi.
- Butterworth, B. (1999). *The Mathematical Brain*: Macmillan, London.
- Geary, D. C. (2004). *Mathematics and learning disabilities*. Journal of Learning Disabilities, 37(1), 4-15.
- Ginsburg, H. P. (1997). *Mathematics learning disabilities: A view from developmental psychology.* Journal of Learning Disabilities, 30: 20-33.
- Kosc, L. (1974). *Developmental Dyscalculia*. Journal of Learning Disabilities, Vol. 7.
- Kumar, S. Praveen and Raja, B.W.D. (2011). *Special Education: Focus on Mathematical Learning Disability,* APH Publishing Corporation, New Delhi.
- Rao, G. Narayana. (2005). *How learning disabilities occur in a child.* Edutracks, 5(3), 10-11.

- Shalev R. S., Auerbach J., Manor O., Gross-Tsur V. (2000), *Developmental Dyscalculia: prevalence and prognosis.* Steinkopff Verlag,
- Wilson, A., Dehaene, S. (2007). *Number sense and developmental dyscalculia. In Human behaviour, learning and the developing brain*: Atypical development, pp. 212-238.
- http//www.understood.org

# Chapter - 11

# Dyspraxia: Understanding the Hidden Disorder

*— Dr Meenakshi Dwivedi*


**Abstract**

*Dyspraxia, also known as Developmental Co-ordination Disorder (DCD), can affect all types of skills, including manual dexterity, balance and motor movement, which is why sufferers tend to have poor physical co-ordination and appear clumsy and awkward. Symptoms of dyspraxia can include behavioural issues, poor balance and sensitivity to noise. It can also, in extreme cases, cause speech impediments. Generally, people with dyspraxia also have difficulties with routine tasks, such as driving or cooking, writing or doing up buttons. Dyspraxia affects each person in unique ways. Students may need support with a range of day-to-day tasks, or they may need support in specific areas. The present chapter deals with the concept, symptoms in different age groups and causes of dyspraxia. There are a number of interventions and strategies that can help students with dyspraxia which are also discussed here. The article can also be useful to provide general and more specific information for parents and teachers on the subject of dyspraxia.*


***Keywords:*** *Dyspraxia, Developmental Co-ordination Disorder, Interventions.*

## Dyspraxia

***"Everyone says I'm stupid but I know I'm not. I wish someone could understand what it's like to be me. I feel so fed up and lonely."***

***Sarah**, an eight years-old girl who has dyspraxia*

Dyspraxia is surprisingly common in both children and adults. It is a hidden condition, which is still poorly understood. Dyspraxia, a form of Developmental Co-ordination Disorder (DCD) is a common disorder affecting fine or gross motor coordination, in children and adults. DCD is often regarded as an umbrella term to cover motor coordination difficulties. Dyspraxia refers to those people who have additional problems in planning, organising and carrying out movements in the right order in everyday situations. Dyspraxia can also affect articulation and speech, perception and thought. Although dyspraxia may occur in isolation, it frequently coexists with other conditions such as Attention Deficit Hyperactive Disorder (ADHD), dyslexia, language disorders and social, emotional and behavioural impairments.

Word dyspraxia came from the Greek word ‘praxis’ which is the learned ability to plan and carry out sequences of co-ordinated movements in order to achieve an objective. Dys is the pre-fix means ‘bad’. Dyspraxia therefore literally means bad praxis and is a term used to describe behaviours that results from an underlying incapacity in praxis.

**A person with dyspraxia has problems with movement, co-ordination, judgement, processing, memory and some other cognitive skills. Dyspraxia also affects the body’s immune and nervous systems.** It is also known as Motor Learning Difficulties, Perceptuo-Motor Dysfunction and Developmental Coordination Disorder (DCD).

According to the National Centre for Learning Disabilities, individuals with dyspraxia have difficulties in planning, coordinating and completing fine motor tasks. This can range from simple motor movements, such as waving goodbye, to more complex ones like brushing one’s teeth.

Individuals with dyspraxia oftentimes have language problems and sometimes a degree of difficulty with cogitation and perception. Dyspraxia, however, does not affect the person’s intelligence, although it can be causation of learning problems in children. Developmental dyspraxia is an immaturity of the organisation of movement. The brain does not process information in a way that allows for a full transmission of neural messages. A person with dyspraxia finds it difficult to plan what to do and how to do the task.

Experts say that about ten per cent of people have some degree of dyspraxia, while approximately two per cent have it critically. Four out of every five children with evident dyspraxia are boys. If the average classroom has 30 children, there is probably one child with dyspraxia in substantially each classroom.

## Symptoms of Dyspraxia

Dyspraxia symptoms may vary based upon the age of the child which is categorised as:

***Very early childhood-***

The child may take longer than other children to:

- Sit.
- Crawl - Many children never go through the crawling stage.
- Walk.
- Speak - The child may be slower in answering questions, finds it hard to make sounds or repeat sequences of sounds or words, has difficulty in sustaining normal intonation patterns, has a very limited automatic vocabulary, speaks more slowly than other kids and uses fewer words and more pauses.
- Stand.
- Become potty trained.
- Build up vocabulary.

***Early Childhood-***

Later on the following difficulties may become apparent:

- Problems performing delicate movements, such as tying shoelaces, doing up buttons and zips, using cutlery, handwriting.
- Many will have difficulties getting dressed.
- Problems carrying out playground movements, such as jumping, playing hopscotch, catching a ball, kicking a ball, hopping and skipping.

- Problems with classroom movements, such as using scissors, colouring, drawing, playing jig-saw games.
- Problems processing thoughts.
- Difficulties with concentration. Children with dyspraxia commonly find it hard to focus on one thing for long.
- The child finds it harder than other kids to join in playground games.
- The child will fidget more than other children.
- Some find it hard to go up and down stairs.
- A higher tendency to bump into things, to fall over and to drop things.
- Difficulty in learning new skills - while other children may do this automatically, a child with dyspraxia takes longer. Encouragement and practice help enormously.
- Writing stories can be much more challenging for a child with dyspraxia, as can copying from a blackboard.

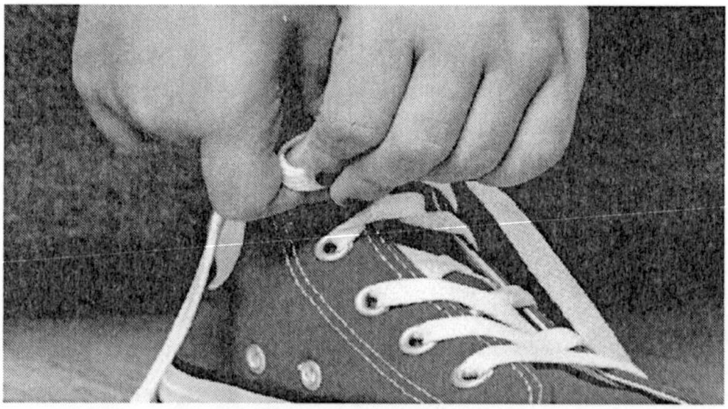

***Tying shoelaces can be a difficult task for children suffering with dyspraxia.***

**The Following are also Common at Pre-school Age**

- Finds it hard to keep friends;
- Behaviour when in the company of others may seem unusual;
- Hesitates in most actions, seems slow;

- Does not hold a pencil with a good grip;
- Such concepts as *in, out, in front of* are hard to handle automatically.

***Later on in Childhood***

- Many of the challenges listed above do not improve, or do so very slightly.
- Tries to avoid sports.
- Learns well on a one-on-one basis, but nowhere near as well in class with other kids around.
- Reacts to all stimuli equally (not filtering out irrelevant stimuli automatically).
- Mathematics and writing are difficult.
- Spends a long time getting writing done.
- Does not follow instructions.
- Does not remember instructions.
- Is badly organised.

## Social and Sensory

Individuals with dyspraxia may be extremely sensitive to taste, light, touch and noise. There may also be a lack of awareness of potential dangers. Many experience moods swings and display erratic behaviour. Researchers say that there is often a tendency to take things literally. the child may listen but not understand.

## Verbal Dyspraxia

Children with developmental verbal dyspraxia have difficulty in making and co-coordinating the precise movements required for the production of clear speech and yet there is no evidence of damage to nerves or muscles. They have difficulty in producing individual speech sounds and in sequencing sounds together in words. As a result their speech is often unintelligible even to family members. The speech disorder is the predominant presentation, but children with developmental verbal dyspraxia may also have poor-motor dyspraxia, affecting their ability to make and co-ordinate the movements of the larynx, lips, tongue and palate and generalised dyspraxia affecting gross and fine body movements. The favoured term in the UK is *Developmental Verbal Dyspraxia*, however it is also sometimes referred to as *Articulatory dyspraxia* and in the USA the usual term is developmental or *childhood apraxia of speech*. Speech and Language Therapists usually diagnose developmental verbal dyspraxia by referring to checklists of characteristics and identifying a symptom cluster of presenting features. In addition to speech characteristics, checklists usually refer to commonly reported language, learning, clinical and motor characteristics.

## Causes

Although the exact causes of dyspraxia are unknown, it is thought to be caused by a disruption in the way messages from the brain are transmitted to the body. This affects a person's ability to perform movements in a smooth, coordinated way. People with dyspraxia have no neurological condition to explain their movement difficulties.

## Strategies

The following strategies may be opted by the teachers in and outside the classrooms to help children with dyspraxia.

- Pre-set students for touch with verbal prompts, "I'm going to touch your right hand."
- Avoid touching from behind or getting too close and make sure peers are aware of this.
- Provide a quiet place, without auditory or visual distractions, for testing, silent reading or work that requires great concentration.
- Warn the student when bells will ring or if a fire drill is scheduled.
- Whisper when working one to one with the child.
- Allow parents to provide earplugs or sterile waxes for noisy events such as assemblies.
- Make sure the parent knows about what is observed about the student in the classroom.
- Refer student for occupational therapy or sensory integration training.

- Be cognisant of light and light sources that may be irritating to child.
- Use manipulative, but make sure they are in students field of vision and don't force student to touch them.

## Helping Dyspraxia Children

In order for a dyspraxia child to perceive themselves as being successful they must actually be successful. Therefore aims for teaching and therapy at home and school must include:-

## Preserve Motivation and Confidence

This is a real disability with performance being unpredictable and inconsistent therefore recognition and awareness of difficulties required in order to leads to understanding and appreciation.

- Modify our responses: reassurance rather than criticism.
- Descriptive praise and encouragement. For example, in class it is important to mark work of a child with Dyspraxia using ticks and descriptive praise and praise on effort rather than performance.
- Make all goals attainable.
- Have feedback sessions at the end of lessons.
- Acknowledge good points of character i.e. kindness, willing to continue trying.

## Upgrade Skill Performance

Upgrade skill performance so that their abilities meet that demanded by the environment. Children can refine and generalise motor skills. However, children with Dyspraxia need time and over learning and steps to learning cannot be assumed. They need motor skills 'hard wired' much more than other children.

## Teaching Techniques

- List all areas of difficulty.
- Place in order of priority.
- Make sure that a skill is developmentally appropriate.

- Make sure you have plenty of time to address difficulty and practice– do not rush!
- Break down task into the sensory-perceptual-motor components and cognitive-verbal steps (Task analysis).
- Teach each component individually either by forward or backward chaining. Upgrade/adapt sensory and meta-cognitive strategies to make motor steps easier, successful and rewarding. Make sure that each step has a 'just right challenge'.
- Gradually build components into whole skill – work forwards.
- Practice skill lots of times.
- Generalise skill i.e. different shoes and different laces.
- Follow through into everyday life i.e. wear laced up shoes to school everyday.
- Openly acknowledge success.

## Modify and Adapt Environment

This helps relieve neurological stress and improves organisation, which results in increased confidence but also improved concentration and attention on the activity and content of work.

## Handwriting and Dyspraxia

One of the primary symptoms of dyspraxia is poor handwriting. This is due to poor motor skills, perceptual dysfunction and erratic organisation and motor planning. Due to the volume of writing required in school today, difficulties in this area have a profound effect on the child's academic performance and subsequent confidence. The following suggestions provide some practical advice to alleviate some of the anxiety and concerns brought about by poor handwriting.

***Posture:*** It is very important that children are seated with feet securely on the floor and knees and hips bent at a 90° angle. The height of the table should equate to the elbow height when seated. Sometimes the furniture in the classroom is required as per the need of dyspraxic children.

***Positioning of Paper:*** The paper should be positioned at a slight angle in alignment with the child's arm be this a left or right diagonal.

## Classroom Guidelines

| *Dyspraxic Difficulties* | *Problems at School* | *Classroom Strategies* |
|---|---|---|
| • Hand to Eye Co-ordination sky | • Hand writing difficulties | • Practice multi-sensory letter formation e.g., sandpaper letters, writing, ricetrays.<br>• Use pencil grips, writing lines, stencils. |
| • Hand to Eye Co-ordination | • Difficulties with dressing and fastening clothes<br>• Using tools, utensils and cutlery | • Suggest loose-fiteasy on/easy off clothing and Velcro fastenings<br>• Break down each task into small sections to be mastered one by one. |
| • Large Muscle Movements | • Difficulty walking in straight line, bumps into people and things<br>• Difficulties running, hopping, jumping, catching/kicking balls | • Provide balance or wobble boards, walking on the line and hand to hand throwing using bean bags or water-filled balloons. |
| • Attention/concentration | • Reacts to all stimuli without discrimination<br>• Attention span is poor<br>• Distracted in open-plan environments<br>• Flits between activities<br>• Disturbs others | • Allow child to choose activities which meet child's own interests.<br>• Avoid disturbing child when on task.<br>• Avoid fluorescent lights, fluttering ceiling displays.<br>• Keep wall displays to a minimum.<br>• Promote a 'no-disturbance' culture showing respect for each child's work space. |
| • Conceptualisation | • Difficulty understanding concepts such as 'in' 'on' 'in front of' | • Playfarm/zoo/journey games with command cards such as 'cow in front of barn' with correct picture on back of card. |
| • Personal Organisation | • Generally poorly organised | • Supply time-tables, daily diaries and instructions for specific activities in sequenced picture cards. |
| • Communication | • Unable to remember and/or follow instructions | • Get the attention of the child before giving instructions.<br>• Use simple language with visual prompts.<br>• Provide time to process the information.<br>• Use activities, demonstrations and pictures. |
| • Speech, Language and communication | • Difficulty in explaining needs or answering a question. | • Provide visual supports to help recollection of personal experiences. |

Children should be encouraged to hold their paper with the opposite hand, if this proves difficult buy a sheet of thin non-slip matting (Dycem) to position the paper and encourage the placement of the opposite hand by drawing a stencil of the ideal position using a permanent marker pen.

***Pencil Grip*:** It is common to see children with dyspraxia holding the pencil awkwardly and struggling to achieve a tripod grip which incorporates the thumb, index and middle finger. Pencils with triangular barrels such as hand huggers should be used. Alternate position of the pencil can be tried out. Place the pencil between the index and middle finger with the main shaft of the pencil on the upper surface of the hand, the pencil is then controlled by the thumb while positioning the wrist on the writing surface. This is effective and comfortable.

***Writing Alignment*:** As many children with dyspraxia struggle to plan and organise their movements, they will also find writing across the page in a left to right horizontal direction very difficult. Guidance is therefore needed to help them with writing alignment. It is advisable to use lined paper rather than a line guide which easily moves. Mark a margin at the left hand side in a clear colour or place starting points at the left margin to reiterate where each line of writing should start.

***Letter Formation*:** To develop an appreciation of form it is important to use variety of multisensory activities to reinforce the child's appreciation of shape and size like play games which reinforce shape and size i.e. sorting boxes, ball games, shape stencils, spirograph etc. Provide a starting arrow to show which way a letter should be produced i.e., the letter c is orientated in an anticlockwise direction and the letter b requires a clockwise orientation.

***Spatial Organisation:*** Spaces between words may be omitted or placed erratically by dyspraxia learners. This results in text becoming increasingly illegible. It is therefore crucial to teach the child how to provide adequate spaces between words and to space letters appropriately. For this, Practice writing on grid paper placing each letter in a square and a space between each word. Place a fingertip after each word before writing the next word. Introduce joined writing pattern very early in the child's education.

***Augmentative Technology*: **As the expected volume of handwriting increases in every year of schooling so too will the child's level of anxiety. It is at this time when a computer may be considered. This may be around the age of eight or nine years. At this point word-processing can be introduced in parallel with handwriting. The child may eventually become more proficient at using a computer over hand skills or vice versa. It is important that the computer or keyboard is carefully selected and that the right scheme is introduced to help the child develop new skills. It is not important that touch typing is achieved with all fingers but that the child's abilities are utilised fully to appreciate the technology available to him.

## Conclusion

Early recognition of dyspraxia enables a child's special educational and social needs to be identified. Action can then be taken to reduce the impact of this condition on their whole family. Although dyspraxia is a lifelong condition, motor co-ordination may improve with age. Symptoms in children and adults can lessen if they are given appropriate treatment and advice on practical actions to minimise the day-to-day difficulties that their dyspraxia can cause. Many people who have Dyspraxia are creative, such as, writers and artists they have a unique way of thinking which can contribute so much to other people's lives. Few famous people who suffered from Dyspraxia are **Albert Einstein** who was unable to tie his shoes laces even as an adult, **Daniel Radcliffe,** the Hollywood actor and **David Bailey** – the photographer, **Cara Delevingne,** the US supermodel.

## References


- Boon, M. (2001). *Helping Children with Dyspraxia*. Jessica Kingsley Publishers, London.
- Guild, A. S. and Vail, T. *What is developmental apraxia of speech*? Retrieved January 23, 2016 from www.tayloredmktg.com/dyspraxia.
- Hapnes, K. (2001). *Developmental Co-ordination Disorders. Special Children*, pp. 28-30.
- http://www.ncld.org.
- http://www.dyspraxiafoundation.org.uk
- Shirberg, L. D., Aram, D. M. and Kwiatkowski, J. (1997). *Developmental apraxia of speech: Descriptive and theoretical perspectives.* Journal of

Speech, Language and Hearing Research, 40, 273-286. Retrieved January 28, 2016 from www.proquest.umi.com.

- Stordy, B. J. and Nicholl, M. J. (2000). *The remarkable nutritional treatment for ADHD, dyslexia and dyspraxia the LCP solution*. New York: Random House.
- Wikipedia, online encyclopedia. *Dyspraxia.* Retrieved January 30, 2016 from www.wikipedia.org.

# Chapter - 12

# Attention Deficit Hyperactivity Disorder and Social Skill Development

*—Ms Waseem Zahra*

**Abstract**

*It is important to lay the foundations of socialisations by teaching the skills at home, school, and/or a social skills programme. Children who lack certain social skills may have great difficulty building a network of supportive friends and acquaintances as he or she grows older and may become socially isolated. Moreover, one of the consequences of loneliness is an increased risk of developing emotional problems or mental disorders. Social skills training have been shown to be effective in treating patients with a broad range of emotional problems and diagnoses. Many children with exceptionalities such as learning disability (LD) and attention deficit hyperactivity disorder (ADHD), lack the necessary social skills to develop good interpersonal relationships. Research shows that these children have difficulties connecting with their peers, establishing close friendships and getting along with their teachers. They often appear to misread social cues, fail to control impulsive desires and have difficulty anticipating the consequences of their actions. In this study researcher tries to explore ways of teaching social skills, parents and teachers can make a difference with exceptional students by being supportive and practicing positive proactive interventions.*

***Keywords:*** *Social skills, Attention Deficit Hyperactivity Disorder, Learning disabilities, Development.*

## Introduction

Social skill is any skill facilitating interaction and communication with others. Social rules and relations are created, communicated and changed in verbal and nonverbal ways. The process of learning these skills is called socialisation. Social skills are not the same thing as behaviour. Rather, they are components of behaviour that help an individual understand and adapt across a variety of social settings. Social skills is "*a set of competencies that (a) allow an individual to initiate and maintain positive social relationships, (b) contribute to peer acceptance and to a satisfactory school adjustment and (c) allow an individual to cope effectively with the larger social environment*". Social skills can also be defined within the context of social and emotional learning recognising and managing our emotions, developing caring and concern for others, establishing positive relationships, making responsible decisions and handling challenging situations constructively and ethically. With this understanding, researchers and educators seek to evaluate and build students' social skills within a variety of social contexts. The classroom is one such environment children must learn to navigate. Successful learning requires students to interact closely with teachers and peers. In addition to their general importance for daily interaction, social skills can have a big impact on a child's ability to succeed in an academic setting. The classroom becomes both a training ground for development of social skills and an arena in which those skills are put to use.

In order to build gratifying human relationships, it is vital that children learn and have the opportunity to practice the social skills considered appropriate by society. It is important to teach children to conduct themselves in ways that allow them to develop relationships with other people. Some find this more difficult than others, because of learning or other cognitive challenges, visual or hearing impairments, or a physical disability that limits their chances to socialise. Acquiring socialisation skills does not happen overnight. These skills are developed through instruction, practice and reinforcement. Some of the most important aspects of socialising that individuals may initially have difficulty grasping include turn-taking during conversations, maintaining eye contact, being polite, maintaining attention, repairing misunderstandings, finding a topic that is of mutual interest and distinguishing social cues (both verbal and nonverbal). These subtleties, however, are not impossible for individuals to learn.

As most children grow older, they interact more and more with people in situations where direct supervision by parents is not possible. Drawing from what they have learned at home and school about socialising, children make friends within their peer group and soon learn more about socialising, hopefully refining their social skills as they grow and mature. These friendships are important for all children to develop, not only because contact, understanding and sharing with others are basic human needs. Friends also serve central functions for children that parents do not and they play a crucial role in shaping children's social skills and their sense of identity.

## Social Skills in the Children with ADHD

Many children with exceptionalities such as learning disability (LD) and attention deficit/hyperactivity disorder (ADHD), lack the necessary social skills to develop good interpersonal relationships. Research shows that these children have difficulties connecting with their peers, establishing close friendships and getting along with their teachers. They often appear to misread social cues, fail to control impulsive desires and have difficulty anticipating the consequences of their actions.

Associated with these social limitations are emotional consequences. These students often feel isolated and lonely. They tend to be anxious and have high rates of depression. Researchers estimate depression rates of 30 per cent in children with Learning disabilities and as high as 75 per cent in the case of ADHD. Normal rates for depression in youth range between 8 and 12 per cent.

Children with poor impulse control are often identified as having behavioural problems in school. They are placed in behavioural programmes where they connect with a peer group that is also marginalised and excluded from the general school community. They feel misunderstood by the adults around them, demoralised by their lack of academic success and deeply hurt by their treatment by peers.

## Understanding Social Skills Problems

On the surface, these children appear to be the same as everyone else. As a result, their inappropriate behaviours are often seen as intentional. They are described as mischievous, oppositional, or just plain odd. Within the research community, there are two schools of thought to explain the social difficulties often associated with Learning disabilities and ADHD. One theory is neurological. This view suggests that children may have a cognitive deficit associated with self-regulation, inattention and language processing. These cognitive functions all play an important role in the development and application of communication skills. These skills, known as pragmatic skills, include the ability to produce and interpret conversations in real time. They become the cornerstone of good social skills. The second theory is social. It suggests that constant peer rejection and school failure undermines students' confidence, limits practice and leads to isolation and loss of motivation to flourish socially. It is probably fair to assume that both theories interact to affect the social and emotional development of children.

Dr. G.L. Flick, Ph.D., author of *Power Parenting for Children with ADD/ADHD*, divided the challenging social skills for children with ADHD into five categories:

1. Listening
2. Following instruction
3. Sharing
4. Working/Playing cooperatively
5. Social graces

Without these social skills, a child may experience difficulty with peers in school and society.

**Identifying Children with ADHD**

*The Diagnostic and Statistical Manual of Mental Disorders (DSM)* has laid down certain guidelines to help identify a child with ADHD. According to the diagnostic manual, children with ADHD display a combination of inattention, hyperactivity and impulsivity.

According to the DSM, signs of inattention include:

- becoming easily distracted by irrelevant sights and sounds;
- failing to pay attention to details and making careless mistakes;
- rarely following instructions carefully and completely;

- losing or forgetting things like toys, or pencils, books and tools needed for a task.

Some signs of hyperactivity and impulsivity are:

- feeling restless, often fidgeting with hands or feet, or squirming.
- running, climbing, or leaving a seat, in situations where sitting or quiet behaviour is expected.
- blurting out answers before hearing the whole question.
- having difficulty waiting in line or for a turn.

People who are inattentive find it difficult to focus on a particular task and get bored quickly. While they may display effortless concentration doing things they enjoy, making a deliberate and conscious effort to organise and complete a task or to learn something new is difficult. Hyperactive people seem to bounce off the walls with energy and just cannot sit still. Impulsive people don't think before they act or speak. They have difficulty waiting for things to take their natural course. Everything must happen right away.

## Teaching Social Skills to Children with ADHD

Especially when working with children with ADHD, teachers should consider social skills just as important as academics. While we used to believe that students should come to school prepared to behave well and interact successfully with peers, we now know that "behave well" means different things to different families. Some students grow up in households that don't prioritise what teachers tend to like in the classroom: sitting quietly, listening attentively and taking notes, or following directions written on the board. But we educators often expect students to behave the way we learned to when we were young and the students who don't often end up either unsuccessful in class or facing constant consequences for their behaviour. Thus, social skills become a "hidden curriculum" — rule that students are held accountable for but are never explicitly explained or taught.

When children are hampered by ADHD or other neurologically based problems, the world may often appear as a vast puzzle that overwhelms their senses and confounds their thinking. Abruptness, inconsistency and sudden disappointment can trigger immense emotional reactions that are disproportionate and extremely troubling to those around them. Children with ADHD and other learning disabilities may need extra help in developing social skills. The Impulsivity and the short frustration tolerance of a child with special needs can lead to poor peer relationships. Children with poor attention and concentration fail to tune in to the social cues in their environment and thus don't learn social skills through experience. Children with learning disabilities may have difficulty processing information from the social environment or have difficulty with self-expression.

Teachers should also realise that research studies looking at the effectiveness of social skills programmes have shown limited success. A 1995 meta-analysis of 52 research studies by *Kavale* and *Forness*, on the effectiveness of social skills training for students with Learning Disabilities, found that these studies showed very little improvement in students' social skills. The same results were found when reviewing social skills programmes for children with behaviour disorders. It is important that teachers review the research before selecting programmes for their students. Though the research is mixed on the success of social skills training programmes, there are following simple things that teachers can do that will benefit the entire class as well as exceptional students:

- ***Immediate feedback*:**

  Keeping in mind the short attention span of children with ADHD, parents need to give them immediate feedback or consequences for their behaviour and activities. This feedback must be clear, specific and occur as close in time after the behaviour that it refers to.

- ***Frequent feedback*:**

  While immediate response is important, feedback must also be frequent. Parents need to tell ADHD children how they are faring in whatever activity they are involved in or how well they are conducting themselves at very short intervals.

- ***Positive feedback*:**

  Positive feedback can be in the form of praise or compliments but should specify exactly what the child has done to earn it. It can also be in the form of physical affection like a hug, extra privileges or occasionally a food treat.

- ***Evaluate the child's individual needs and strengths:***

  Assess the unique educational needs and strengths of a child with ADHD in the class. Working with a multidisciplinary team and the child's parents, consider both academic and behavioural needs, using formal diagnostic assessments and informal classroom observations. Assessments, such as learning style inventories, can be used to determine children's strengths and enable instruction to build on their existing abilities. The settings and contexts in which challenging behaviours occur should be considered in the evaluation.

- ***Select appropriate instructional practices:***

  Determine which instructional practices will meet the academic and behavioural needs identified for the child. Select practices that fit the content, are age appropriate and gain the attention of the child.

- ***Explain how conversations are like taking turns at telling something about you***

  Conversational tools include volunteering information without being asked, pausing to allow others to speak, asking questions that are related to the topic being discussed and bringing up subjects that have been covered in the past. Suggest that they observe how others blend these elements together to form satisfying conversations. Once they develop some proficiency, try recording the discussions so that they can listen to their success and identify areas for improvement.

Because no two children with ADHD are alike, it is important to keep in mind that no single educational programme, practice, or setting will be best for all children.

## Parenting Advice for Teaching Social Skills

For one reason or another, some children do not develop social skills as easily as others. There is probably nothing so painful for a parent as the rejection of his child. Parents need to take the long view of social problems and to map out a plan to solve them quite as carefully and thoughtfully as they would consider academic or health problems. There are guidelines which if followed, will help these children if the parent is willing to take time and initiative. Sometimes, ADHD children need help making and keeping friends. Parents can make a big difference without stepping on toes by helping an ADHD child with following strategies:

- **Get to the root of the problem.** ADHD children often have little sense of how they're perceived by their peers and will commit social blunders without realising it. Help them by discussing what went wrong, why it happened and what your child could (not should) do differently next time. Be as sensitive with your attention deficit child as you would be with a close adult friend, too much negative feedback can hurt your child's self-esteem. On the flip side, when your child has a successful interaction, congratulate him.
- **Watch your child closely.** Whenever he's playing with other kids, make sure you can see and hear what's going on. Be ready to intervene if he picks a fight, starts telling fibs, or does something dangerous in an effort to impress others.
- **Consider team sports.** Joining a team can help ADHD children realise about them. The lessons learned in sports can overflow into their social lives and you may see your child start to develop healthy friendships.
- **Consistency in discipline.** Parents should strive to react in the same manner over a period of time to the child's behaviour whenever it occurs. In addition, they will need to be persistent when dealing with an ADHD child, as they are not exactly the most obedient kind. Even if parents feel that their efforts are going to waste, they need to stick to the disciplinary programme or they will not see the fruits of their hard work.
- **Communication.** Keep the conversations flowing with your children. Since she is more comfortable with you, incorporate good communication and social skill when talking to her. Keep good eye contact, show emotion and ask questions to drive the conversation along. Listening and showing interest in her when she talks helps teach her good listening skills.
- **Enhance their powers of inference by using television and real life observations.** Explain how the ability to infer

meaning essentially means picking up on clues and figuring out what is going on in a situation. Facial expression, body posture, tone of voice, eye contact and other clues should be identified and referred to when watching television and/or observing others from a distance. When appropriate, suggest that you can watch a show together with the volume muted and attempt to infer what it going on between the characters. Another variation is to watch the first half of a show, turn it off and discuss what may have happened during the final sequences.

- **Help your child remember.** Make lists of the tasks that the child has to accomplish. Highlight important dates on the calendar. Verbal reminders are also necessary.
- **Provide outlets for the release of excess energy.** Encourage the child to participate in creative constructive activities like a sport or a hobby.
- **Accept your child's limitations.** An ADHD child is never going to be a model child. So don't hit your head against a brick wall trying to make him one. Try to see the virtues in your child and help him make the most of them.

## Conclusion

Children with ADHD and Learning Disabilities are less likely to form healthy intimate relationships as adults, more likely to experience peer rejection and have a higher likelihood of running into trouble either with the juvenile or adult legal system. Social skills in schools impact safety as well as interpersonal interactions, because students with poor social skills are more likely to demonstrate aggressive or violent behaviour, are less likely to be able to self-regulate their behaviour and have trouble asking or accepting help from others, which makes violence a more likely response to conflicts. In summary, social skills are pivotal to successful transition to adult life for youth with disabilities. Cooperative learning, communication, role-playing and participation in social and emotional learning programmes foster the acquisition of these skills. In addition, a positive school and home climate supports social learning by providing an environment in which all students are valued and respected.

## References


- Alexander-Roberts, C. (1994). *The ADHD parenting handbook: Practical Advice for Parents from parents,* Texas: Taylor Publishing company retrieved on 15/09/15 from www.healthcommunities.com/adhd/.../improve-social-skills_bht.shtml
- Flick, G.L. (1996). *Power Parenting for Children with ADD/ADHD: A Practical Parents Guide for Managing Difficult Behaviours,* New York: The Centre for Applied Research in Education retrieved on 17/09/15 from www.healthcommunities.com/adhd/.../improve-social-skills_bht.shtml
- Forness, S.R. and Kavale, K.A. (1996*). Treating social skill deficits in children with learning disabilities: A meta-analysis of the research.* Learning Disability Quarterly, 19, 2-13.
- Kavale, K.A., and Mostert, M.P. (2004). *Social skill interventions for individuals with learning disabilities.* Learning Disability Quarterly, 27(1), 31-43.
- Kendall, J, Hatton, D, Beckett, A, Leo, M. *Children's accounts of attention-deficit/hyperactivity disorder.* Advances in Nursing Science. 2003; 26(2): 114-130.
- La Greca, A.M. and Mesibov, G.B. (1979). *Social skills intervention with learning disabled 7 children: Selecting skills and implementing training.* Journal of Clinical Child Psychology, 8, 8 234-241.
- McConnell (Eds.). *Social competence in young children with disabilities,* Baltimore, MD: Paul H. Brookes, 93-109.
- Odom, Samuel L., et. al., (1992). *Social competence of young children with disabilities: Issues and strategies for intervention.* Baltimore: Paul H. Brookes Publishing Co.
- Olmeda, R.E. and Trent, S.C. (2003). Social skills training research with minority students with 4 learning disabilities. Learning Disabilities, 12(1), 23-33.
- Sainato, D. and Carta, J. (1992). *Classroom influences on the development of social competence in young children with disabilities.* In W.H. Brown, S.L. Odom and S.R.

# Chapter - 13

# Psychological Problems of Pre-adolescent Learning Disabled Students

*— Dr Arpana Godbole and Rashmi Tiwari*

**Abstract**

*Pre-adolescence is a phase in the life span when critical development starts relative to identity, autonomous social relations. If we talk about the children with learning disabilities the scenario is more critical as when they go through school they begin to understand and note various differences between themselves and their abled classmates. By using social comparisons, learning disabled children start learning to judge whether they are better or worse than normal classmates in different activities. These comparisons play an important role in moulding the child's self-esteem and influence the development of positive or negative feelings they have about themselves. This chapter throws the light on the psychological problems of pre-adolescents learning disabled students and suggests some measures for their parents and teachers to help them for the better prospects.*

***Keywords:*** *Learning disability, Pre-adolescents, social relations, self-esteem.*

***"I live in a cocoon of social making***
***Peeping out at the world from behind a curtain."***

## Learning Disability

A learning disability can be described as a state of arrested or incomplete development of mind leading to significant impairment of intellectual as well as adaptive and social functioning. Children with a general learning disability find it more difficult to learn, understand and do things as compared to other children of the same age as their brain is not able to receive and process information in the same way as others. They may have trouble performing certain tasks or displaying certain skills. They may also struggle with social skills and interaction, potentially leaving them vulnerable in dangerous situations. The degree of disability can vary greatly. Some children will never learn to speak and so are likely when they grow up to need help with looking after themselves - feeding, dressing or going to the toilet. On the other hand, the disability may be mild and the child will grow up to become independent. A general learning disability is not a mental illness. However, children with learning disability are more likely to develop mental health problems, for example anxiety, or have additional developmental disorders, such as Autism Spectrum Disorders and Attention Deficit Hyperactivity Disorder (ADHD).

## Types of Learning Disabilities

Learning disabilities usually fall within four broad categories:

- Spoken language - listening and speaking.
- Written language - reading, writing and spelling.
- Arithmetic - Calculation and concepts.
- Reasoning - Organisation and integration of ideas and thoughts

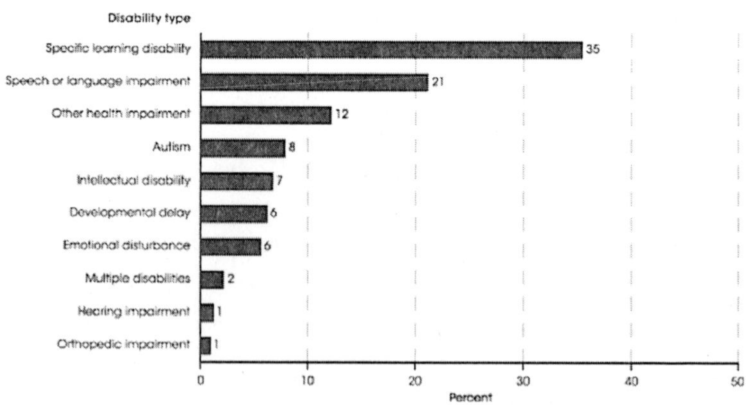


***The percentage distribution of children aged 3-21 served under the Individuals with Disabilities Education Act (IDEA) in school year 2012-13***

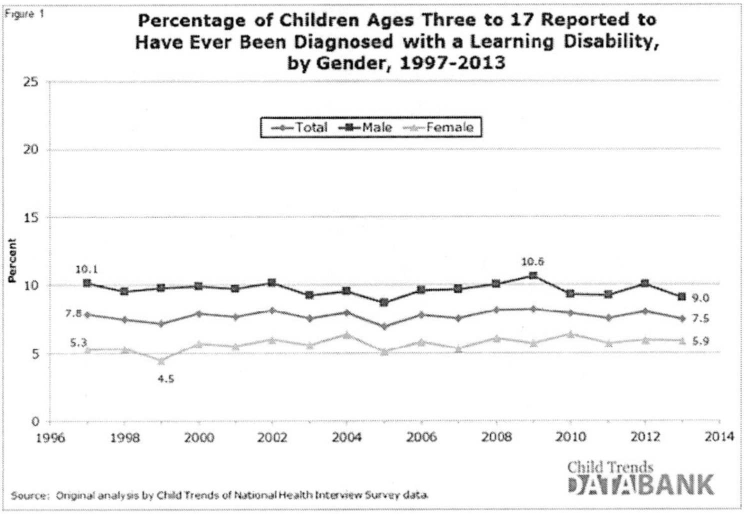


Alternatively, learning disabilities can be divided into three broad categories: developmental speech and language disorders, academic skills disorders and other (such as coordination disorders). Some commonly used terms for LD are dyslexia, dyscalculia and dysgraphia, dyspraxia, dysphasia, ADHD.

The percentage of children who are identified as having a learning disability increases with the increase in age. In 2013, three per cent of three- to four-years-old, eight per cent of five- to eleven-years-old and nine per cent of 12- to 17-years old had been diagnosed as having a learning disability.

## Why Pre-adolescents with Learning Disabilities a Big Challenge?

Problems faced by Pre adolescents are a stage of human development following early childhood and preceding adolescence. It generally ends with the beginning of puberty, but may also be defined as ending with the start of the teenage years. Pre-adolescent children in fact have a different view of the world from younger children in many significant ways. Typically, theirs is a more realistic view of life than the intense, fantasy-oriented world of earliest childhood. Pre-adolescents have more mature, sensible, realistic thoughts and actions: "the most sensible" stage of development- the child is a much *less emotional being* now. Pre-adolescence can bring its own challenges and anxieties. Things become even more complicated if a pre-adolescent child has some learning disability. They are aware of what goes on around them. However, their ability to understand and communicate may be limited and they can find it hard to express themselves. Speech problems can make it even harder to make other people understand their feelings and needs. They can become frustrated and upset by their own limitations. When they compare themselves to other children, they can feel sad or angry and think badly of themselves.

The effects of having a learning disability or learning difference are not limited to educational outcomes only. Rather individuals with learning disabilities may experience social problems as well. As recently as five years ago, very little information on the emotional well-being of pre-adolescents with learning disabilities (LD) was available. However, a great deal of research has been conducted recently and some of the implications are unnerving. Research on self-concept, attributions, anxiety, depression and suicide among pre-adolescents with LD is examined for the purpose of detecting consistency of indicators concerning these emotional and developmental variables. The research indicates that the emotional development of many pre-adolescents with LD is not notably positive and these students appear to be at increased risk for severe depression and suicide.

- Pre-adolescent children with learning disabilities often have clusters of difficulties that lead to academic failure or low achievement.
- Pre–adolescent children with learning disabilities experience several problems in their everyday life. Some children with attention problems, high levels of anxiety or impulsive or aggressive behaviour are at greater risk of difficulties at school. This is because they find it harder to adapt to the demands of the classroom setting or difficulty in concentrating during classroom tasks and teachers' instructions. But it is also true that not every child with special needs faces academic problems.They are more likely to be rejected or isolated by their classmates and peers.

- Formalised researches support the concept that children with learning disabilities have deficient or ineffective social skill. They are more likely to choose socially unacceptable behaviours in social situations and are less able to solve social problems. However, it would be incorrect to say that all individuals with learning disabilities experience social skill difficulties. Research and observation indicate that some learning disabled students have a degree of social competence that is equal to or superior to their peers. However, social skill deficits create major obstacles for a significantly large subgroup of learning disabled students.

## Outlook of Teachers, Parents and Society

- For parents, it can be distressing to find out that their child has a general learning disability. It may be hard for them and other members of the family to understand why the child is like this. It can also be hard to communicate with the learning disabled child, difficult to manage their behaviour and hard for other people to understand. **Children with learning disabilities puzzle parents because of their many abilities and disabilities. It can also be difficult to understand how much of their behaviour the nature of the condition and how much is oppositional is.** It **takes time for both children and parents to embrace the concept that being different does not mean being inferior.**
- Parenting approaches that include clear, concise instructions; structure without rigidity; nurturing a child's gifts and interests; and constant approval of positive behaviour help parents feel better and help children feel safe.
- Parents need to be nurtured and praised to help them nurture and praise their children. Most parents use almost every resource they have to help their children flourish and still, they worry they are not doing a good enough job.
- Students with disabilities tend to disrupt the classroom with behaviour issues. Because they are not as cognitively developed as their peers, the teaching-learning process is not as effective as it could be. It is difficult to serve the needs of every student who is normally in the regular education class and with the

special needs students the job becomes even more of a struggle for the teacher and someone draws the short in of the stick, usually the special needs students. Teachers have to treat special needs students differently based on standards are on their learning level. Special needs students are deprived of a suitable education when they are taught at a mismatched level with students how are significantly above their level.

- Since almost five per cent of all students in our nation's public schools are classified as having specific learning disabilities (SLD), every teacher can expect to find students with learning disabilities in the classroom. Success for these students requires a focus on individual achievement, individual progress and individual learning. Despite obstacles, recent research tells us that we can teach these students how to learn. We can put them into a position to compete!
- During the past 40 to 50 years there have been numerous changes in our society with respect to the management and treatment of children with disabilities. Prior to the twentieth century, social attitudes reflected the view that children with disabilities were unhealthy, defective and deviant. For centuries, society as a whole treated them as objects of fear and pity. However, the attitude and outlook of society has changed over the period of time.

## Remedies/Cures

Learning disabilities cannot be cured and for parents, it can be a difficult and stressful time trying to help their child through education and making sure they receive the best support possible for their needs. It is indeed very important to understand that handling pre-adolescents with learning disabilities requires a lot of patience, research and integrated effort of parents and other family members and teachers.

- It is important to recognise, as soon as possible, that a child is learning and developing slowly. It is only when the problem is recognised that the child and his/her family can be offered the help and support they need.
- The severity of learning disability of children decides the level of support required by them. On one hand, some with a

mild learning disability may need only a little support while on the other hand some with a severe learning disability may need full-time care and support in every aspect of their life.

- As the child gets older, a number of people can help the child's particular needs. They often work together in a group known as the Child Development Team. This team includes specialists such as community pediatricians, nurses, psychologists and speech therapists.
- School can be a particular challenge for children with learning disabilities because of both, learning and as well as social demands. Local education departments can make special arrangements to meet the educational needs of each child. However, there is an expectation that most children will receive their education in a mainstream inclusive environment, especially those who are able to cope comfortably with other people. On the other hand, a child with a more severe disability may go to a special school.
- Respite care and holiday play schemes can extend the learning and social opportunities for the child. Parent support groups can put families in touch with other people who are coping with similar problems.
- Disability does not stop a child from having a full and enjoyable life. The aim of all the specialist services is to help children with a general learning disability to have lives that are as enjoyable and fulfilling as those of other people.
- There are many tests that can help ascertain if a child has learning difficulties, including psychometric tests to measure IQ and the Adaptive Behaviour Scale.
- There are many facilities available to support both parents and children through the process of diagnosing a learning difficulty and providing the best course of action and support for the child.
- Parents should make sure the child eats and sleeps well and gets regular exercise that will help him/her to focus and teaches them good habits for life.
- Parents and teachers of children with learning disabilities can help them by providing clear structuring of time and space.

Parents can also assist their children by engaging them in planning activities.

- While children with learning disabilities face challenges academically, a problem that many parents find more troubling than difficulties are relationships. This affects family life and peer relationships. Parents need to coach them through common social situations until they develop appropriate interpersonal behaviours.
- Parents can provide their children with practice in anticipating what might happen in various social situations.
- Parents and teachers must boost children's self-esteem by seeking out what they can do well and fostering and supporting these areas to the hilt.
- Teaching children that many people have overcome difficulties to become successful is another valuable parenting strategy.
- Children with learning disabilities and ADHD often feel powerless and inadequate. They tend to be passive learners and need to be totally involved in activities to make them active learners. Parents can encourage hands-on activities, which have their own additional benefit.

## Further Suggestions

- Learning disabilities are treated educationally, preferably with early intervention. An educational specialist can teach effective learning strategies to help a child overcome his or her learning problems. In addition to ensuring that schools provide diagnostic testing, federal laws require that remedial services be provided to all children who qualify for them. Private tutoring may also be beneficial to maximise progress. Repeating a grade is typically not recommended and may be associated with poor long-term outcomes.
- Children and their families may benefit from psychological counselling. Understanding and emotional support are needed for children with learning disabilities so they can feel good about themselves. It is also essential to provide opportunities

for success in areas where the child may shine. Finally, children with learning disabilities sometimes have problems with peer relationships and may benefit from counselling to help improve their social skills.

- Learning disabilities are not treated medically; however, children with learning disabilities who are also diagnosed with a co-existing disorder such as ADHD may benefit from medication. Physicians should follow the academic progress of their patients as part of their overall medical management.
- Parents should make sure that their child receives help for his or her learning problems. They should also monitor the child's progress to make sure adequate improvement is being made in skill development. Parents should foster communication between outside specialists, school personnel and the child's physician. It is also critical that parents provide an atmosphere at home that encourages learning.

## Conclusion

A learning disability can be a life-long condition, affecting many aspects of life, including education and employment, family life and daily routines. Children with learning disabilities are far more likely than other children to be enrolled in special education and to use healthcare services. Despite their limitations, persons with learning disabilities can learn if given the opportunity. Academic supports and accommodations can help with the learning process, as can medical treatment for certain disorders. It is the moral responsibility of schools and educators to take care of all the needs of students with learning disabilities. The educational institutions should be equipped with all those facilities which are required to take care of these children, keeping in mind that students **with disabilities get the same educational opportunities and choices** as all other students. Also, it is necessary for schools to be in constant touch with parents of these children. Society and its people should not consider children with learning disabilities as a social stigma. They should rather make efforts to provide them equal opportunities to be a part of the society and live their life to the fullest like any normal person does.

## References


- Bryan, T. (1999). *Assessing the personal and social status of students with learning disabilities.* Learning Disabilities Research and Practice, 12, 63-76.
- Cooper and Patricia, S. (1993). *Self-esteem and facial attractiveness in learning disabled children.* Child Study Journal, 23, 79-88.
- Heyman, W. (2000). *The Self-Perception of a Learning Disability and its Relationship to Academic Self-concept and Self-esteem.* Journal of Learning Disabilities, 23, 473-475.
- Orton, S. (1937). *Reading, writing and speech problems in children.* New York: W. W. Norton.
- Patil, M., Saraswathi, G. and Padakannaya, P. (2009). *A study on Self-esteem and Adjustment among Children with Reading and Writing Difficulties.* Study Home Communication Science, 3, 91-96.
- Serafica, F. and Harway, N., (2002). *Social Relations and self-esteem of children with learning disability.* Journal of Clinical Child Psychology, 227-233.
- Swanson, H.L. and Hoskyn, M. (1998). *Experimental intervention research on students with learning disabilities: A meta-analysis of treatment outcomes.* Review of Educational Research, 68, 277-321.

## Chapter - 14

# Auditory Problems and Remedial Measures for Children with Learning Disabilities

***— Dr Sita Ram Pal***

### Abstract

*Learning disability is an umbrella term for a wide variety of learning problems. A learning disability is not a problem with intelligence or motivation. Kids with learning disabilities aren't lazy or dumb. In fact, most are just as smart as everyone else. Their brains are simply wired differently. This difference affects how they receive and process information. Children and adults with learning disabilities see, hear and understand things differently. This can lead to trouble with learning new information and skills and putting them to use. The most common types of learning disabilities involve problems with listening, reading, writing, math, reasoning and speaking. Children and adults who have Central Auditory Processing Disorder (CAPD) are a heterogeneous group of people who have difficulty using auditory information to communicate and learn. CAPD is not a specific problem or disease; rather it is a set of problems that occur in different kinds of listening tasks. Often children with CAPD are first diagnosed with learning disabilities. Later, an audiologist may render a diagnosis of CAPD. American Speech and Hearing Association (ASHA) 1996, has focuses audiological assessment of CAPD on Sound localisation and lateralisation, Auditory discrimination, Auditory pattern recognition, Temporal aspects of audition, Auditory performance decrements with competing acoustic signal and Auditory performance with degraded acoustic signals. According to Chermak and Musiek (1998), the incidence of CAPD has been estimated to be as high as three to five per cent and is more common than the incidence of hearing loss. Several strategies are available to help children with auditory processing difficulties. Some of these are commercially available, but have not been fully studied. Any strategy selected should be used under the guidance of a team of professionals and the effectiveness of the strategy needs to be evaluated. Researchers are currently studying a variety of approaches to treatment. It can be improved with support from parents, speech-language pathologists, Audiologist, teachers and tutors.*

***Key Words**: Auditory problem, remedial measures, Learning Disabilities.*

## Auditory Process

Auditory is the sense by which sound is perceived. Auditory processing is a natural process of taking in sound through the ear and having it travel to the language area of the brain to be interpreted. To have a breakdown in this process is called an auditory processing disorder or "delay". This deficit is present despite having normal hearing. Auditory processing is "what our brain does with what the ear hears" (Katz). When one is faced with an auditory processing deficit, his or her ears can pick up the sounds, words, etc., but his or her brain is not able to process the sounds properly the auditory information becomes jumbled up or confused and therefore, misunderstood.

Auditory Processing Disorder (APD) may be defined as a reduced or impaired auditory processing ability to discriminate, recognise, or comprehend auditory information. This problem will be most pronounced when the auditory signals are compromised by distortion, competition, poor acoustic environments, or other reduction in signal clarity, strength, or information content. In other words, the individual with APD will experience greater problems when the acoustic environment is less than ideal, such as in an open classroom or when the signal is poor due to interference, intensity, or content.

Auditory processing disorder (APD), also known as central auditory processing disorder (CAPD), is a hearing problem that affects about five per cent of school-aged children. Kids with this condition can't process what they hear in the same way other kids do because their ears and brain don't fully coordinate. Something interferes with the way the brain recognises and interprets sounds, especially speech. CAPD usually shows up in the early grades, when children are required to become active listeners. Even before school age, however, there may be warning signs. A young child with CAPD is fidgety at story time and overwhelmed in noisy settings. Sound discrimination problems may cause him to mispronounce words. Later, he may have trouble with reading, which involves the manipulation of sounds. These are signs of central auditory processing disorder (CAPD), a learning disability that impacts the brain's ability to filter and interpret sounds. Children with CAPD have a hard time receiving, organising and using auditory information. They're able to hear, but fall short at listening.

If you suspect a problem with auditory processing, first have your pediatrician rule out hearing loss. Identifying CAPD requires tests by an audiologist, typically performed after age seven, when kids can understand the instructions. An evaluation should distinguish CAPD from ADHD and other disorders that share some of its symptoms. In some children, these disorders coexist - and learning more about learning disabilities is a must.With the right therapy, kids with APD can be successful in school and life. Early diagnosis is important, because when the condition isn't caught and treated early, a child can have speech and language delays or problems learning in school. An expert who believes auditory processing is part of the whole person; he/she will refer you or your child to Vision Services, Neurotechnology Services, Outpatient Rehabilitation Services, including Occupational and Speech Therapy.

## Incidence and Etiology of CAPD

According to Chermak and Musiek (1998), the incidence of CAPD has been estimated to be as high as three to five per cent and is more common than the incidence of hearing loss. Gravel, Wallace and Ruben reported a study in 1996 in which they followed children with and without early ear infections (otitis media) from the first year of life through nine years of age. They found that these children, who experienced the mild, fluctuating hearing loss associated with otitis media, had long-term problems with higher-order auditory-processing skills and learning. Thus, not only do many more children have auditory learning impairment from CAPD than from hearing loss, but the former may be a more "hidden" deficit because hearing impairment is usually recognised more easily and associated more directly with a marked effect on speech and language.

## Trouble in Understanding Speech

Kids with APD are thought to hear normally because they can usually hear sounds that are delivered one at a time in a very quiet environment (such as a sound-treated room). The problem is that they usually don't recognise slight differences between sounds in words, even when the sounds are loud and clear enough to be heard. Such kinds of problems usually happen when there is background noise, which is often the case in social situations. So kids with APD can have trouble understanding what is being said to them when they're in noisy places like a playground, sports events, the school cafeteria and parties.

## Difference between Hard of Hearing and Auditory Processing Disorders

Hearing impairment and auditory processing disorders can look very similar on the surface. To understand the difference, it helps to know what hearing is. We learn as kids that hearing is one of the five senses. But it's a complex process picking up sound and attaching meaning to it. Hearing loss, or hearing impairment, is a problem with one or more parts of the ear that interrupts the way sound travels through the hearing system up to the brain. Someone who has hearing loss might be able to hear most sounds, hear only some sounds or possibly nothing at all.To understand hearing loss, it helps to know how the ear works. Auditory Processing Disorders (APD) is not the inability to hear. It's the inability to interpret, organise, or analyse what's heard. All the parts of the hearing pathway are working well. But parts of the brain are not. Some symptoms of APD in children are very similar to the symptoms of a hearing loss. So they're often confused. But they're not the same thing.

Hearing loss can be detected very early. Some infants can be diagnosed right after birth. Some **symptoms of childhood hearing loss:**

- Child does not react to loud sounds.
- Child is unable to detect where a sound is coming from, for example, turning the head toward the person speaking.

- Child is not responding to his own name by six months.
- Babbling does not develop into recognisable speech sounds or into words by age two.
- Child may start showing frustration and acting out aggressively.
- Child frequently asks "what?" when spoken to.

Unlike hearing loss, APD cannot be diagnosed in infancy. Experts have different opinions on when a child's brain is mature enough to be diagnosed with APD. Some say as early as four years and others say not until 12. But the majority of experts say six is the earliest and that it's best to wait until a child is seven or eight years old. This is because children develop at different rates.

### Symptoms of APD include

- Unusual sensitivity to loud sounds.
- Difficulty understanding speech in noisy environments.
- Difficulty following directions, especially directions with more than one step.
- Difficulty telling the difference between similar-sounding speech sounds such as pat and bat.
- Difficulty with spelling, reading and understanding information presented verbally.
- Frequently saying "huh?" or "what?" when spoken to.

It's important to remember that neither hearing loss nor APD can be accurately diagnosed by checking through a list of symptoms. Diagnosing either hearing loss or APD requires a multidisciplinary team of consultants:

- The **pediatric ear, nose and throat** (ENT) doctor will assess any medical problems with the hearing pathway, such as ear infections, etc.
- An **audiologist** will test hearing sensitivity to determine if there is a hearing loss. She will administer the series of tests that will determine if APD is present.
- The **speech-language pathologist** (SLP) will test developmental milestones in speech and even written language.

- The **teacher** or an **educational expert** will look at academic difficulties.
- A **psychologist** will evaluate cognitive functioning.

Hearing loss and APD may have some symptoms in common. But the treatment options are very different. That's why it's a good idea to work with professionals who are trained to recognise the difference. The National Center for Learning Disabilities (NCLD) lists four types of auditory skills needed for a child to properly process what he or she hears:

1. **Auditory discrimination** is the ability to notice, compare and distinguish the distinct and separate sounds in words. If a child has difficulty with auditory discrimination, he or she may confuse similar words like seventy and seventeen have trouble learning to read and be unable to follow directions even when the child appears to be paying attention.
2. **Auditory figure-ground discrimination** is the ability to pick out important sounds from a noisy background. A child who struggles with auditory figure-ground discrimination may be unable to filter background conversations and noises to focus on what is important. For example, a child may miss lessons in class if he or she can't filter extraneous background noise in the classroom.
3. **Auditory memory** is the ability to recall what is heard after a period of time and includes both short-term and long-term memory. Difficulties associated with auditory memory may include remembering people's names, memorising telephone numbers, following multi-step directions and recalling stories or songs.
4. **Auditory sequencing** is the ability to understand and recall the order of words. Difficulties with auditory sequencing may include confusing numbers like 93 for 39 and confusing lists and sequences. For example, a child with auditory sequencing problems may not be able to complete a series of tasks in the right order. He or she may fail to be able to do so even when appearing to have heard and understood the directions. Our non-medical, whole-child approach to improving brain

function can reduce or eliminate symptoms of auditory processing disorder and other neuro-developmental disorders.

## Diagnosing Auditory Processing Disorders

Children with APD may exhibit a variety of listening and related complaints. For example, they may have difficulty understanding speech in noisy environments, following directions and discriminating (or telling the difference between) similar-sounding speech sounds. Sometimes they may behave as if a hearing loss is present, often asking for repetition or clarification. In school, children with APD may have difficulty with spelling, reading and understanding information presented verbally in the classroom. Often their performance in classes that don't rely heavily on listening is much better and they typically are able to complete a task independently once they know what is expected of them. However, it is critical to understand that these same types of symptoms may be apparent in children who do not exhibit APD. Therefore, we should always keep in mind that not all language and learning problems are due to APD and all cases of APD do not lead to language and learning problems. APD cannot be diagnosed from a symptoms checklist. No matter how many symptoms of APD a child may have, only careful and accurate diagnostics can determine the underlying cause.

A multidisciplinary team approach is critical to fully assess and understand the cluster of problems exhibited by children with APD. Thus, a teacher or educational diagnostician may shed light on academic difficulties; a psychologist may evaluate cognitive functioning in a variety of different areas; a speech-language pathologist may investigate written and oral language, speech and related capabilities; and so forth. Some of these professionals may actually use test tools that incorporate the terms "auditory processing" or "auditory perception" in their evaluation and may even suggest that a child exhibits an "auditory processing disorder." Yet it is important to know that, however valuable the information from the multidisciplinary team is in understanding the child's overall areas of strength and weakness, none of the test tools used by these professionals are diagnostic tools for APD and the actual diagnosis of APD must be made by an audiologist.

To diagnose APD, the audiologist will administer a series of tests in a sound-treated room. These tests require listeners to attend to a variety of signals and to respond to them via repetition, pushing a button, or in some other way. Other tests that measure the auditory system's physiologic responses to sound may also be administered. Most of the tests of APD require that a child be at least seven or eight years of age because the variability in brain function is so marked in younger children that test interpretation may not be possible.

Once a diagnosis of APD is made, the nature of the disorder is determined. There are many types of auditory processing deficits and, because each child is an individual, APD may manifest itself in a variety of ways. Therefore, it is necessary to determine the type of auditory deficit a given child exhibits so that individualised management and treatment activities may be recommended that address his or her specific areas of difficulty.

## School Strategies

These academic accommodations can be included in your child's Individualised Education Programme. A teacher can:

***Improve classroom acoustics.*** CAPD makes it hard to screen out background noise. Adding bookshelves, carpeting and drapes to a classroom absorbs the extra sound.

***Provide attention prompts.*** Seat a child away from windows, doors and other sources of distraction. Periodically touch her shoulder to remind her to focus.

***Streamline communication.*** Establish eye contact and insert pauses to allow time for sorting information. Ask questions to see if the child is following the lesson and rephrase material that has been misunderstood.

***Use visual aids.*** Jot instructions or key words on the board and provide simple written or pictorial outlines.

***Build in breaks.*** Children with CAPD have to work harder than other kids to pay attention and may need more frequent downtime to consolidate information.

***Use a microphone and headset.*** The teacher's voice is amplified through a microphone connected to the student's headset. This helps to focus attention on the teacher.

## Role of Teachers

Students with auditory processing disorder (APD) can't process the information they hear in the same way as others because their ears and brain don't fully co-ordinate.

Kids with APD often have difficulty recognising subtle differences between sounds in spoken words, even when the sounds are loud and clear enough to be heard. This usually happens when there's background noise, like in a typical classroom. In addition, loud or sudden noises can easily distract or bother students with APD.

Teachers also can help students with APD by:

- reducing background noise, when possible;
- having them sit in the front of the class or near you to hear better;
- encouraging use of assistive devices in class, such as a personal FM system;
- having them take tests or work on assignments in an area away from distractions.

## Role of Parents

Many of the techniques described above are helpful at home as well as at school. Try these strategies, too.

- **Boost auditory attention with games and tapes.** Games like Simple Simon teach a listening strategy and provide a chance to practice.
- **Look ahead.** Go over the basic concepts and help your child learn any new words in upcoming lessons.
- **Develop routines.** Provide a structure to help your child focus in chaotic environments. Before going to his school locker, for instance, have him check his assignment book and list what he needs to take home. Above all, teach your children to create the conditions he needs for optimal listening. By the time he heads for high school, he should be well-armed with coping strategies.

## Auditory Processing Disorder Checklist

Although Auditory Processing Disorder originates in the brain, neurological dysfunction is not observable. APD tends to manifest as poor listening skills or an inability to process auditory information and is often accompanied by motor problems. **The checklist below is designed to help you assess whether your child has CAPD.** Several other conditions and learning disabilities share similar characteristics.

## Listening

- Has difficulty locating a sound source.
- Has difficulty hearing in noisy background.
- Has difficulty listening when there is more than one person talking.
- Is very sensitive to loud noises or feels uncomfortable in noisy places.
- Has severe difficulty comprehending degraded speech (unfamiliar accent, muffled etc.).
- Is suspected of having a hearing loss even though hearing is well within the normal range.
- Finds it difficult to hum along with a tune.
- Confuses similar sounding words.
- Has difficulty making sense of distorted speech signals.
- Often asks for repetition or clarification (e.g., may often say 'huh?' for more information).
- May often ask for instructions to be repeated.
- Has difficulty understanding the emotional status of a speaker.
- Has difficulty making sense of what others are talking about.
- Often misunderstands what others have said.
- Has difficulty following spoken instructions especially multi-step directions.
- Has difficulty following and participating in conversation or discussion.

- Does not understand the tone of voice, has difficulty comprehending a spoken message based on the prosodic (rhythm, syllabic stress and intonation) aspects of speech.
- Finds neutral sounds unpleasant or painful.
- Puts volume of music or television unusually high or unusually low.

**Speaking**

- Has difficulty answering open-ended questions.
- Has difficulty finding words to express themselves.
- Prefers the use of gestures and facial expressions to words.
- May speak in a flat, monotonous, expressionless manner.
- May speak with words out of order or muddles sentences (e.g., 'Daddy car red').
- May speak in oversimplified short sentences with difficulties in syntax (e.g., 'dog eat' instead of 'dog is eating').
- Mispronounced words, especially long words.
- Is slow in responding to verbal questions.
- Responds inconsistently and inappropriately in conversations.

**Phonological Awareness**

- Has difficulty in speech-sound discriminations.
- Does not appreciate rhymes.
- Has difficulty blending sounds together.
- Has difficulty manipulating the sounds in words.
- Has difficulty applying phonetic skills in reading and spelling.
- (Title / Subheading) High-order processes: Attention, memory and learning.
- High-order processes: Attention, memory and learning.
- Diagnosed as having attention deficit disorder (ADD/ ADHD).
- Is easily distracted by noises.
- Has a short attention span.
- Has difficulty focusing during conversations.
- Forgets information that is easily heard. Is delayed in learning to talk.

- Has difficulty in acquiring correct grammar especially for second language.
- Gets tired of listening and tunes out after a while.
- Performs better in a one-to-one setting.
- Has difficulties taking notes in class.
- Has difficulty with dictation.
- Has difficulty with reading.
- Has difficulty with spelling.
- Has poor musical ability.
- Appears messy and disorganised.

**Language**

- Doesn't speak fluently or articulate clearly.
- Has poor vocabulary, sentence structure and grammar usage.
- Displays illogical flow of stories or ideas.
- Uses vague words such as 'thing', 'stuff', 'whatever'.
- Problems with receptive language?
- Needs to hear instructions/directions more than once.
- Appears overwhelmed when there is a lot of auditory activity.
- Misinterprets verbal messages.
- Confuses similar words or sounds.
- Seems distracted or unable to sustain attention when receiving verbal messages.

**Family and Developmental History**

- Has a history of recurrent or on-going ear infection.
- Has family members with speech or language disorders.
- Has family members with learning difficulties.
- Talks or likes T.V. louder than normal.
- Interprets words too literally.
- Often needs remarks repeated.
- Difficulty sounding out words.

- "Ignores" people, especially if engrossed.
- Unusually sensitive to sounds.
- Asks many extra informational questions.
- Confuses similar-sounding words.
- Difficulty following directions in a series.
- Speech developed late or unclearly.
- Poor "communicator" (terse, telegraphic).
- Memorises poorly.
- Hears better when watching the speaker.
- Problems with rapid speech.

## Conclusion

In recent years, there has been a dramatic upsurge in professional and public awareness of Auditory Processing Disorders (APD), also referred to as Central Auditory Processing Disorders (CAPD). Unfortunately, this increase in awareness has resulted in a plethora of misconceptions and misinformation, as well as confusion regarding just what is (and isn't) an APD, how APD is diagnosed and methods of managing and treating the disorder. The term auditory processing often is used loosely by individuals in many different settings to mean many different things and the label APD has been applied (often incorrectly) to a wide variety of difficulties and disorders. As a result, there are some who question the existence of APD as a distinct diagnostic entity and others who assume that the term APD is applicable to any child or adult who has difficulty listening or understanding spoken language. In this regard Gail Chermak, Frank Musiek and Jay Hall have written extensively on various techniques and procedures for clinical management of CAPD. Dr. Hall (2000) has emphasised the importance of classroom modifications for children diagnosed with CAPD. Some of Dr. Hall's recommendations include- Education of teachers and other school personnel about teaching strategies, modification of environment and recognising at-risk children, Preferential seating so the child can see the teacher as he or she speaks, see the board easily and have some distance from distracting noises, documentation and when possible, reduction of classroom noise levels and echoes, reduction of noise, when possible, by use of acoustic ceiling tile, soft furniture, wall panels and so on.

At last I would like to say that once CAPD identified, Additional support from parents, speech-language pathologists, teachers and tutors may also be needed. Research in neuroplasticity (the ability to change how the brain functions with appropriate stimulation) indicates that brain function can be improved by the appropriate stimulation.

## References


- American Speech-Language-Hearing Association Task Force on Central Auditory Processing Consensus Development. (1996). *Current status of research and implications for clinical practice.* American Journal of Audiology, 5 (2), 41-54.
- Chermak, G., Somers, E. and Seikel, J.A. (1998). *Behavioural Signs of Central Auditory Processing Disorder and Attention Deficit Hyperactivity Disorder.* J Am Acad Audiol, 9, 78-84.
- Dr Hall (2000). *Relationships between tests of central auditory function and receptive language.* Seminars in Hearing, 5 (3), 243-250.
- Gravel, J., Wallace, I. and Rubin, R. (1996). *Auditory Consequences of Early Mild Hearing Loss Associated with Otitis Media.* Acta Otolaryngol, 116, 219-221.
- Chermak, G. and Musiek, F. (1997). *Central Auditory Processing Disorders: New Perspectives.* Singular Publishing Group, Inc.
- Pal, Sitaram and Vishwakarma, B. (2011). *Hearing and Speech Management*: N. Publication, Ahmedabad.

## Chapter - 15

# Learning Disabled vs Low Achievers

*—Dr Arpana Godbole and Ms Priyam Shukla*

### Abstract

*Being an educator, the greatest plight of a teacher lies in the failure of her learners. It is so because for every teacher, her each and every student is a pupa who is lying in its cocoon waiting to come out in the world and show his talent to the world, the talent which has been nurtured and polished by the teacher herself. When the teacher goes into her classroom and sees any of her student suffering with one or the other problem, she feels pined about it and wants to change the whole scene and right here comes the revolution, the change when the learner becomes the epicenter for the teacher and she brings out a change in the life of her learners. But in the absence of the knowledge regarding the problems of these learners, the objective cannot be achieved in wholesome manner. The present paper deals with the concept of learning disabled learners and low achievers. Along with the differences and similarities between these two are discussed in detail.* **Failure is not falling down, it is not getting up again.**

***Keywords:*** *Learning Disability, Low Achievers, differences, similarities.*

## Introduction

***Failures repeated, failures are finger posts on the road to achievement. One fails forward toward success.***

**C.S. Lewis**

Every teacher who enters a classroom faces the same challenge- the challenge to develop such a teaching methodology that enable one to meet the educational demands of every individual present in the classroom. As a teacher, one has to be equipped with various teaching strategies which are apt for each learner. But the biggest obstacle in this objective's fulfillment is the great variance of IQ level of the learners present. The biggest problems come from those learners who are not able to achieve the desired educational achievement and are regarded to be *below average* learners of the class. The greatest irony is that no one is able to understand the plight of such learners as the teachers declare them unfit for that particular level whereas the parents take it as a result of sheer negligence and the society regards them to be withdrawn ones. But none of them takes the pain to enquire about their problems which are the root cause of their low academic achievements. There is a chance that the learner may be a sufferer of mental retardation, is learning disabled, low achiever or a backward child. The educator has to understand the problem of the individual and develop the teaching strategies in accordance to the particular problem diagnosed.

## Low Achievers

Every classroom has some learners who are classified as 'Low Scorers' or 'Under Achievers' of that particular class. Simply they are declared to be the 'Below Average Learners' of the class. But no one bothers to know about the reason behind their performance. They might be the pupils who have limited ability due to different reasons in the education process. They might be the 'Low Achievers' who are better known as 'Backward' or 'School retarded' and 'Educationally deteriorated' individuals. Technically, the term 'Low Achievers' is used for those individuals who leave their schooling either without qualifications or with qualifications of a level that might be considered to reduce employment perspectives. Low Achievers typically do not qualify for special education services because they do not meet the 70 or below IQ requirement for mentally retarded or the IQ achievement discrepancy for learning disabled classification.

## Learning Disability

"Learning Disability" or "Learning Disorders" is an umbrella term for a wide variety of learning problems. A learning disability is not a problem with intelligence or motivation. Kids with learning disability are not lazy or dumb. In fact, most are as just as smart as everyone else. Their brains are simply wired differently. The difference affects how they receive and process information. In 2000, the US Department of Education Office of Special Education Programme (OSEP) convened a group of 18 educators to reexamine, the problems of defining learning disabilities with the purpose of providing a basis for future legislation. In 2001, the group reaffirmed the concept of learning disabilities as follows:

The central concept of *Specific Learning Disabilities (SLD)* involves disorders of learning and cognition that are intrinsic to the individual. SLD are specific in the sense that these disorders each significantly affect a relatively narrow range of academic and performance outcomes. SLD may occur in combination with other disabling conditions but they are not due primarily to other conditions, such as mental retardation, behavioural disturbances, lack of opportunities to learn, or sensory deficits.

## COMMON TYPES OF LEARNING DISABILITIES

| | | |
|---|---|---|
| **Dyslexia** | Difficulty with reading | Problem in reading, writing, spelling, speaking |
| **Dyscalculia** | Difficulty with math | Problem in doing math problems, g time, using money |
| **Dysgraphia** | Difficulty with writing | Problem with handwriting, spelling, organising ideas |
| **Dyspraxia** | Difficulty with fine motor skills | Problem with hand–eye co-ordination, balance, manual dexterity |
| **Dysphasia/ Aphasia** | Difficulty with language | Problem in understanding spoken language, poor reading comprehension |
| **Auditory Processing Disorder** | Difficulty in hearing differences between sounds | Problem with reading, comprehension, language |
| **Visual Processing Disorder** | Difficulty in interpreting visual information | Problems with reading, math, maps, charts, symbols, pictures |
| **ADHD–Attention Deficit Hyperactivity Disorder** | Difficulty in learning | Problem in sitting still, staying focused, following instructions, staying organised and completing homework |

Learning disabilities greatly vary from one child to another. One child may struggle with reading and spelling, while another loves books but can't understand math. Still another child may have difficulty understanding what others are saying or communicating out loud.

The problems are very different, but they are all learning disorders. It's not always easy to identify learning disabilities. Because of the wide variations, there is no single symptom or profile that can be looked upon as proof of a problem. However, some warning signs are more common than others at different ages. One needs to be aware of what they are, in order to be able to catch a learning disorder early and quickly and take steps to get the child help.

## Causes of being a Low Achiever

- **Emotional growth:** Whatever one feels about oneself whether positively or negatively is termed as emotional growth. Emotional growth is closely related to social growth of an individual because in the primary stages an individual develops the feelings of trust, fear and love while later on the feelings of friendship, pride and relationship also strengthen gradually which ultimately leads to the social-emotional development of the individual. The individual starts to develop negative emotions if he is ignored in this stage and gradually avoids trust initially on parents and later on others. The consequence of such negative emotions is his isolation from the outer world, as he has started feeling neglected, rejected and unsecured.
- **Environment:** Environment plays a crucial role in the development of any individual as the child reacts to the environment in early stages and consequently learns a lot while growing up.
- **Growth and opportunities of learning:** Every cognitive ability and development requires the maximum scope of opportunities of learning so that they start learning new things and enhance their thinking skills.
- **Absenteeism:** Absenteeism affects a child's ability to learn. Being frequently absent a child fails to cope up with the lessons and is unable to catch up with his peer group. It results in the child's isolation and becoming a low achiever.
- **Defective vision:** A poor or defective vision might lead to low achievement as it hinders a child's proper growth and development and the social functioning skills.

- **Psychological problems:** Sometimes high expectations from families and absence of guidance result in psychological stress for both the parents and the students. Such problems lead to retarding effect on the learners' educational development.

## Causes of Learning Disability

Generally the under given three factors are found to be responsible for causing learning disabilities:

(i) **Geneticor hereditary factors:** Sometimes, this factor is found to be the major cause for generating learning disabilities among the children. It is said 'like begets like' pattern is followed and the disability is transmitted from generation to generation.

- About 20 to 25 per cent of hyperactive and impulsive children have been found to have at least one parent of this nature.
- A greater degree of concordance for reading disabilities and speech and language disorders has been found more in the monozygotic twins than the dizygotic twins.
- Studies have revealed that heredity may account for at least some family linkage with dyslexia.
- Researches have proved that the emotional imbalances, disorders of memory and thinking, speech and learning are hereditary in nature.
- There are creditable evidences that genes connected to chromosomes 6 and chromosomes 15 play an important role in transmitting reading disabilities hereditarily.

(ii) **Organic or physiological factors:** Some professionals opine that children with learning disability suffer from some types of brain injury or dysfunction of central nervous system (CNS) as any factor that can cause neurological damage to the central nervous system may lead to its malfunctioning and subsequent learning disabilities.

- Learning abilities get affected by any neurological difficulty, viz. and brain damage before or after birth.

- Any damage to the spinal cord and message carrying nerves leads to their malfunctioning and subsequent learning disabilities.
- Consumption of artificially coloured or flavoured food items may cause hyperactivity, impulsivity, emotional imbalance, etc. leading to malfunctioning of the CNS.
- Vitamin deficiency may cause inability of a child's bloodstream to synthesise a normal amount of vitamins required for normal functioning of the CNS.
- Sometimes medical problems like diabetes, meningitis, cardiac arrest, pediatric AIDS proves to be a potent factor of the neurological dysfunction.
- Intake of teratogens by the expecting mothers or the infants results in neurological dysfunction to the growing foetus and children.

**(iii) Environmental factors:** It is believed that sometimes improper and uncongenial factors and conditions present in any child's physical, social, cultural and educational environment are also responsible for generation of learning disabilities.

- Poor nourishment and defective environment received by foetus in the mother's womb.
- Pre-mature delivery, uncongenial and improper settings at the time of birth or a defect in the CNS.
- Diet deficiency and poor medical care and attention are also an important reason behind CNS dysfunction.
- Insufficient early experiences and simulation in terms of learning and acquisition received on account of defective educational set up.
- Inadequate and improper development of language skills, lack of concentration and adequate attention, lack of motivation, skill and ability on part of teachers also leads to malfunctioning of the child's physiological processes.
- Social and cultural deprivation, use of drugs and intoxicating substances is also responsible for learning disabilities.

- Imitation and company of defective learning models present in one's cultural, social and educational environment is also responsible for the rise of learning disabilities.

## Remedial Measures

Every disability can be minimised by early intervention and proper care, hence under given are some remedial measures which if taken care about can bring a lot of change in the lives of such individuals.

### *For Low Achievers:*

- **Emotional Growth:** The changes being rapid ought to be dealt most carefully with positive feelings about oneself and trust building with others.
- **Environment:** Environment must be safe for the child so that he is stress free. If the child is suffering from physical threat in the environment that should also be removed immediately. Such safe and secure environment flourishes their abilities in positive direction leading to better confidence in life and education.
- **Growth and Opportunities of Learning:** Parents must ensure a rich learning environment for their children so that the new opportunities are available up to its maxim for every individual.
- **Absenteeism:** Absenteeism can be avoided by ensuring that the child trying to be regular to school at one's best. Teachers must give such children some extra homework so that he can cope up with the learning level. Parents must ensure that the child is doing extra homework and must be able for any kind of assistance in its completion so that he is able to minimise his shortcomings, a failure to which results in isolation.
- **Defective Vision:** Proper check up must be done regularly and parents must ensure whether the child has a vision problem, if so proper medical attention must be provided.
- **Resources:** Parents can provide better resources of learning by providing their children good books and other learning materials which are helpful in the child's better learning.

- **Illiteracy:** In case of illiterate parents, teachers need to provide careful treatment to the child so that one can develop the skills which are helpful in the later age in the school and college.
- **Teachers' Training:** There should be trained teachers in the school so that they might help in understanding the child and his learning and psychological problems resulting in a better outcome.
- **Class Size:** There should be an ideal class size i.e. 20 – 30 students per class so that the teacher can give due attention to each and every student and evaluate them equally leading to 'no student left behind' concept.
- **Parents' Involvement:** Working parents should manage their working hours in such a way that the child's development is not hindered at all, especially those who are between 3 to 6 years of age as it is a very crucial stage of life.
- **Violence in School:** It must be ensured that there is no violence with any child whether in school or anywhere else because violence affects a child's cognitive, psychological and learning process.
- **Family Size:** Family members especially parents must ensure that the child is getting their maximum attention for his proper development and they are also able to provide the best available resources to their children.
- **Health:** Parents must take proper care of their child's physical fitness too as if the child is in good health, he will be able to perform better in both the fields whether curricular or co-curricular.
- **Culture:** Culture and background should be nourished by the parents and teachers as culture is essential to nourish the child well.
- **Teaching Staff:** Adequate teaching staff should be made available by the concerned authorities as its shortage affects whole teaching-learning process.
- **Leadership:** Appropriate and motivating leadership plays a pivotal role in shaping any child's future. So the availability

of good teachers, parents and head-teachers becomes an essential for the all-round development of any individual.

- **Teaching Methods:** A good teacher never uses a single teaching method as this methodology leads to more low achievers in the class. Every individual being different, an effective teacher uses different methods in class so that each and every child in the class learns and understands.
- **Course:** Course needs to be designed in such a way that it adopts the easy to difficult approach, which enables the learner to understand what is being taught in a much easier way.
- **Transfer of Teachers:** The teachers' transfer should not be quiet frequent as it affects the students' psychology and trust. The concerned authorities must ensure a long term of job for every teacher.
- **Fear Complex:** Teachers must develop a positive and supportive attitude towards the learners. There should be no fear in the learners' mind as this fear might hinder the positive development of the child.
- **Psychological Problems:** There should be adequate and timely counselling of both the parents and the students so that the psychological problems should not develop at all and the children are mentally free and healthy.

### *For Learning Disabled*

It is essential to seek advice from the specialist because it's not always easy to know what to do. But any specialist is not just enough, one as a parent need to work with the child and his school to make accommodations for the child and get specialised academic help. But parents' role cannot be overlooked as they know their child better than anyone else, so they have to take the lead in looking into the options, learning about new treatments and services and overseeing the child's education.

- Reading and learning about the child's type of learning disability must be done. One as a parent must try to find out how the disability affects the learning process and what cognitive skills are involved. It becomes easier to evaluate learning techniques if one understands how the learning disability affects the child.

- Along with knowing about the type of learning disability the child has, one must get knowledge about the most effective treatment options available. This can help to advocate for the child at school and pursue treatment at home.
- Even if the school doesn't have the resources to treat the child's learning disability optimally, one can pursue these options at home or with a therapist or tutor.
- Even though children with learning disabilities struggle in one area of learning, they may excel in another. Attention must be paid to the child's interests and passions. Helping children with learning disorders develop their passions and strengths will probably help them with the areas of difficulty as well.
- The children may have trouble expressing their feelings, calming themselves down and reading nonverbal cues from others. This can lead to difficulty in the classroom and with their peers. As a parent, one can have a huge impact in these areas.
- Learning disabilities and their accompanying academic challenges, can lead to low self-esteem, isolation and behaviour problems, which can be countered by creating a strong support system for children with learning disabilities and helping them learn to express themselves, deal with frustration and work through challenges.
- By focusing on the child's growth as a person and not just on academic achievements, one as apparent can help him learn good emotional habits that set the stage for success throughout life.

## Similarities between Learning Disabled and Low Achievers

- **Positive Outlook:** Both of the disabilities require a positive approach as if the individual suffering with any of the disability gets a positive response and support from the parents, teachers and the society, an appreciable change is observed.

## Comparison between Learning Disabled and Low Achievers

| *S.No.* | *Factors* | *Learning Disabled* | *Low Achievers* |
|---|---|---|---|
| 1. | **Nature** | Learning disability is entirely intrinsic | Low achievement is basically extrinsic |
| 2. | **IQ** | No relation with IQ level | Possess low IQ level i.e. below 70 |
| 3. | **Emotional support** | If provided with positive reinforcement and assistance significant changes can be seen | If provided with positive reinforcement and assistance wonders can be seen |
| 4. | **Teachers** | Teachers trained in Special Needs Education are more effective | Trained teachers are required to provide relevant teaching method |
| 5. | **Approach** | Specialised approaches and techniques are required | Only growth and opportunities of learning are required |
| 6. | **Parents** | Parents' involvement is significantly effective | Parents' involvement is significantly effective |
| 7. | **Society** | Society plays a noticeable role | Society has a crucial role |
| 8. | **Teaching method** | Specialised instructions are required | Sequencing of instructions is required |
| 9. | **Curriculum** | Special curriculum planning is required | Regular curriculum with directional instructions is required |

- **Teaching Methods:** Both require separate and one to one approach while receiving the teaching learning instructions.
- **Directional Guidance:** Both do not require any kind of sympathy from anyone, they require a directional guidance which can provide them an easy access to learning.
- **Trust:** Individuals suffering from both the problems need trust from their parents, peer group, teachers and society. As this mutual trust gives a strong base to the personality development and a sense of being confident and independent to such individuals.
- **Acceptance:** Any individual who is either a Low Achiever or Learning Disabled needs a social acceptance as the negligence works as a negative catalyst in their growth.
- **Inclusive Education:** Both kind of individual can raise the bar of their performance if are educated in Inclusive Educational system as in such a system they get the opportunity to be with other children of their age group and learn how to interact and behave socially.
- **Quality Time:** A dying need of quality time with others whether parents, teachers or the peer group is always with both the Low Achievers and the Learning Disabled ones.
- **Feedback:** Feedback to their actions or work and if it is positive, works as a booster for both type of individuals.
- **Early Intervention:** If any of the two disabilities diagnosed at its earliest, the maximum possible betterment can be done for the individual.

## Teaching Methods

Teachers play an important role in shaping the personality of any learner, so it becomes an essential demand of the situation that teachers as educators provide the most appropriate teaching adapting the best available methodology for the individual.

### *For Low Achievers*

- Teachers must make sure that they are able to get the students' attention fixed before starting the lesson.
- Vocabulary should be updated from time to time.

- Use of simple language and slow pace of speaking proves to be effective.
- Concrete to abstract explanation should be adopted.
- Open ended questions should be avoided as close ended or precise ones enable the teacher to attain the teaching objectives.
- One instruction at a time enables the individual to understand it better.
- In order to meet all learning styles, teachers must vary their teaching methods.
- Explicit instructions are beneficial for low achievers as they are not good problem solvers.
- Repetition, revision and recycling should be done by the teachers on regular basis.
- Key points should be written on the board and use of coloured markers also proves to be effective.
- If the teacher provides a checklist, it becomes easier for the learners to learn on their own.
- New information should be presented in form of tables, charts, pictures, etc.
- Whenever any important point is presented, the teacher must ensure that its importance is told to the learners repeatedly.
- Key points must be summarised at the end of every lesson.
- Assignment can be of different forms, viz., an interview, a questionnaire or even a role play.
- If some pictures and descriptions are added to the written text, it makes the content interesting for the learners.
- The learners should be provided with sufficient to ask and answer the questions.
- Controlled and guided tasks prove better than the free tasks for low achievers.
- Teachers' focus should be on quality rather than quantity, so amount of task allotted should be reduced.
- Large amount of work should be split into smaller parts.
- Teachers should be open for the assistance to the low achievers.

***For Learning Disabled***

- The learners should be trained self-monitoring, which enables them to be aware of their own learning process.
- Teachers should give direct instructions, as they help in seeking proper corrective, remedial as well as developmental measures for the learners.
- Visual displays and graphic organisers provide the needed information in an easy to understand manner to the learners.
- Guided notes prove helpful in guiding the students for proper understanding and comprehending the curriculum contents covered in an entire lesson.
- Mnemonic devices prove helpful in improving the learners' ability to recall specific content.
- Cooperative learning strategy proves helpful in getting rid of their learning deficits and problems related to academics.
- Individualised instructional approach helps the learners rectify their learning deficiencies.
- Self-instructional approach is required for these learners as it enables them to adopt self-learning and self-improvement measures for treating their learning deficits and deficiencies.
- Multisensory approach proves beneficial as it appeals the learners' multiple senses i.e. visual, auditory, touch, smell and taste, etc. depending upon the content to be taught.
- Advanced technology like audiotapes, videos or computer assisted instruction should be used to provide remedial instruction programme to the learners.
- Teachers should make an attempt to provide opportunities of modifying the behaviour.
- Teachers should adopt psychoanalytic approach to analyse the behaviour of the learner and find out the root cause of the learning deficiencies.
- If required some medical assistance should also be provided (clinical or medical approach).

## Conclusion

The power of perspective taking can reach its prime or simply can be a failure if the teacher fails to fulfill the requirements of her students. If teacher really takes the pains about these low achievers and the learning disabled ones, she is ready to change their world and the change starts right from this initiative.

## References


- Chauhan, S.S. (2011). *Advanced Educational Psychology*, Seventh Edition, Reprint,Vikas Publishing House Pvt. Ltd. New Delhi.
- http://iris.peabody.vanderbilt.edu/module
- https://www.shef.ac.uk
- https://www.researchgate.net
- http://ldaamerica.org/types-of-learning-disabilities
- https://en.wikipedia.org/wiki/Learning_disability
- Solomon, A. (2014). *Far From the Tree Parents, Children and the Search for Identity.* London: Vintage Random House Grp. Ltd.
- www.ldaofky.org

# Chapter - 16

# Learning Disability and Assistive Technology

*— Ms Priyanka Srivastava*

**Abstract**

*The child learns to talk walk and play and to do many other things during the crucial period. All these are possible because of the interaction between the child's biological capacities and the environment. Infrastructural facilities, trained professionals and supportive materials are the prerequisites of such rehabilitation. Assistive technology plays an important role to overcome the disability of students with disability. Assistive technology for students with Learning Disability is defined as any device, piece of equipment or system that helps bypass, work around or compensate for an individual's specific learning deficits. Learning disabilities look very different from one child to another. One child may struggle with reading and spelling, while another loves books but can't understand math. Still another child may have difficulty understanding what others are saying or communicating out loud. But for every problem there is an assistive device. An assistive device acts as a supplement to the student with learning disability. This article will focus upon the different types of assistive technologies available for student with learning disabilities. It must be beneficial for the parents of student with learning disabilities, special educators, other teachers and school authorities.*

***Keywords:*** *Learning Disability, Assistive Technology, High-tech device, Low-tech device.*

## Introduction

***"When an individual or a team is empowered with technology, transformation to higher potential for achievement is assured."***

— Dr A.P.J. Abdul Kalam

The advances in aeronautical, space and defense technology, developments in microelectronics and material science, spurt in information technology together with boom in human rights movement all over the world have led to Virtual Reality Technology (i.e., negligible gap between invention of a technology and its application to disability rehabilitation) in disability rehabilitation. Technology, techniques, manpower development and approaches to service delivery are the four independent variables that directly influence the outcome of disability rehabilitation efforts. Each influences the other. The extrinsic variables that affect the outcome are economics, level of awakening (includes spread of information, elimination of beliefs, ignorance and superstition) and priority attached to the activity.

## Learning Disability

Representatives of organisations committed to the education and welfare of individuals with learning disabilities are known as National Joint Committee on Learning Disabilities (NJCLD). In the 1980s, NJCLD therefore defined the term learning disability as:

> *A heterogeneous group of disorders manifested by significant difficulties in the acquisition and use of listening, speaking, reading, writing, reasoning or mathematical abilities. These disorders are intrinsic to the individual and presumed to be due to Central Nervous System Dysfunction. Even though a learning disability may occur concomitantly with other handicapping conditions (e.g. sensory impairment, intellectual disability, social and emotional disturbance) or environmental influences (e.g. cultural differences, insufficient/inappropriate instruction, psychogenic factors) it is not the direct result of those conditions or influences.*

The 2002 LD Roundtable produced the following definition:

> "Concept of LD: Strong converging evidence supports the validity of the concept of specific learning disabilities (SLD).

This evidence is particularly impressive because it converges across different indicators and methodologies. The central concept of SLD involves disorders of learning and cognition that are intrinsic to the individual. SLD are specific in the sense that these disorders each significantly affect a relatively narrow range of academic and performance outcomes. SLD may occur in combination with other disabling conditions, but they are not due primarily to other conditions, such as intellectual disability, behavioural disturbance, lack of opportunities to learn, or primary sensory deficits."

## Challenges for Student with Learning Disability

Learning disabilities look very different from one child to another. One child may struggle with reading and spelling, while another loves books but can't understand math. Still another child may have difficulty

understanding what others are saying or communicating out loud. The problems are very different, but they are all learning disorders. It's not always easy to identify learning disabilities. Because of the wide variations, there is no single symptom or profile that you can look to as proof of a problem. However, some warning signs are more common than others at different ages. These are as follows:

- **Reading**

  Children face the problem in decoding, reading fluency and comprehension.

- **Writing**

  They have problem in proper spelling, punctuation, grammar, word usage and organisation.

- **Listening**

  Some students have problem in difficulty in processing and remembering spoken language.

- **Calculations**

  Many students have problem in computing, organising, aligning and copying math problems down on paper.

- **Organisation and memory**

  Some children face the problem in planning, organising, managing, storing and retrieving information.

**Assistive Technology:** Assistive devices and assistive technologies are important in enabling persons with disabilities to 'live independently'. However, the kind of devices that are needed can best be accessed through synergetic interaction between those involved in community based rehabilitation, technologists and the advocates of equal opportunity.

***Learning Disabled learners***

Assistive technology refers to the devices and services that are used to increase, maintain, or improve the capabilities of a student with a disability (Dell, Newton and Petroff, 2012). While the phrase assistive technology may make us think of computers and computerised devices, assistive technology can also be very low-tech. For example, pencil-grips (the molded plastic grips that slip over a pencil) are considered assistive technology. Assistive technology that helps students with learning disabilities includes computer programs and tablet applications that provide text-to-speech (e.g., Kurzweil 3000), speech-to-text (e.g., Dragon Naturally Speaking), word prediction capabilities (e.g., WordQ) and graphic organisers (e.g., Inspiration).

In comparison to other interventions, assistive technology may have a significant effect in helping students with disabilities progress towards the goals outlined on their Individual Education Plans (Watson, Ito, Smith and Andersen, 2010). Assistive technology helps in two ways: it can help the student learn how to complete the task and it can help to bypass an area of difficulty. For example, when a student decides to listen to a digital version of a book, they are bypassing an area of difficulty. However, if the student focuses on the computer screen as highlighted words are read aloud, they can learn unfamiliar words. It can be categorised as low-tech technology and high-tech technology.

## Benefits of Assistive Technology

- **Portable and lightweight:** Laptop computers and tablet devices are beneficial for students with learning disabilities because they are portable and lightweight. For students with handwriting difficulties, being able to take notes on a laptop or computerised device (such as an iPad) can improve the quantity and quality of the notes (Vaughn and Bos, 2009).
- **More organised and less spelling errors:** Using a word processor can help students to complete work that is more organised and includes less spelling errors than handwritten work (Hetzroni and Shrieber, 2004).
- **Correct more errors:** In addition, students may identify and correct more errors when using spell check than when editing by hand (MacArthur, Graham, Haynes and De La Paz, 1996; McNaughton, Hughes and Ofiesh, 1997).
- However, obtaining personal access to laptops and computerised devices does not ensure engagement and increased academic success (Donovan, Green and Hartley, 2010).

– For many students, laptop computers and computerised devices can be too distracting. Teachers and students need to be trained in how to meaningfully integrate technology into academic contexts so that the devices don't detract from learning (Dell, Newton and Petroff, 2012).

Besides these some other benefits are as below:

- Could be used as a supplement, not a replacement.
- Fosters teaching / learning.
- Saves time and the instructions can be retrieved at any point of time.
- Used generally for drill and practice.

## Types of Assistive Technology

We can categorise the devices in many ways. Here the division takes place on the basis of quality of the devices i.e. low-tech and high-tech and further uses of the devices i.e. for reading, writing, listening, calculations, reasoning, speaking and to enhance the memory.

### 1. Low-tech Technology

Low-tech devices are not very much advance in technology but it helps the children with learning disability in many ways. Some devices of low-technology are as follows:

### Assistive Devices for Reading

- ***Pentop computers –***

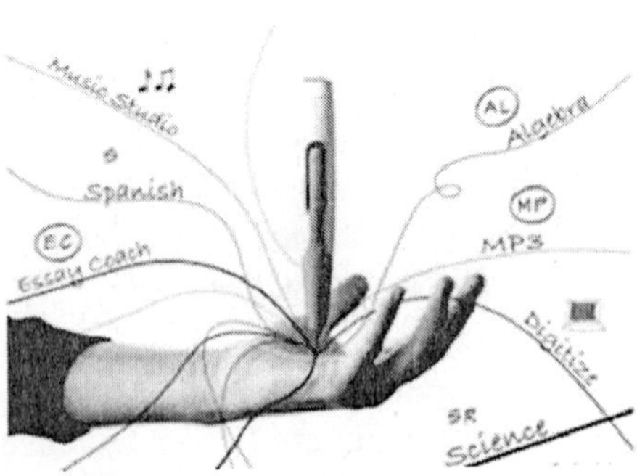

Pentop computers, such as Live Scribe smart pens, are cheaper than high-tech devices like iPads but can provide text-to-speech, strategy feedback and other organisational functions. As cost-effective and self-regulated reading aides, pentop computers may be a useful tool for students with reading disabilities (Schmitt, McCallum, Hennessey, Lovelace and Hawkins, 2012). Pentop computers are also useful because they utilise instruction strategies such as providing auditory feedback during composition or math work. Handheld computerised devices that provide feedback have shown to be helpful for students with learning disabilities for essay composition (Bouck, Bassette, Taber-Doughty, Flanagan and Szwed, 2009) and receptive note-taking and multiplication skills (Bouck, Flanagan, Miller and Bassette, 2009). For example, pentop computers are able to provide reminders such as "don't forget to carry" during multiplication questions (Doughty, Bouck, Bassette, Szwed and Flanagan, 2013).

- ***Highlighter strips –***

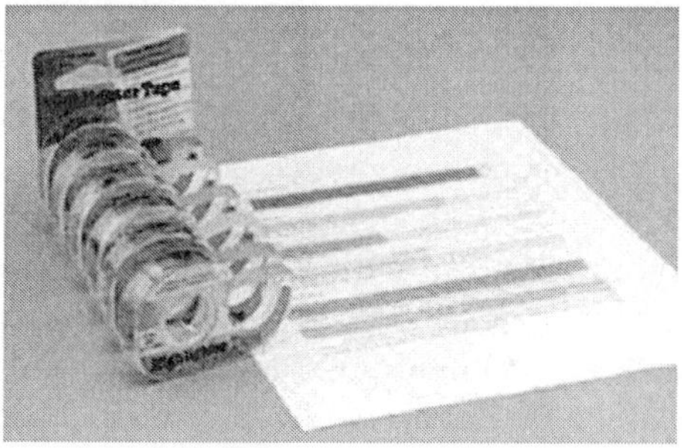

Translucent rectangles of colour can help eliminate extra visual clutter by blocking out the rest of the text. Sticky notes – Students with LDs may find it useful to summarise the main ideas of the text with sticky notes which can be stuck directly on the page.

- ***Pencil grips –***

For students who struggle with handwriting, pencil grips can provide a surface that is easier to manipulate.

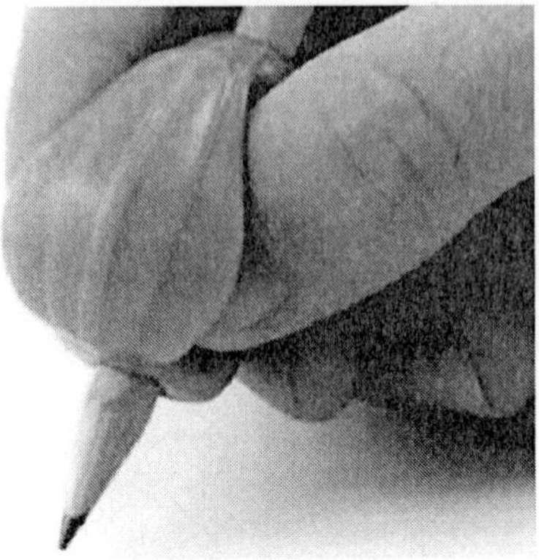

## Assistive Devices for Writing

- ***Graphic Organisers –***

  Graphic organisers benefit individuals who experience difficulty expressing their thoughts on paper as well as visual learners who need to see their ideas mapped out. While graphic organisers completed without technology can help students with learning disabilities to improve the quality of writing (Institute for the Advancement of Research in Education, 2003), electronic versions, such as Inspiration, allow students to arrange their thoughts on the computer screen without worrying about order, level of importance or categories because the text can be easily manipulated. Graphic organisers provide an organisational framework to help writers generate topics and content for writing projects and can assist with the planning and organisational stages of writing and using concept mapping software can increase the quality and quantity of writing (Sturm and Rankin-Erickson, 2002). Using a web-based graphic organiser with procedural prompts enabled students to produce better organised and higher quality papers, than they could produce with handwritten organisers (Englert, Wu and Zhao, 2005; Englert, Zhao, Dunsmore, Collings and Woblers, 2007). Being taught a strategy to plan and organise writing can improve the compositions of students with learning disabilities (MacArthur, 2009).

- **Computerised pens –**

  These pens can automatically transmit handwriting into digital text. Some computerised pens have audio-recording functions that allow the writer to listen to specific sections of the audio file by tapping on the written notes.

## Assistive Devices for Calculations

Students with learning disabilities may have a history of academic failure, which contributed to their development of learned helplessness in math. For some students, a fear of failure and low academic self-concept can lead to math related anxiety.While the use of calculators can level the playing field for students with learning disabilities, some research has shown that calculators may provide unfair advantage (Bouck and Flanagan, 2009).

Graphing calculators may be particularly effective because they provide visual conformation of the graph-shape. The added advantage of visual data can be highly motivating for students with learning disabilities (Bethell and Miller, 1998). Math drill programmes can be an effective way for students to learn to mentally solve math questions (Adcock *et. al.,* 2010), they are also effective in increasing motivation and the addition and subtraction skills of students with dyscalculia (Amiripour, Bijan-zadeh, Pezeshki and Najafi, 2011).

- ***4-function calculator*** – Depending on the type of work being done, a 4-function calculator can be a great help without providing disproportionate advantage to students with LDs.

## Assistive Devices for Memory

- ***Notepad*** – Notepads are an excellent way to record information. Students with learning disabilities (LDs) may appreciate having the information colour-coded based on the purpose, topic, or function of the information.

## Assistive Devices for Speaking

- ***Cue cards*** – Cue cards provide helpful hints for the oral presentation of information and the process of composing cue cards can help organise the information before-hand.

## 2. High-tech Technology

It mainly refers to as computer assisted technologies. It is also known as Computer-assisted instruction. Computer-assisted instruction refers to software and applications that have been designed to provide instruction and practice opportunities on a wide range of devices (e.g., computer, laptop, iPad, mobile technology). Computer-assisted instruction provides immediate and dynamic feedback and students with learning disabilities can benefit from this nonjudgmental computerised drill and practice (Stetter and Hughes, 2010). Computer-assisted instruction has been shown to be helpful for students with learning disabilities in spelling and expressive writing skills (Wanzek *et. al.,* 2006) as this software can reduce distractibility (Hecker, Burns, Elkind, Elkind and Katz, 2002) and can help students learn to read (Lee and Vail, 2005) and achieve other academic outcomes (Chiang and Jacobs, 2009). Computer-assisted instruction is also an effective way for students with learning disabilities to practice math drills (Bouck and Flanagan, 2009), as students who used computer-assisted instruction to practice math skills were able to memorise math facts more easily and developed a more positive attitude towards math than students who did not use computer-assisted instruction (Adcock *et. al.,* 2010).

### Assistive Devices for Reading

- ***Optical character recognition***

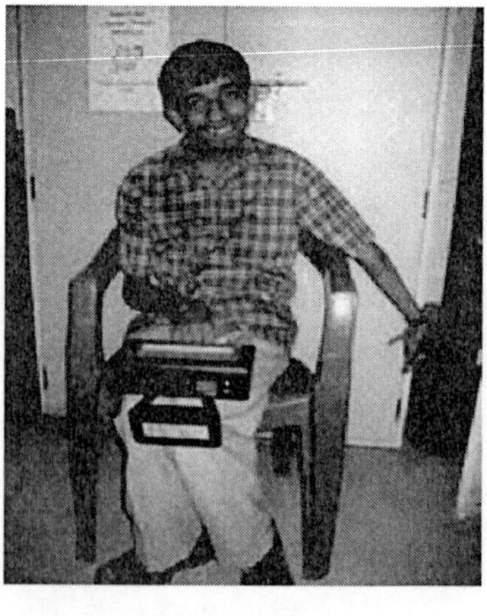

This technology allows a user to scan printed material into a computer or handheld unit. The scanned text is then read aloud via a speech synthesis/screen reading system. Optical Character Recognition (OCR) is available as stand-alone units, computer software and as portable, pocket-sized devices.

- ***Speech synthesisers/screen readers***

These systems can display and read aloud text on a computer screen, including text that has been typed by the user, scanned in from printed pages (e.g., books, letters), or text appearing on the Internet.

- ***Kurzweil 3000*** – Text-to-speech software, such as Kurzweil 3000, can read aloud digital or printed text.
- ***Storyline Online*** – A free online streaming video programme featuring books read aloud. Each book includes accompanying activities and lesson ideas.
- ***Project Gutenberg*** – Over 45,000 free e-books.

## Assistive Devices for Writing

- ***Abbreviation expanders***

Used with word processing, these software programmes allow a user to create, store and re-use abbreviations for frequently-used words or phrases. This can save the user keystrokes and ensure proper spelling of words and phrases he has coded as abbreviations.

- ***Alternative keyboards***

  These programmable keyboards have special overlays that customise the appearance and function of a standard keyboard. Students who have LD or have trouble typing may benefit from customisation that reduces input choices, groups keys by colour/location and adds graphics to aid comprehension.

- ***Freeform database software***

  Used in conjunction with word processing or other software, this tool allows the user to create and store electronic notes by "jotting down" relevant information of any length and on any subject. He can later retrieve the information by typing any fragment of the original note.

- ***Graphic organisers and outlining***

  Graphic organisers and outlining programmes help users who have trouble organising and outlining information as they begin a writing project. This type of programme lets a user "dump" information in an unstructured manner and later helps him organise the information into appropriate categories and order.

- ***Portable word processors***

A portable word processor is lightweight device that is easy to transport (e.g., from classroom to home). It can be helpful to kids who may have trouble writing by hand and prefer to use a keyboard. Word processing allows the user to edit and correct his written work more efficiently than doing so by hand.

- ***Proofreading programmes***

  Students who struggle with writing (e.g., spelling, grammar, punctuation, word usage and sentence structure) may benefit from software programmes (included in many word processing systems) that scan word processing documents and alert the user to possible errors.

- ***Talking spell checkers and electronic dictionaries***

  Talking spell checkers and electronic dictionaries can help a poor speller select or identify appropriate words and correct spelling errors during the process of writing and proofreading. Talking devices "read aloud" and display the selected words onscreen, so the user can see and hear the words.

- ***Word-prediction programmes***

  Word prediction software can help a user during word processing by "predicting" a word the user intends to type. Predictions are based on spelling, syntax and frequent/recent use. This prompts kids who struggle with writing to use proper spelling, grammar and word choices, with fewer key.

## Assistive Devices for Calculations

- *Electronic math work sheets*

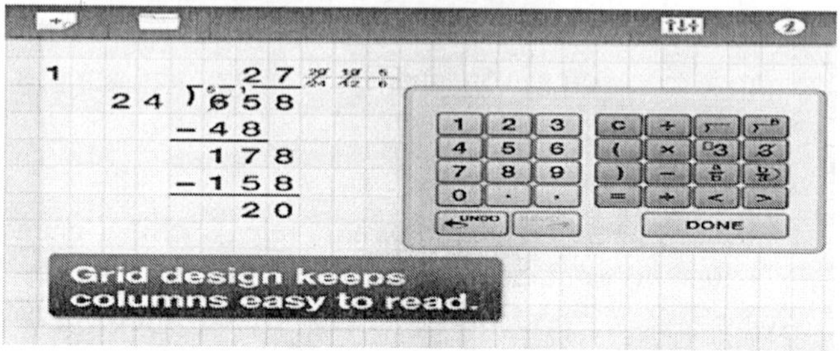


Electronic math worksheets are software programmes that can help a user organise, align and work through math problems on a computer screen. Numbers that appear onscreen can also be read aloud via a speech synthesiser. This may be helpful to people who have trouble aligning math problems with pencil and paper.

- *Talking calculators*

A talking calculator has a built-in speech synthesiser that reads aloud each number, symbol, or operation key a user presses; it also vocalises the answer to the problem. This auditory feedback may help him check the accuracy of the keys he presses and verify the answer before he transfers it to paper.

- ***Graphing calculator –***

Graphing calculators can solve complex equations and the dynamic display screen allows the student to verify the results before solving on paper.

- ***Math Dictionary for Kids*** – An animated, interactive online math dictionary that explains over 600 common mathematical terms in simple language.
- ***IXL Math*** - IXL's math practice skills are aligned with pre-K through Grade 8 provincial curricula and students' performance is assessed on each objective.
- ***Sumdog –***

Sumdog's learning engine adapts its math questions to each student's ability. Covering number operations through to simple algebra, it is designed for students age 6 to 14.

## Assistive Devices for Listening

- ***Audio books and publications***

  Recorded books allow users to listen to text and are available in a variety of formats, such as audiocassettes, CDs and MP3 downloads. Special playback units allow users to and search and bookmark pages and chapters. Subscription services offer extensive electronic library collections.

- ***Personal FM listening systems***

  A personal FM listening system transmits a speaker's voice directly to the user's ear. This may help the listener focus on what the speaker is saying. The unit consists of a wireless transmitter (with microphone) worn by the speaker and a receiver (with earphone) worn by the listener.

- ***Variable-speed control (VSC) tape recorders***

  Tape recorders/players allow a user to listen to pre-recorded text or to capture spoken information (e.g., a classroom lecture) and play it back later. Variable speed control (VSC) tape recorders speed up or slow down the playback rate without distorting the "speaker's" voice.

## Assistive Devices for Speaking

- ***Speech-recognition programmes***

  A speech recognition programme works in conjunction with a word processor. The user "dictates" into a microphone and his spoken words appear on the computer screen as text. This can help a user whose oral language ability is better than his writing skills.

- ***Prezi***

  A free 3D graphic organiser which can be used to create presentations. Prezis can be collaborative as students can comment and build upon other Prezis.

## Assistive Devices for Memory

- ***Information/data managers***

  This type of tool helps a person plan, organise, store and retrieve his calendar, task list, contact data and other information in electronic form. Personal data managers may be portable, hand-held devices, computer software, or a combination of those tools working together by "sharing" data.

- ***Freeform database software***

  Used in conjunction with word processing or other software, this tool allows the user to create and store electronic notes by "jotting down" relevant information of any length and on any subject. He can later retrieve the information by typing any fragment of the original note.

- ***Braining Camp*** – Animated lessons and interactive activities to assess student understanding.

## Assistive Devices for Reasoning

- ***Inspiration*** – This software helps students organise ideas visually without the challenge of handwriting or spelling requirements. The content can be instantly translated into outlines for essays or compositions.
- ***Spark-Space*** – This software supports the writing of students who are visual learners through the use of functions such as idea mapping essay writer tool.
- ***Audacity*** – Audacity is a free software programme which allows you to record and edit sounds.

## Apps for Mobile Devices

There are some apps for mobile devices which are useful for children with Learning Disability. Some of these are listed below:

- ***Audiobooks*** – Provides a simple way to listen to many of the best classic books and modern titles.
- ***Show Me Interactive Whiteboard*** – In order to reduce anxiety, students may opt to record presentations on their iPad beforehand. Video recordings can be uploaded on YouTube or a more private domain.
- ***Speak Selection*** – Located in the accessibility features of Apple devices, Speak Selection can be used to read aloud electronic text.
- ***Free Books*** – This app contains more than 23,000 free booksNotes, highlight option; bookmark and dictionary tools are provided.
- ***Good Reader*** – This PDF reader allows you to add sticky notes, highlight and take notes.
- ***Pages*** – The Pages app allows you to compose, edit work and share. It also includes word prediction, speech-to-text and spell check functions.
- ***iWordQ*** – iWordQ provides reading assistance, word choice and proof reading functions.
- ***Dragon Dictation***–This easy-to-use voice recognition application allows you to speak and instantly see your text or e-mail messages. You must be connected to the Internet for this application to work.
- ***Simple Mind+*** – This app allows you to brainstorm and organise your ideas. Completed concept maps can be automatically converted to an outline.
- ***ShowMe and ScreenChomp*** – These apps provide an interactive whiteboard interface to solve problems. The actions on the screen and audio can be recorded and shared as a video file.

## Conclusion

While student with Learning Disability present significant instructional challenges, there is reason to be optimistic about the magnitude of gains that they can make if they are taught using validated interventions with fidelity and intensity. Additionally, there is a distinct and important role for both assistive technologies and special educators to play in the educational process. Collectively, these factors and conditions can result in positive outcomes for older students with Learning Disability. A sobering reminder that these conditions and factors are not as commonly adhered to as they should be is the fact that an unacceptably large number of student with Learning Disability still drop out of school.

***As David Werner has said "physical technology, when not available could be compensated with human assistance, as well".***

## References


- Ault, M. J., Bausch, M. E. and McLaren, E. M. (2013). *Assistive technology service delivery in rural school districts. Rural Special Education Quarterly,* 32(2), 15-22. Retrieved from http://search.proquest.com/.
- Batorowicz, B., Missiuna, C. A. and Pollock, N. A. (2012). *Technology supporting written productivity in children with learning disabilities: A critical review.* Canadian Journal of Occupational Therapy, 79(4), 211-224. doi:10.2182/cjot.2012.79.4.3
- Bethell, S. and Miller, N. (1998). *From an E to an A in first year algebra with the help of a graphing calculator. Mathematics Teacher*, 91, 118-119.
- Blackhurst, A. (2005). *Perspectives on applications of technology in the field of learning disabilities.* Learning Disabilities Quarterly, 28, 175-178.
- Bouck, E. C., Bassette, L., Taber-Doughty, T., Flanagan, S. M. and Szwed, K. (2009). *Pentop computers as tools for teaching multiplication to students with mild intellectual disabilities. Education and Training in Developmental Disabilities*, 44, 367-380.
- Stanberry, Kristin and Raskind, Marshall H. (2009). *Assistive Technology for Kids with Learning Disabilities: An Overview,* Retrieved from info@readingrockets.org.

# Chapter - 17

# Learning Disabilities Worldwide

*— Dr Meenakshi Dwivedi*

**Abstract**

*Children with learning disabilities are one of the most marginalised and excluded groups of children and remain invisible to the mainstream population and education officials. The 1963 conference in Chicago articulated the cornerstones on which the field of Learning Disabilities is based. After that there have been lots of changes globally through the years in how people with a learning disability have lived their lives. This is influenced by the concern about the guaranteed right of education in every country like USA, Canada, Korea, China, UK, India. Here it is presented the status of learning disabilities in some countries where societies adapt their structures to ensure that all children, irrespective of age, gender and disability, can enjoy their basic human rights without discrimination of any kind.*

***Keywords:*** *Learning Disability, USA, Canada, Korea, UK, China, India.*

The term 'learning disability' was first coined in 1963 by ***Dr Samuel Kirk***, a psychologist, while delivering a speech at an education conference named ***Exploration into the Problems of the Perceptually Handicapped Child*** held in Chicago. Learning disabilities are lifelong disabilities, so they affect adults in college and the workforce, too. In the 2010 U.S. Census, 4.6 million Americans reported having Learning Disabilities far more than the numbers who disclose their disability in college and the workplace.

In 1964, USA government started financing the training of teachers to provide 'remedial education' to help children with learning disabilities continue their education in regular mainstream schools. Subsequently, in 1969, the USA government passed "*The Children with Specific Learning Disabilities Act*" which for the first time officially acknowledged Learning Disabilities as a disability and ensured their entitlement to "publicly funded" remedial education services and the benefit of provisions (accommodations) in their school curriculum. In 1977, the USA government further strengthened this law by empowering these children with a "legal right to continue education in regular mainstream schools". This was done to protect them from discrimination in education.

The public's attitude also plays an important role in what happens to kids with Learning Disabilities. In a 2012 online survey by *National Centre for Learning Disabilities*, most who responded (84 per cent) see Learning Disabilities as a growing concern in the US. And about two-thirds of them know someone who has Learning Disabilities. The same survey found:

- 92 per cent have heard of dyslexia, but 66 per cent don't know about dysgraphia, dyscalculia and dyspraxia.
- 76 per cent know genetics can be a cause of Learning Disabilities.
- The most positive finding: eight out of 10 people agree that children with Learning Disabilities are just as smart as you and me.

A survey data shows that only 24 per cent of young adults with learning disabilities inform post-secondary schools about their needs. seventeen per cent get accommodations and support at the post-secondary level and 41 per cent of young adults with learning disabilities complete post-secondary education within eight years of leaving high school, as compared to 52 per cent of young adults without learning disabilities. The US Department of Education recently introduced new profiles of students with disabilities in each state called "Data Displays". These handy profiles provide a snapshot of student demographics, assessment performance, educational environments, graduation rates and post-school outcomes.

Talking about the learning disables in the workforce it is noticed that 46 per cent of working-age adults with learning disabilities report being employed, as compared to 71 per cent of adults without any learning disabilities. Sixty-six per cent earned $25,000 or less per year within eight years of leaving high school. nineteen per cent say their employers are aware that they have learning disabilities. Five per cent have accommodations in the workplace.

The following statistics are drawn from the Statistics Canada report on the 2006 *Participation and Activity Limitation Survey* (PALS). The survey measures the prevalence of learning disabilities among Canadian children and adults.

- According to Statistics Canada, more children in this country have a learning disability than all other types of disabilities combined.
- According to Statistics Canada, of all the children with disabilities in this country, more than half (59.8 per cent) have a learning disability.
- Statistics Canada reports that 3.2 per cent of Canadian children have a learning disability – that's the equivalent of one child in every school bus full of children.
- Statistics Canada reports that as children make the transition from home to school, the number diagnosed with a learning disability grows by nearly 25 per cent. These transition years are a key time during which we need to assess children and begin accommodating those with learning disabilities so they can reach their full potential.
- According to Statistics Canada, more than half a million adults in this country live with a learning disability, making it more challenging for them to learn in universities and colleges and on the job.
- According to Statistics Canada, learning disabilities increased considerably between 2001 and 2006 among Canadians aged 15 and over by almost 40 per cent to 631,000 people, making it one of the fastest growing types of disabilities in Canada that isn't related to aging.

**Korea** has a short history for education of learning disability but same as other countries, learning disability is considered as a disability which needs some helps in education. Korean special education came from basis on other foreign countries and had short time for having special classes focusing on learning disabilities. The development of special education in Korea has been influenced by theories and practices from other countries, especially the United States, United Kingdom, France, Germany etc. The concept of learning disability was introduced to Korea in the latter half of the 1970s. Special education for students with learning disability has been limited by the lack of a conceptual definition of learning disability.The education for children with Learning Disability started when special classes were established in 1971. Special classes began as an effort to the right of education for students with learning problems who had been scattered in general classes. It became a turning point for children with learning disability, mental retardation and speech disorders who had not been provided with special education. In some years, number of students attending schools with learning disability had been increased. But, there are more students who attend general classes with learning disability.

By having associations for learning disabilities, Korean education focuses on learning problems and facilitates students with learning disabilities to overcome their disabilities. Through giving them good backgrounds on learning with special schools, Korean special education gives new ways to live for people with learning disability. Since Koreans see people with learning disabilities as not stupid people but as slow learners who need few helps for learning. Korean education provides people with learning disabilities special classes in special schools to give them few helps. And, there are associations studying and researching learning disability to provide better education and backgrounds for learning disability. Korean education emphasises on futures of the students and ***ways for them to live their lives by themselves with their disabilities***. By having effort continuously on giving better conditions for learning disability, people with learning disability try to get opportunities to work and live in society.

It is estimated that in **UK** in 2011 approximately 11,91,000 people have learning disabilities. This includes 2,86,000 children (1,80,000 boys, 1,06,000 girls) age 0-17 and 9,05,000 adults aged 18 + (5,30,000 men and 3,75,000 women), of whom 1,89,000 (21 per cent) are known to learning disabilities services. Overall, 90 per cent of children with moderate learning difficulty, 27 per cent of children with severe learning difficulty and 18 per cent of children with profound multiple learning difficulty are educated in mainstream schools.

The Public Health Observatory and the Confidential Inquiry have been set up by the Department of Health to provide knowledge and information that will enable health and social care agencies improve the health and well-being of people with learning disabilities in UK. The *British Institute of Learning Disabilities* (BILD) want people with learning disabilities to be valued equally, participate fully in their communities and be treated with dignity and respect. Its services help to develop the organisations that provide services and the people who give support. BILD uses its books and journals, conferences and events and membership information and networks to encourage the exchange of new ideas and good practice.

Students with learning disabilities form a large significant group in **China**. Research has shown that the prevalence rate in young people upto the age of 18 ranges from a low of 4.86 per cent to a high of 31.62 per cent (He, 2005; Liu, 2000; Wang, 2003; Yao, 2009). A major reason for such a wide discrepancy is the plethora of definitions and diagnostic criterion, none of which have been widely adopted across China. The more simplified the criterion used, the higher the rate of identified students. However, no matter which rate is referred, given such a large country, the population of students with learning disability will always be large. In China, over the past two decades, learning disability has increasingly received attention from many research fields such as education, psychology and medicine. According to a study by *East China Normal University*, 82.6 per cent teachers feel lacking achievability toward students with special needs (including learning disability) and 81.8 per cent have some awareness of these students but feel incapable to teach them (Li, Li and Fan, 2002). It is, therefore, essential for teacher training institutions in China to better prepare pre-service teachers with perceptions, knowledge and skills to teach students with learning disability.

In **India**, around 13 to 14 per cent of all school children suffer from learning disorders. Unfortunately, most schools fail to lend a sympathetic ear to their problems. As a result, these children are branded as failures. The past decade has witnessed a sudden spurt in the recognition of learning disabilities in India. This sensitivity has benefited some children who have to cope with the invisible learning disability. Besides the growing awareness, there are still a number of misconceptions that are associated with the term 'learning disabilities'. The reasons for these misconceptions are manifold. Learning disabilities are heterogeneous with different manifestations. The hard fact is that learning disability is real and a stumbling block for a nation's development process. The question is why and how it affects development? A person can be of average or above-average intelligence, without any sensory problems (like blindness or hearing impairment) and yet struggle to keep up with people of the same age in learning and regular functioning.

The learning disability movement in India is of a recent origin and is today comparable with that of its Western counterparts. Reports of lower incidences of learning disability in the Eastern world were attributed by Western scholars to the general lack of awareness and sensitivity among educationists to the specific difficulties faced by children learning to read in overcrowded classrooms. *The Nalanda Institute* report has highlighted that in India during the last two-decade or so, there has been an increasing awareness and identification of children with learning disability. Despite this growing interest, India still does not have a clear idea about the incidence and prevalence of learning disability. Unfortunately, epidemiological studies of learning disability are fraught with difficulties ranging from the very definition of learning disability, identification, assessment, to socio-cultural factors unique to India. More districts and states are implementing a policy of inclusion for children who before might have been in separate classes yet assistance or resources are lacking for teachers who are working with children with so many different ability levels.

Despite the fact that learning disability is a known classroom disorder, it has not reached its optimum awareness levels in the schools in the country. Teachers either ignore the deficiency or blame it on the child's personality branding it as laziness, attitude or aggression. The child continues to graduate from one class to the other totally inept at handling the pressure of the higher classes. This leads to behavioural problems.

Ironically, policy related to learning disability is yet to see the daylight. In absence of such a policy and incongruous environment, children with learning disability cannot be rehabilitated in regular schools. Though isolating such children from regular schools for training at special schools is not a good precedent, it is the best available option in the prevailing conditions and inevitable too.

During the past three decades, *Rehabilitation Council of India* and *Ministry of HRD, Ministry of Social Justice and Empowerment, Government of India* with the help and intervention of country's strong academic community and specialists studied the instructional techniques, strategies and conditions that best enable students to learn critical skills, especially in the area of reading. The first step in this strategy should be early detection, acceptance by parents and broad awareness among the academic community and above all a mature handling of the problem. At the government level, there is a need to formulate a constructive policy in this regard.

Nevertheless, there are several agencies in government and non-government sector working in the field and contributing for elimination rather detection of this classroom disorder. Interestingly, many institutions facilitate early intervention in the child's academic life so that he/she learns the strategies and skills necessary to cope with it better and in some cases, overcome it altogether. Early intervention reduces incidence of extreme steps such as repetition of a class or even expulsion, which, needless to say, could have an adverse effect on the child's self-esteem and leave an indelible scar on their psyche. Children with special needs have a right to be relaxed and confident about them and we must, as responsible adults, try our best to help them remain that way.

The multidisciplinary clinics are also intended to provide remedial services to children with special needs. Classroom situations present various forms and degrees of difficulties and problems relating to phonetics, comprehension, general study skill, computation, speech and language development and visual perception skills. These areas require special care and individual strategy and skills.

In India, *SAMVEDA Research and Training Centre, Kolkatta,* the brainchild of Surendranath P Nishanimut, a young entrepreneur, is another such responsible effort in rehabilitating children with learning disability in India. Furthermore, *The Tata Interactive Learning*

*Disability Forum 2008*, held in Mumbai and Kolkata focuses on urgent need to address learning disability issues. Focusing on the theme of 'Special Deeds for Special Needs', the TLDF underlined the importance of early remedial action to help learners with special needs.

Specific learning disability afflicts 5-15 per cent of school-going children. Over the last decade; awareness about this invisible handicap has grown in India. However, much needs to be done to ensure that each afflicted child gets an opportunity to achieve his or her full academic potential in regular mainstream schools. In order to achieve this ideal scenario, all regular classroom teachers should be sensitised to suspect and trained to screen for this disability when the child is in primary school. School managements should become proactive to set up resource rooms and employ special educators to ensure that these children receive regular and affordable remedial education; and be diligent in ensuring that these children get the mandatory provisions both during school and board examinations. Once specific learning disability is recognised as a disability by the Government of India, these children with the backing of the *Right to Education Act*, would be able to benefit significantly.

The nation's commitment towards achieving the goal 'education for all' remains unfulfilled and will remain so if educational opportunities is not extended to all school-going children including children with learning disability. More attention to these children by extending support to institutions and schools that help children with learning disability will certainly improve the scene. There are institutions which have trained personnel who could help assess the extent of damage and treat these children accordingly. Government of India should envisage a national debate on the rehabilitation issue of learning disabled children in the classroom.

## References


- http://www.improvinghealthandlives.org.uk
- He, Er-Shi. (2005). *Review on the researches of cognitive characteristics of children with learning disability.* Chinese Journal of Special Education (Monthly), 57, 85-89.
- Liu, Lin. (2000). *Research on factors of children with learning disabilities (in translation).* Chinese Journal of School Health, 21: 4, 329-330.

- Li, Jie., Li Zhi-Min. and Fan, Jing-Jing. (2002). *The research on the school building environment for limb and trunk disables: An analysis causes preventing limb and trunk disables from entering schools.* J.Xi'an Univ. of Arch. and Tech. (Natural Science Edition), 34:4, 313-316.
- http://ro.uow.edu.au
- https://en.wikipedia.org/wiki/Learning_disability
- http://www.rehabcouncil.nic.in
- *The Right of Children to Free and Compulsory Education Act, 2009* [Internet]. New Delhi: Ministry of Law and Justice (IN), Legislative Department; 2009 Aug. 27. Available from: http://education.nic.in/Elementary/free%20and%20 compulsory.pdf. Accessed on February 5, 2016.

# Index

## D



## E

**T**



**U**